IMAGINING MIAMI

D1739118

RACE AND ETHNICITY IN URBAN POLITICS

Luis Fraga and Paula McClain, *Editors*

IMAGINING MIAMI

ETHNIC POLITICS IN A

POSTMODERN WORLD

SHEILA L. CROUCHER

UNIVERSITY PRESS OF VIRGINIA

CHARLOTTESVILLE AND LONDON

Acknowledgments for previously published material appear on pages ix and x.

The University Press of Virginia

©1997 by the Rector and Visitors of the University of Virginia

Printed in the United States of America

First published 1997

♾The paper used in this publication meets the minimum requirements of the American National Standard for Information Sciences—Permanence of Paper for Printed Library Materials, ANSI Z39.48-1984.

Library of Congress Cataloging-in-Publication Data

Croucher, Sheila L.

    Imagining Miami : ethnic politics in a postmodern world / Sheila L. Croucher

      p. cm.—(Race and ethnicity in urban politics)

    Includes bibliographical references (p.) and index.

    ISBN 0-8139-1704-2 (cloth : alk. paper).—ISBN 0-8139-1705-0 (pbk. : alk. paper)

     1. Miami (Fla.)—Ethnic relations—Anecdotes. 2. Miami (Fla.)—Race relations—Anecdotes. 3. Minorities—Florida—Miami—Anecdotes. 4. Ethnicity—Florida—Miami—Anecdotes. 5. Cuban Americans—Florida—Miami—Politics and government. 6. Afro-Americans—Florida—Miami—Politics and government.

    I. Title. II. Series.

F319.M6C76   1997

305.8'009759'381   DC20   96-41357

                                          CIP

CONTENTS

List of Illustrations   vii

Acknowledgments   ix

1. POSTMODERN MIAMI   1

2. FROM "MAGIC CITY" TO "PARADISE LOST"
The Evolution of Ethnic Conflict in Miami   24

3. THE DISCOURSE OF DISPLACEMENT
Constructing the Threat of an Immigrant Takeover   61

4. THE SUCCESS OF THE CUBAN SUCCESS STORY
Cuban American Ethnicity and the Politics of Identity   102

5. MANDELA IN MIAMI
The Globalization of Ethnicity in an American City   142

6. CONTESTED REALITIES/SHIFTING TERRAIN
Toward a Theory of Ethnicity in the Postmodern World   172

Appendix 1. Labor Market Analysis   199

Appendix 2. Methodological Strategy   201

Appendix 3. Interview Schedule for Community Informants   204

Notes   207

References   215

Index   231

ILLUSTRATIONS

1.   Ethnic profile of Dade County   33

2.   Responses to interview question on ethnic hostility in Miami   53

3.   Responses to interview question on job displacement in Miami   98

4.   Five waves of Cuban immigration   107

5.   Responses to interview question on ethnic divisions in Miami   161

A1.   Occupational dissimilarity between whites and blacks in Miami   199

ACKNOWLEDGMENTS

Throughout this project I have received valuable professional and personal support from various individuals. I am particularly indebted to Charles Wood, Steve Sanderson, and Jim Button for their wise guidance and intellectual enthusiasm. They have, at every turn, helped me to "re-imagine" as opportunities what I often "constructed" as obstacles to the completion of this manuscript.

The fieldwork component of this research was invaluable, and in that regard I wish to thank the many individuals in Miami, Florida, who invited me into their offices and homes and shared with me details of their professional and personal lives. Lloyd Major, executive director of the Dade County Community Relations Board, Maurice Ferre, former mayor of Miami, and Drs. Johns Stack and Kevin Yelvington of Florida International University were particularly gracious.

At the University Press of Virginia, editor Richard Holway and the reviewers assigned to the manuscript offered helpful advice and encouragement; so, too, have many of my current colleagues and friends at Miami University. Michael Pagano, Jeanne Hey, Walt Vanderbush, Patrick Haney, and Judith Zinsser provided constant support.

Finally, I wish to thank my family, Sam, Mary Lou, and Lisa, whose own individual commitments to intellectual growth have been a lifelong source of inspiration; and my other family, Sherry and Gertrude, whose friendship and support have been unending.

Chapter 5 originally appeared under the same title, "Mandela in Miami," in *Journal of Developing Societies.* Substantial portions of chapter 4 originally appeared in "The Success of the Cuban Success Story," *Identities* 2:351–84 (Gordon and Breach Publishers, © OPA [Overseas Publishers Association] Amsterdam B.V.). My thanks to both publishers for granting republication.

IMAGINING MIAMI

POSTMODERN MIAMI

Every major national transformation the United States is undergoing—from the postindustrial revolution to the aging of America, and from the third great wave of immigration into the United States to the redefinition of American sexual relationships—has converged on Miami. How Miami solves, or fails to solve, those problems cannot but provide clues as to how the whole country will cope with the massive changes—full of both peril and opportunity—that are transforming the lives of us all.

T. D. Allman, *Miami*

For the past thirty years Miami has captured the world's imagination in powerful and contradictory ways. Images of tourists strolling leisurely along sandy beaches compete with images of the dark bodies of Haitian refugees washed up along those same shores. Never too far removed from the glitz and the glitter of an "American Riviera" are the burning buildings and broken glass of a "Paradise Lost." The multitude of metaphors that have been used to characterize Miami facilitate little more than the understanding that Miami is a city not easily understood. Yet, frequent references to Miami as a "city of the future" or the "prototypical city of the 21st century" suggest that if the rest of the United States, if not the world, is to confront and cope with the numerous social, cultural, economic, and political trends that have converged, sometimes violently, on South Florida in recent years, then Miami is a city that must be understood.[1]

Some of the contradictory images of Miami may be attributed to the city's youth. Relative to other large metropolitan areas in the

United States, Miami is a new city—a city without a long, rich history, a city not comfortably situated within established social, economic, and political traditions of the United States, a city without a firm or deeply rooted identity. In fact, the vagaries of history and geography have precluded both Miami and the state of Florida from being characterized as stereotypically "southern" or as a part of the span of states in the West and Southwest that make up the Sun Belt. The oldest state in the union in terms of European settlement, ranking first in the nation in its proportion of foreign born, boasting a longer seaboard than any state except Alaska, with several counties registering one of every three residences as a mobile home, and just ninety miles from a communist country, Florida and the city of Miami share little with neighboring states or cities (Whitfield 1993).

These circumstances or peculiarities lead some observers to conclude that Miami is a city without true substance, a state of mind instead of a state of being.[2] Or as author John Rothchild has argued about the state as a whole, "Florida is spiritually unclaimed. On this higher level, it does not seem to exist" (Whitfield 1993, 418). Many of Miami's residents and supporters respond, sometimes defensively, that the city is merely suffering from growing pains (along with too much bad publicity from the likes of the television program *Miami Vice*). One high-level administrator of a university in Dade County, and a founding member of Miami's Spanish American League Against Discrimination (SALAD) said that "the 1980s was a decade of awareness for Miami, cultural awareness. This community has evolved tremendously, and we are now experiencing growing pains. The natives complain about crime, and about crowds, but you have other cities in the U.S. with the same problems, but without an influx of immigrants. People confuse growing pains with ethnic tension" (interview, 30 September 1992).[3] In other words, what appears to be superficiality could also be interpreted as a reflection of an understandable identity crisis in the face of rapid social, political, and economic change.

This book examines the issues of image and identity in Miami, but from a new direction. The metaphors associated with Miami are used not as literary devices but as raw data for analysis. And the fluctuating images that have characterized Miami over the past fifty years are used not only as descriptive tools but also to provide insight into the nature and complexity of social and political reality. At one level, this book analyzes ethnic politics in a culturally diverse urban arena. At a more profound level it uses ethnic politics in Miami to illustrate the need for dramatic changes in contemporary social science techniques. Rather than attempting to prove which image of Miami is the true one, this book looks at how the images themselves have been socially and politically constructed. Instead of attempting to distinguish empirically between substance and superficiality in Miami, it looks at how different actors and interests, variously situated within the city's social and political structure, actively promote competing images of Miami and its inhabitants, some of which achieve greater currency than others.

In Miami, the most prominent and persuasive public images are those associated with ethnicity, race, and cultural conflict. This book reconfigures those popular concepts in a manner that provides valuable insight into Miami and has important implications for the study of other geographic areas and other forms of social and political identity as well. Miami provides the laboratory, but the implications extend far beyond the confines of South Florida. Similarly, although the focus is on ethnicity and ethnic group relations, the analysis also suggests implicit points of comparison with other socially constructed identities—race, gender, nation, and sexual orientation. My goal is to lay the foundations of a framework for understanding the form and content of social images and identities, why some become more or less salient at particular points in time, and how and why changes occur over time. A fundamental purpose of this approach is to illuminate dimensions of power and urban politics that tend to be otherwise obscured by conventional frameworks.

THE EVOLUTION OF THE INQUIRY

This book began as an attempt to explore the roots of an urban rage that has plagued U.S. metropolitan areas, Miami in particular, for decades. But the exploration quickly encountered various methodological challenges, theoretical constraints, and epistemological ambiguities that prompted a reconfiguration of the inquiry itself, not only of the questions asked but also of the findings sought. While some of the initial questions remain unanswered, the outcome of this reconfiguration is a more original and potentially more valuable contribution to the topic at hand.

As stated above, one of the most prominent and unfortunate images associated with Miami is that of inner-city violence and racial strife, and it is an image with much to sustain it. In May 1980, twelve years after the devastating Watts riots of 1968 and twelve years before Los Angeles again would erupt after the acquittal of the police officers accused in the beating of Rodney King, Miami was engulfed in the flames of one of the worst racial upheavals in U.S. history. Over a three-day period entire neighborhoods were destroyed, fires set, windows broken, and homes and businesses looted. In addition to severe property damage estimated at more than $200 million, eighteen human lives were lost, some through astonishing displays of hatred and disgust. The following account of a brutal attack on two brothers who were driving through Liberty City, a neighborhood on the north side of Miami, the evening the 1980 riots began illustrates a level of horror and hostility seldom captured by academic analyses of urban conflict:

The Kulp brothers, from all accounts, were beaten continuously by a variety of people for about fifteen to twenty minutes. They were punched, karate-kicked and struck with rocks, bricks, bottles and pieces of concrete, one of which . . . later recovered by homicide detectives . . . weighed 23 pounds. At one point, someone picked up a yellow *Miami Herald* newspaper dispenser and brought it down on Jeffrey Kulp's head. They were shot several times with a revolver and run over by a green Cadillac, whose driver then came over and stabbed them with a screwdriver. (Dunn forthcoming)

Sergeant Patrick Burns, one of the first police officers to arrive, described the scene as follows: "I ran over and grabbed one Kulp brother, . . . he was still fibrillating, sort of jumping, you know. His head had been split open with an ax it looked like. I ran over and rolled the other brother over. His head was looking up but his body was so mutilated it was like all out of the natural way of lying down. He had his head split open too, and he had a rose coming out of his mouth" (Dunn forthcoming).

The public reaction was one of shock, bewilderment, and disbelief. Residents of Dade County were faced with the startling reality that the devastation that surrounded them was the result, not of hundred-mile-an-hour winds, torrential rains, or some freak occurrence of nature, but of human outrage. People outside of Miami were equally shocked to learn that such an urban nightmare had befallen a city best known as America's favorite playground. Although the Liberty City riots seemed to take the city and the nation by surprise, even the most cursory overviews of Miami's history reveal severe ethnic tensions dating back to the founding of the city in 1896. The Liberty City riots were only the latest—and the most destructive—in a series of social upheavals that had begun in 1968. It was also easy to see that many of the conditions that blacks in Miami had begun to complain about in 1968—poverty, unemployment, police brutality—remained unchanged in 1980; and for many residents of Miami's black ghettos they persist to this day.

As is often the case for public crises such as a large-scale urban race riot, politicians, government officials, the media, and casual observers need not look far to understand the level of hopelessness and despair that overtook Liberty City in May 1980 or Los Angeles in 1992. Yet, as is also often the case, they do not look far enough. Where politicians, government officials, the media, and casual observers did or did not look for answers to the riots in Miami and which elements of the story did or did not receive substantial public attention reveals more about the nature and causes of ethnic conflict than do the voluminous reports produced by the various committees and commissions charged with studying civil unrest. For example, whereas many blacks in Miami continued to live in desperation and despair, what had changed by 1980, and changed dramatically, was the broader social, political, and economic context surrounding neighborhoods like Liberty City, Overtown, or Black (Coconut) Grove. It was around these changes that the explanations for the 1980 Liberty City riots and those that would follow coalesced.

Almost every account of what had happened in Liberty City on 18 May 1980 called attention to the impact of immigration on metropolitan Miami. Miami was portrayed as a city that continually suffered the effects of social and political turmoil throughout the Third World and had frequently fallen prey to foreign invasion. Reports of this nature emphasized the particularly devastating consequences of the immigrant influx for the native black

interesting language — an invasion across impermeable borders?

population in Miami. The anger and hostility of blacks was attributed specifically to a loss of jobs to incoming Cuban refugees. As racial disturbances continued to plague Miami throughout the 1980s, this particular explanation appeared to gain credence.

The claim that Cuban immigrants had taken jobs from African Americans in Miami prevailed despite the lack of empirical evidence to substantiate it. This gap in the literature was puzzling given the amount of local, national, and international attention focused on the city in recent years. Thus, labor market substitutability presented itself as a promising area for further research on urban ethnic conflict in Miami. Armed with a multitude of statements defining "the problem" as one of fierce competition between immigrants and the native minority over scarce economic resources, I saw my project as a straightforward attempt to measure the economic impact of Hispanic immigration on black Americans in metropolitan Miami's labor market.

Several facts became apparent immediately. First, there is nothing straightforward about measuring labor market displacement of one individual or group by another. This is likely to be the case in any geographic area at any time and between any groups. It is particularly true in cities like Miami, which have undergone very rapid demographic and economic changes. Miami's local economy is in a state of flux that continues to transform an area once dependent on the tourist trade into a major center of international banking and commerce. Furthermore, the labor pool comprises individuals from very diverse backgrounds, including an unknown but purportedly substantial population of undocumented workers. Obtaining accurate longitudinal labor market data by race and ethnicity is itself a trying task.

Second, the results of a preliminary empirical analysis did not appear to support the displacement thesis (see appendix 1). Although limited in scope, the findings were sufficient to challenge the strength and validity of the job displacement claim in Miami. Further investigation revealed that other analysts had reached similar conclusions.[4] Yet the public perception of immigrants' taking over jobs in Miami and in other U.S. border cities persists. No definitive statement on labor market substitutability can be based on this or any other existing analysis of metropolitan Miami; and labor market competition between natives and newcomers remains an interesting area for research. What the existing set of circumstances did unequivocally suggest was the need for an alternative, or at the very least amended, explanation for ethnic conflict in Miami.

When the results of the labor market analysis did not support my original hypothesis—that Cuban immigrants had taken jobs from black Americans—one possible response was to simply discount the negative findings. The puzzle remained, however, why there was widespread and seemingly uncritical acceptance of the truth of the hypothesis in Miami in the absence of empirical evidence to support it. An alternative response, and the one presented here, was to acknowledge that perhaps the research question itself was flawed and therefore the methodological strategy was an improper one. The more appropriate focus of analysis, in other words, was not the *reality* of job displacement but rather why and how this particular theme gained prominence on Miami's public agenda. cultural studies

Upon closer examination of the history and nature of social and political turmoil in Miami, a variety of situations surfaced that, like the job displacement debate, were characterized by an incongruity between subjective perceptions and objective facts. It appeared that *Miami Herald* columnist Juanita Greene's observation during the Cuban refugee influx almost thirty years prior—that "Miami is dealing with a situation in which feelings are as important as facts"—was still accurate (Greene 1965b). On the basis of that realization, the entire focus of my analysis shifted away from unemployment rates and wage differentials and toward the sociopolitical mechanisms by which "facts" and "images" are created and the role these "imagined realities" play in determining social outcomes. As suggested earlier, this new analytical focus not only provides needed insight into an issue of great relevance for metropolitan Miami but also suggests critical changes for the study of urban politics, ethnicity, race, and, more generally, identity.

THE STATE OF THE FIELD

Race and ethnicity are now popular topics of discussion and debate, and there is no shortage of material, scholarly or otherwise, that attempts to elucidate these complex social phenomena. In spite of the amount of attention focused on ethnicity, social scientists still lack an accurate framework for explaining the persistence and diversity of ethnic identities and ethnic group conflict. This is the case not only in the United States but throughout the rest of the world as well. Observers from all backgrounds have been caught off guard by the continued force of ethnicity as a critical factor in social and political mobilization worldwide. Similarly, analysts and policy makers alike seem ill prepared to explain or cope with the emergence and resurgence of what has conventionally been viewed as an archaic form of cultural attachment.

Much of the inability of social scientists to explain and predict contemporary ethnic political behavior stems from attempts to apply conventional theories, concepts, and methodological strategies to a postmodern, postindustrial, post–Cold War world. The nature of ethnicity, for example, has been obscured by various assumptions deeply rooted in the theoretical and epistemological foundations of both liberal pluralism and Marxism, the two intellectual frameworks that have dominated Western thought since the Enlightenment. In the United States theories about ethnic and race relations have focused primarily on assimilation, or the adaptation of one group to the core culture and structures of another group. This perspective, still influential in many respects, dates back to the work of Park and Burgess, who defined assimilation as "a process of interpenetration and fusion in which persons and groups acquire the memories, sentiments, and attitudes of other persons or groups, and, by sharing their experience and history, are incorporated with them in a common cultural life" (1924, 735). Milton Gordon's seminal *Assimilation in American Life* built on Park's framework to delineate a series of stages through which groups adapt to a core society, including cultural assimilation, structural assimilation, marital assimilation, and ideological assimilation (1964, 71).

These and the works of other assimilation theorists portray interaction between different ethnic and racial groups as a relatively peaceful process, a smooth progression through established and universal stages of adaptation to a core or common culture. This perspective, heavily laden with the assumptions of liberal pluralism, ignores the role of power, conflict, and inequality in the relations between ethnic and racial groups and assumes that in the final stage of intergroup interaction social, cultural, economic,

How about "borders" vis a vis
Boston?

and political distinctions based on race or ethnic group identity will fade or "melt" away.

The assimilationist framework has been attacked by various Marxist analyses that emphasize the interactions between class, race, and ethnicity.[5] Rather than viewing the United States as a "melting pot" that creates a new amalgamation of relatively equal and culturally homogeneous peoples, these analysts point to the persistence of power and resource inequalities between whites and nonwhites. They emphasize the conflict, subordination, and exploitation that characterizes intergroup relations. This neo-Marxist challenge recognizes differences between ethnic and racial groups but does not view them as truly distinct forms of group identity or social stratification. Instead, racial and ethnic divisions are considered to be a product of the class stratification of modern capitalism, or, in Marxist terminology, a form of false consciousness.[6]

In the 1960s, when modernization theorists began to use the United States and other Western countries as models for understanding, predicting and promoting world development, they conceptualized ethnicity as a "traditional" form of social identity that would pass away with the advent of "modernity."[7] This development literature came under attack by more radical scholars for its ethnocentricity, Western value biases, and inattention to power and conflict. Many of modernization theory's harshest critics were scholars influenced by Marxist modes of inquiry, who argued against a smooth progression from traditional societies based on affectivity, ascription, and particularism to a modern world in which functionally specific interest groups interact in a free and open market (Parsons 1951). They posited instead a revolutionary progression in which class consciousness would prevail and the mass of workers would rise up to overthrow the world capitalist system (Parkin 1979; Tucker 1978). *- Does she (and I) think that this is just the way things will be?*

Although liberalism and Marxism are often portrayed as diametrically opposed, these two schools of thought share many views and commit similar errors as well. Both tend to present social change as deterministic and unilinear, both downplay the role of race and ethnicity in social stratification and political mobilization, and both have been shown, by recent world events, to be inaccurate or at the very least incomplete. Many schol-

a mess of ambiguities! Where is her goes, "where do we go from here?"

ars from both schools of thought remain unwilling to concede defeat and continue to interpret world events in a light favorable to their own academic discourse. In his 1990 presidential address before the American Political Science Association Lucian Pye talked about the crisis of authoritarianism brought about by a world culture of modernization (1990, 3). Pye explicitly interpreted this "great transformation" as a vindication for modernization theory, pointing out that as early as the 1950s and 1960s he and his colleagues had predicted that economic growth, the spread of science and technology, and the acceleration and spread of communications would bring about democratic transitions worldwide (1990, 7). But whereas Pye and others celebrate events in Eastern Europe and elsewhere as the "end of history,"[8] groups such as the Serbs, Croatians, and Muslims in the former Yugoslav Republic and the Hutus and Tutsis in Rwanda engage in daily struggles that will go down in history as among the bloodiest, most violent, and most destructive human pillage known to the modern world.[9]

The unanticipated persistence and resurgence of ethnic group conflict in a postmodern, postindustrial, post–Cold War world has renewed scholarly interest in the subject of ethnicity and ethnic relations. Many of these analyses directly challenge the optimistic assumptions about a "new world order." Samuel Huntington (1993) argues, for example, that the apparent triumph of liberal democracy brings with it not the end of history but the beginning of an era in which culture rather than ideology or economics will be the primary source of conflict. Huntington also cautions that this "clash of civilizations" may be even more devastating and destructive than the ideological conflicts of earlier eras. In a similar vein, Benjamin Barber (1992) argues that the universalizing, homogenizing, or centripetal forces of modernization have been accompanied by equally powerful centrifugal forces (primarily in the form of ethnic conflict) that threaten division, disassociation, and disintegration among the diverse groups that inhabit the global village.

In spite of the recent proliferation of studies on ethnicity, many current approaches remain beholden to assumptions that obscure the nature of ethnic identity and ethnic conflict. Huntington's analysis is illustrative of a primordialist approach that views ethnicity as an unchanging and deeply rooted historical fact. This approach assumes that there are real differences between ethnic groups and that ethnic political behavior can be attributed to cultural, psychological, and affective ties. An alternative set of assumptions often categorized as mobilizationist or instrumentalist argue that ethnicity is not an ancient, affective tie but results instead from the "conscious efforts of individuals and groups mobilizing ethnic symbols in order to obtain access to social, political, and material resources" (McKay 1982, 399).[10] Take, for example, current debates over the rise of ethnonationalism in the former Soviet Union. Did the collapse of communism permit the reawakening or resurgence of ancient animosities and historical blood ties, or did the Soviet system over a seventy-year period actually invent, construct, or assign meaning and legitimacy to identities and cultural groupings that were only loosely formed or connected prior to 1917?[11] And when Barber juxtaposes "Jihad" and "McWorld," to what extent does he overlook the ways advances in world capitalism and global trends in science and technology have actually constructed or reconfigured an ethnic, or "Jihad," response? This tension between the view of ethnicity as a primordial identity and the view of ethnicity as a form of false consciousness is likely to persist. Yet neither primordialism nor instrumentalism adequately explains the multitude and diversity of contemporary ethnic conflicts or provides sufficient foundation for a comparative analytical framework.

though I would say "instrumentalism" has shades of a social-constructionist argument

NEW DIRECTIONS

Social relations in Miami resemble and perhaps foreshadow, although in a relatively less tragic fashion, the ethnic strife now occurring worldwide. Miami also illustrates the inability of existing analyses to grasp the complexity of social relations in a dynamic and interdependent world. Primordial attachments in Miami have not vanished. And despite the prevalent portrayal of social tensions as rooted in economic competition between ethnic groups, the origins of such claims cannot be traced directly to the material conditions to which they purport to refer. In fact, at any point in time a variety of competing claims coexist in and about Miami whether or not they are based on empirical fact.

What emerges is a discrepancy between public portrayals and material realities that is not restricted to the issue of an immigrant job takeover or any other single variable. Several accounts of race and ethnicity in Miami acknowledge the significant role that perception has played in generating tension and hostility, but no attempt has been made to bridge the gap between private perceptions of a "problem" in Miami and public issues of ethnic conflict. This book addresses the issues of ethnicity and ethnic conflict from a new direction. It assumes that collective images of the social world are the outcome of various cultural, political, and economic processes deeply embedded in history. The focus is on how these processes construct explanations for social phenomena that become widely accepted independently of their basis in fact. The relevance of such a perspective to understanding racial and ethnic conflict in Miami or elsewhere is aptly captured by W. I. Thomas's well-known maxim: "If people define situations as real, they are real in their consequences" (1924, 584).

A substantial body of literature provides a strong theoretical foundation for this approach. Analysts from diverse disciplines have challenged the assumption of "a world of facts with determinable meaning and a world of people who react rationally to the facts they know" (Edelman 1988, 1). The result is an epistemological shift away from many of the tenets of positivist thought that have long dominated social science research. This shift is embodied largely, but not entirely, in the writings of postmodern and poststructuralist philosophers. Although the terms *postmodernism* and *poststructuralism* refer to a broad and diverse body of scholarship and, as one author correctly points out, "there are probably as many forms of postmodernism as there are postmodernists" (Rosenau 1992, 15), it is possible to identify some basic themes that characterize the approach. In general, these works reject established boundaries and existing definitions of what constitutes reality and emphasize instead the ambiguous, subjective, and relative nature of meaning itself. Postmodernists and poststructuralists seek, among other things, to expose how structures of power and domination are embedded not only in political and economic systems but also in social discourse. They point to a world in which "the production of meaning has become as important as the production of labor in shaping the boundaries of human existence" and view as essential the need to "challenge those mystifying ideologies that separate culture from power and struggle while simultaneously treating difference as a technical rather than a political category" (Giroux 1991, 226).

nice definition
concise of post-modernism.....

Political scientist Murray Edelman (1988) draws explicitly on the work of poststructuralist scholars in his conceptualization of politics as a "spectacle" that continuously constructs and reconstructs social problems, crises, enemies, and threats. He cautions observers that the claims that make up the political spectacle are to be viewed not as factual statements but as devices for creating disparate assumptions and beliefs about the social and political world. Charles Lindblom, in his recent book *Inquiry and Change,* raises similar questions about the epistemological assumptions that have long dominated the social sciences, although he chooses consciously to distance himself from the "abstractions of Marcuse, Gramsci and Habermas" (1990, ix). And, as early as 1960 E. E. Schattschneider's *The Semisovereign People* emphasized the importance of image, symbolism, and the "mobilization of bias" in constructing political realities.

The study of agenda setting also provides insight into the inherently political and contextual nature of the social definition of reality. The public agenda consists of a range of issues, popular concerns, priorities, and values that are salient to a given community at a particular point in time. In an attempt to predict which sets of issues from myriad conflicting disputes will gain the attention of the polity, agenda-setting theorists seek to understand "how problems develop, how they are defined, the courses of action formulated . . . and the legitimation of one course of action over the other" (Hoppe 1969, 2). This approach challenges the narrow focus on decision making within institutions and contends that the battle over policy may well be decided in the preliminary stages of issue emergence.[12] By concentrating only on the institutional agenda, scholars have tended to overlook the equally influential process of "nondecision making," by which demands for change in the existing allocation of benefits and privileges in the community can be suffocated before they are even voiced (Bachrach and Baratz 1970; Jones 1984).

Sociologists, and social problem theorists in particular, also have focused their attention on the subjective nature of social problems. According to Howard Becker, "If any set of objective conditions, even non-existent ones, can be defined as a social problem, it is clear that the conditions themselves do not either produce the problem, or constitute a necessary component of it" (1966, 6). Herbert Blumer argues that "knowledge of the objective

- when is all of this going?

makeup of social problems is essentially useless" (1971, 305); and Armand Mauss contends that "individuals and interest groups will simply generate a social problem out of their own interests, with or without the data from objective reality" (1975, 45). In *Constructing Social Problems* (1987) Malcom Spector and John Kitsuse build on the theoretical foundation of these earlier works to present an analytical framework that requires researchers to concentrate on the processes by which certain conditions in society come to be defined as social problems. The analysis of social problems, according to Spector and Kitsuse, need not address "actual conditions" themselves, but rather how they are defined by members of society. It is the "claims-making activity" of various actors—journalists, politicians, social workers, union organizers—that defines a social problem (75).

These analysts focus their attention on social and political discourse but recognize that discursive interaction occurs in a context characterized by an unequal distribution of power, influence, and material wealth. This is important, because as Joseph Gusfield cautions,

> The public arena is not a field on which all can play on equal terms; some have greater access than others and greater power and ability to shape the definition of public issues. . . . The social construction of public problems implies a historical dimension. The same "objective" condition may be defined as a problem in one time period, not in another. But there is more to the analysis of public issues than the idea of historicity. At any specific moment, all possible parties to the issue do not have equal abilities to influence the public; they do not possess the same degree or kind of authority to be legitimate sources of definition of the reality of the problem. (Gusfield 1981, 8)

Agenda-setting theorists issue a similar caveat when emphasizing that the public agenda is formed through the normal struggle of social forces and that "at any point in time, it will reflect the existing balance of those forces, or the mobilization of bias within a community" (Cobb and Elder 1972, 161).

CONSTRUCTING THE ETHNIC SPECTACLE

The aforementioned works, drawn from political science, philosophy, sociology, and policy analysis, share the view that objective conditions are seldom so compelling or so unambiguous that they set the public agenda or dictate the appropriate conceptualization of the "problems" with which a given society grapples (Majone 1989, 24). Instead, issues, circumstances, identities, and events (i.e., realities) acquire meaning based on the context in which they occur and the actors or interests by whom they are interpreted or defined. "Discourse," says Stephen Tyler, "is the maker of this world, not its mirror" (1987, 171). This realization has profound implications for the study of ethnicity, and many scholars have applied the relativity, fluidity, and multiplicity of meaning to their analyses of ethnic group relations.

In *The Invention of Ethnicity* Werner Sollors emphasizes the "cultural constructedness" of the modern world. He argues that "the forces of modern life embodied by such terms as 'ethnicity,' 'nation,' or 'race' can indeed be meaningfully discussed as 'inventions.'" Sollors cautions, however, that "this usage is meant not to evoke a conspiratorial interpretation of a manipulative inventor who single-handedly makes ethnics out of unsuspecting subjects, but to suggest widely shared, though intensely debated, collective fictions that are continually reinvented" (1989, x). In a similar vein, K. N. Conzen et al. argue that ethnicity should not be viewed as ancient, unchanging, or inherent in a group's blood, soul, or misty past; nor should it be reduced to a rational means-ends calculation by those intent on manipulating it for political or economic ends: "Rather ethnicity itself is to be understood as a cultural construction accomplished over historical time. Ethnic groups in modern settings are constantly recreating themselves, and ethnicity is continuously being reinvented in response to changing realities both within the group and the host society. Ethnic group boundaries, for example, must be renegotiated, while the expressive symbols of ethnicity (ethnic traditions) must be repeatedly reinterpreted" (1990, 38). *"Ethnic" Conflicts*

These theoretical statements have inspired numerous case studies having to do with the construction or invention of ethnic identity among particular groups but have tended not to generate general propositions for comparative analysis. In this regard, Joane Nagel's "Political Construction of Ethnicity" (1986) has been particularly useful. Nagel accepts the fluidity of ethnic identities and the permeability of ethnic group boundaries but looks to various political factors and processes to explain how and why mobilization occurs along ethnic lines. She posits, for example, that ethnic

The problem being that ethnicity as inherent i.d. causes these "conflicts" (middle East, Serbia, etc)

Bt this would stay organized along ethnic lines?

mobilization is likely to increase when the structure of political access and participation is organized along ethnic lines.[13] Similarly, Yancey, Ericksen, and Juliani (1976) examine the social forces that promote the crystallization of ethnic identity and argue that the development and persistence of ethnicity is dependent upon structural conditions such as common occupational position, residential concentration, and reliance on common institutions and services.

By focusing on the structural forces and factors that produce political mobilization along affective lines these works succeed in advancing the study of ethnicity beyond static debates between primordialism and instrumentalism. The model is still incomplete, however. Similar structural conditions do not produce universal outcomes with regard to ethnic mobilization. And from the standpoint of interethnic conflict, structural conditions themselves tend to be less important than the social perceptions or definitions of those conditions. This book addresses these analytical gaps by recasting the research problem to emphasize image and identity construction.

Central to understanding the invention or construction of ethnic identities and ethnic conflicts is understanding the role of language, or discourse. The actual meaning of the word *discourse* is widely debated (D'Amico 1982). At some level, discourse refers simply to the "circulation of words," but those words "bring together persons occupying multiple and disparate sites in the socio-institutional structure and organizes them into cohesive, stable groups, by infusing them with a common vocabulary, a unified set of interests, and a collective identity" (Forment 1989, 50). This definition is consistent with Michel Foucault's treatment of how discursive practices "formulate their own objects of knowledge and their own subjects; they have their own repertoire of concepts, are driven by their own logics, . . . constitute their own way of acknowledging what is true and excluding what is false within their own regime of truth" (Hall 1988, 51).

Most research on ethnic relations and ethnic conflict sets out to document and empirically evaluate certain conditions about which grievances have been expressed—job loss, income differentials, or language discrimination, for example—and in doing so takes categories such as "black," "white," or "Hispanic," and the collective identities to which they purport to refer, as givens. This study of ethnic relations in Miami focuses on the processes that transform private perceptions into public images. In other words, it assumes that whether a particular "problem" is recognized to exist, whether it qualifies for consideration, and how it is to be considered are functions of the sociopolitical nature of the claims-making process itself (Spector and Kitsuse 1987). Similarly, this book argues that it is discourse, or the circulation of words, that constructs ethnic identities. But discourse is part of a broader framework of power and knowledge that determines what is rational, what is right, and what is true (Foucault 1972; Hall 1988). As Carlos Forment explains, "Discourses become credible only to the extent that they have been infused with power. And yet, the control over power resources is by itself inadequate. Access to power, after all, does not lead automatically to the formation of collective interests and identities, nor to the creation of institutions and structures. Power will remain impotent unless it is also infused with discourse" (1989, 50).

This approach necessarily calls for a methodological strategy that is different from conventional survey techniques. The analyst need not compete with members of society as an arbiter of accurate knowledge but rather must study how members of society "define, lodge, and press claims; how they publicize their concerns, redefine the issues in question in the face of political obstacles, indifference, or opposition; and how they enter into alliances with other claims-makers" (Best 1989, xiii). The information presented in the following chapters is based on an ethnographic analysis of claims-making activity in and about metropolitan Miami from 1960 to the present. Data are drawn from a variety of sources, including in-depth interviews with community leaders, politicians, journalists, and business people in Miami; a thorough review of the periodical and popular literature on Miami, including the *Miami Herald,* the black-owned and operated *Miami Times,* and the Latin *Diario Las Americas;* analysis of public documents; and participant observation (see appendix 2).

Although the methodological approach employed here is clearly more appropriate for the proposed framework than a quantitative analysis of ethnic voting behavior or a labor market study of occupational distribution in Miami by race and ethnicity, it presents certain challenges. Bryan Palmer offers "a blunt reminder" of one such challenge when he states that "those who suggest that texts construct can also engage in their own acts of construction, often ones that skew and distort the very language they are deconstructing" (1990, 84). This dilemma has also been referred to as the Mannheim Paradox: "observers who postulate that the meanings of observations vary with the social situation or with something else must take the same skeptical and tentative position with respect to their own relativism" (Edelman 1988, 4). Many of these concerns and objections are not likely to be allayed by this or any other postpositivist analysis, but Murray Edelman offers an insightful response when he says that

> critics of relativist positions charge that the latter make it impossible to test their own assumptions and conclusions because these conclusions are also relative to something else; but that claim should not be mistaken for an affirmation that relativist positions are false. The claim is only that they cannot be conclusively established as true. But the same must be said of the positivist position. There is reason for tentativeness about all forms of explanation. Relativist positions are not uniquely vulnerable with respect to verification or falsification. Reasons for support or for doubt are all mortals can hope for. (Edelman 1988, 5)

The chapters that follow examine specific discursive formations. In doing so, they present what may appear to be contradictory "evidence" or competing "facts"—an obvious inconsistency for an analysis that explicitly rejects the positivist notion of facts as separable from values, or of observations as verifiable or falsifiable. The presentation of counterclaims, however, is not intended to provide a "truer" version of reality; rather, it is meant to illustrate, particularly for the still dubious reader, that certain definitions of social reality that are widely accepted as true actually compete with and contradict other definitions. Any attempt to prove that one interpretation is more compelling empirically than another would be to pursue a very different line of questioning than that presented here and would inevitably yield very different results. The question such an empirical analysis would not answer is why and how certain images, issues, and identities capture the public imagination and others do not. This question forms the central focus of the current inquiry. It is best answered through an in-depth analysis of the claims-making activity of individuals and groups in a given locale, or what Michael Smith refers to as postmodern urban ethnography (Smith 1992).

THE CASE FOR THE CASE STUDY

Many of the contemporary challenges to mainstream social science remain at the level of theoretical discussion and debate. Much less common is the attempt to examine the empirical applicability of these various philosophical insights.[14] What is new in the present approach is an effort to systematically bring together a wide range of theoretical insights and to apply them to a large body of observations from a single case study. In a recent volume, *A Case for the Case Study* (Feagin, Orum, and Sjoberg 1991), several scholars call for the restoration of the case study as a methodological tool in social science inquiry. Through theoretical discussion as well as empirical application the contributors illustrate the utility of the case study not only as a supplement to other methodologies but as a distinctive means of providing valid social knowledge: "We contend that the case study method is essential if social science is to grapple with major social issues on both the historical and the contemporary scenes. Such matters lie beyond the grasp of the natural science model" (Sjoberg et al. 1991, 28).

Orum and Feagin specifically bemoan the strikingly "small number of theoretically informed, relatively comprehensive, in-depth analyses of major U.S. cities" and conclude their studies of two Texas cities, Austin and Houston, by remarking that "there is no substitute, particularly in realms where one seeks, as we did, some fresh understanding of an old issue, for the intensive study of a single case. Our research alerted us to the role of growth visions and other critical matters in a way that no research, using census or other quantitative evidence, could have" (1991, 121, 145).

Certainly ethnicity qualifies as an "old issue" in need of some "fresh understanding"; and in the terminology and criteria used by case study advocates Miami undoubtedly constitutes a "critical case" for any analysis of contemporary ethnic phenomena (Yin 1984). A former four-term mayor, Maurice Ferre, once characterized relations among ethnic and racial groups in Miami by referring to the city as the "Beirut of the West" (Warren, Stack, and Corbett 1986, 632); and *Miami Herald* political editor Tom Fiedler recently warned of the "Balkanization" of Miami, stating that "we as a community, and as a state—if not as a nation—seem to have forgotten the essence of America. We are behaving instead like Serbs or Croatians or Azerbaijanis or Russian Georgians. We must stop before we start shooting like them" (1992, 4).

There are factors that make the Miami case unique; but given predicted demographic, political, and economic trends, Miami is likely to serve as a model for future social and political relations nationwide. Some analysts have gone so far as to argue that the rapid quantitative and qualitative changes taking place in Miami over the last several years have resulted in a political and social system that in many ways is more akin to that of "new" or developing nations than to the established patterns of more advanced states (Maingot 1986, 87). Finally, postmodernism, as an intellectual current that seeks to expose the elusiveness, dynamism, and "intertextuality" of social phenomena, resonates well with metropolitan Miami's image as a city of illusion. In fact, in a recent critique of postmodern analysis one author made specific reference to Miami as "that enclave of postmodernism" (Palmer 1990, 171).

The present analysis promises to shed light not only on issues of critical relevance to Miami but also on elements of social and political interaction that have heretofore been obscured by the epistemological and methodological premises of conventional analytical techniques. Analysts should begin to ask, for example, whether it is in fact accurate to characterize social tensions in terms of *ethnic* conflict. If it is, then why does conflict manifest itself in terms of ethnicity rather than in terms of some other form of political identity, such as class, race, or gender? And what, in fact, constitutes ethnicity? In other words, rather than accepting ethnic identities as distinctions or differences rooted in historical and experiential factors, this approach interprets ethnic identities and imagery as socially constructed and politically contested phenomena. The methodological strategy employed in this study of ethnic relations in Miami shares Bahr and Caplow's contention that "the construction of social reality produces structures too intricate and multifaceted to be adequately described from any single perspective" (1991, 86) and answers the call for holistic analyses, more interdisciplinary work, and greater recognition of multiple contexts and historical transitions (Yin 1984).

A final point to be made about the relevance of Miami as a critical case study of ethnicity and ethnic conflict concerns a growing body of literature that recognizes the central role of cities in a rapidly changing global environment. In *The Global City* Saskia Sassen (1991) analyzes the relation of cities, specifically New York, London, and Tokyo, to the international economy. She points out that although the world economy has always shaped the lives of cities, since the 1960s a combination of rapid internationalization and industrialization has altered that relationship and created a new strategic role for the metropolis. This and other studies of the global city focus primarily on economic restructuring and the role of cities in the world economy. Less frequently explored is the role of cities as the physical space in which social and political identities are being reconfigured in consequential ways, or as the spectacular crash sites of those forces Benjamin Barber identified as "Jihad" and "McWorld." Miami is one such crash site, and a case that has not been thoroughly examined by scholars of the global city.[15]

In the following chapters metropolitan Miami becomes, in the jargon of postmodernists, "the text." The analysis is organized around different discourses—sets of publicly stated claims, grievances, beliefs, perceptions, attitudes, opinions, and concerns—that depict Miami's urban environment at particular points in time. The objective is to explain the origins and the processes that construct the competing narratives and to show how and why they change over time. Chapter 2 provides a historical overview of the transformation of Miami from a "Magic City" to a "Paradise Lost." Chapter 3 documents a variety of grievances associated with immigration to Miami, from the loss of jobs to the threat of the city's moral decline. These claims are shown to be situated within a broader discourse that defines immigration to Miami as a foreign threat and the immigrants themselves as unwelcome invaders. Chapter 4 traces the emergence and legitimation of the Cuban "success story" as it relates to the changing character of power and politics in Miami as well as in Washington. Nelson Mandela's visit to Miami in 1991 is discussed in chapter 5; it serves to highlight both the symbolic nature of ethnicity and ethnic politics and the need to place local-level analyses in a global context.

The material covered in these substantive chapters may sometimes overlap—in references to specific time periods, actors, issues, or events. This is because the proposed analytical framework indicates that ethnicity, power, and politics in Miami are most accurately approached through the study of discursive formations rather than through quantitative analysis, through historical description, or from the standpoint of distinct (or at least what are defined as distinct) ethnic and racial groups. In other words, a particular issue or event, such as the Mariel boatlift of 1980, may provide content for a variety of different, even contradictory narratives, depending on how it is interpreted and defined. Events surrounding the boatlift may be presented as proof of an immigrant takeover in Miami, as evidence of solidarity among the Cuban exile community, or as a clear indication of racist U.S. immigration policies that welcome white victims of Cuban communism but refuse black refugees from a Haitian military dictatorship. This study is not designed to offer a definitive interpretation of the Mariel boatlift or to enter into already overcrowded debates on related issues ranging from immigration politics to U.S. foreign policy in the Caribbean to the impact of congressional redistricting on minority representation in Florida. These various issues and debates are relevant only to the extent that they constitute the weapons in an ongoing battle to define social reality in Miami. In other words, how these issues are defined, appropriated, and reconfigured provides insight into the exercise of power and into the potential sites of opposition or resistance to domination and control.

The concluding chapter summarizes the insights to be gleaned from this approach to ethnic relations and the broader implications of this case study for future analyses of social and political relations in the United States and abroad. In doing so, it outlines the framework for a theory of ethnicity and introduces new concepts that may help bridge the divide between modern and postmodern approaches to identity, power and politics.

CONCLUSION

Miami is widely accepted as an arena of fierce competition among ethnic groups, competition that frequently translates into social conflict. And historians such as Raymond Mohl (1990, 40) have accurately pointed out that the current tension between blacks and Hispanics in Miami is superimposed on a much longer history of racial conflict that dates back to Miami's origin as a city in 1896. This book argues that a historical analysis of intergroup relations in Miami must not only serve as a backdrop for understanding the contemporary turmoil but also be seen as the raw material with which ethnic identities and ethnic conflicts have been socially constructed. It was this long history of conflict and political struggle in South Florida that produced the definitions of social reality that now circulate in and about Miami, definitions that both create and sustain tensions between ethnic groups.

A recognition that social and political processes define "reality" need not deny the existence of referents for meaning nor degenerate into an endless spiral of relativity (Edelman 1988, 4–6). My intent is merely to expose the boundaries and conditions within which, and the processes through which, meaning is produced. Unemployment, for example, is real; Castro and Mandela are real; riots, death, and destruction are real. But the ways these issues, actors, and events are defined, expressed, interpreted, responded to, and explained are all distinct from empirical conditions themselves. It is these processes, embodied in social and political discourse, that construct "reality," or "realities," as the case may be.

The title, *Imagining Miami,* acknowledges that Miami is a composite of images none of which are devoid of material referents but all of which are constructed through processes distinct from the content or conditions they appear to reflect. This research is guided by the proposition that these images can, with the proper methodology, be traced to the tug and pull of vested interests and community politics. Once constructed, however, these images, perceptions, or constructed realities take on a significance independent of their basis in "fact." In other words, images of reality reinforce as well as reflect established configurations of political, economic, and social power. Explaining the processes that construct these images will illuminate the nature of power and politics in Miami but may also indicate ways in which the "city of the future" can offer suggestions for a more peaceful future not just in Miami but throughout the world.

2

FROM "MAGIC CITY" TO "PARADISE LOST"
The Evolution of Ethnic Conflict in Miami

Before the Miami riot of 1980, in order to find instances in American history where blacks had set out intentionally to kill white people, one would have had to go back to the days of Nat Turner and a few slave rebellions of the pre–Civil War South. When the ashes finally cooled, Miami awakened to an old reality; all was not well in the bowels of the city.

Marvin Dunn, *Black Miami*

On 18 May 1980 billows of gray-black smoke darkened the sky over Liberty City as Miami experienced what one observer described as "the worst rioting in any of the nation's cities since the upheaval in Detroit in 1967" (Levine 1985, 59). The specter of burning buildings seemed as strangely out of place under the sun-drenched palms of Miami as did a 1960s-style urban race riot at the beginning of the 1980s. Politicians, local leaders, and the media were left scrambling to explain how such a violent, destructive uprising could transpire in one of America's favorite resorts.

The so-called McDuffie riot of 1980, named for the man whose beating sparked the riots, was not the first such disturbance in Miami, nor was it the last. By the end of the decade Miami had become synonymous with social upheaval. The predominant tendency, however, was to view these events, if not Miami itself, as an aberration. Yet, as Los Angeles showed in April 1992, the turmoil that plagued Miami throughout the 1980s more accurately qualified the city as a harbinger and not an outlier in race and ethnic relations.

Social rebellion cries out for immediate and comprehensible explanation, but on-the-spot analysis frequently produces fragmented and superficial interpretations of extremely complex cultural, political, and economic variables. Although exacerbated by the convergence of contemporary events, ethnic and racial conflicts must be viewed as multifaceted phenomena whose origins are deeply rooted in historical events. This chapter traces major social, political, and economic trends, highlighting significant events and introducing relevant actors, in order to present a historical interpretation of the evolution of ethnic conflict in Miami from the late 1950s to the present. An analysis that rejects openly the epistemological and methodological assumptions of positivist social science, as this one does, must also acknowledge that "even in a democracy, history always involves power and exclusion, for any history is always someone's history, told by that someone from a partial point of view" (Appleby, Hunt, and Jacob 1994, 11). This historical overview, like the substantive chapters that follow, seeks not to convey some kind of objective truth about the past, but to introduce the images and themes that have dominated public portrayals of Miami and to provide background information about demographic, cultural, political, and economic factors that helped to shape, sustain, and in some cases reconfigure those public images and themes. —I think she overstated this

The journalist Stanley Crouch's response to the 1980 riots was typical: "I used to think of Miami as primarily a Mafia bastion and a Jewish burial ground in Deep South resort trappings, but it is actually a modern border town where black people live in an impoverished Southern past as the future takes place around them" (Whitfield 1993, 417). This common portrayal of Miami as a sleepy, southern town just recently come to life belies the fact that the geographic area at the edge of the Everglades has always been the uneasy meeting ground of peoples of strikingly different cultural backgrounds. In fact a truly comprehensive overview of ethnic relations in Miami would have to begin much further back in South Florida history than the 1950s.[1] Such an overview would have to begin, for example, with the interaction between Spanish explorers and native inhabitants, primarily Seminole Indians, throughout the seventeenth and eighteenth centuries. It would have to examine the relations between immigrants from the Bahamas and settlers who migrated from the North. A truly comprehensive account of the impact of the Cuban influx in South Florida would likewise have to begin long before Castro's overthrow of Fulgencio Batista in 1959. Communities of Cubans were scattered from Key West to Tampa, working in thriving cigar industries, drinking *cafe cubano,* and arguing politics well before Castro and his comrades launched their attack on the Moncada barracks, and well before Miami's Eighth Street was referred to as Calle Ocho. Indeed, as far back as the Cuban revolution of 1933, and almost fifty years before the first "Marielito" ever set foot on Miami's shores, Anglo residents were complaining about the "infiltration of Cubans" (Boswell and Curtis 1984; Dunn forthcoming; Parks 1981).[2] The history of Miami is a history of social cooperation and social conflict along ethnic and racial lines. These lines have been more firmly drawn in some time periods than in others, but the divisions have never remained constant. From the beginning, ethnic relations in Miami have been remarkably fluid in terms of both the social identity of individuals and groups and the relations between groups.

Until the late 1800s, Indians were a fierce and prominent force in South Florida. Blacks were also a growing presence in the region, and throughout the first half of the nineteenth century these two groups maintained a close and pragmatic alliance. The Dade Massacre of 1835 saw blacks and Seminoles join forces to wage a bloody attack against the advancing U.S. military. The severity of the attack, in terms of the number of soldiers killed, ranked second only to General Custer's infamous battle forty years later (Allman 1987, 150; Kearney 1986). Today, the only sizable American Indian population residing in Dade County are the Miccosukee, who live a fairly destitute existence in the Everglades and have limited interaction with or connection to any other ethnic group (Rodrigues 1990).

Unlike the Indians, the black population continued to expand throughout the twentieth century, sometimes at a rate that surpassed that of whites (Mohl 1991, 112). Much of the growth in Miami's black population can be attributed to immigration from the West Indies. In 1920, for example, black immigrants from the Bahamas made up 52 percent of Miami's blacks; and Miami had a larger population of black immigrants than did any other city in the United States with the exception of New York (Mohl 1987; 1991, 137). Since that time blacks have consistently composed approximately 15–20 percent of the population in Dade County and have represented diverse regional, cultural, and linguistic backgrounds. This diversity has been a source of fragmentation within the black community, but the factors separating one element of the black population from another have not remained constant. At the turn of the century, for example, a great deal of tension existed between Bahamian blacks and American blacks, many of whom were former slaves migrating from North Florida and Georgia. Both groups came seeking better economic opportunity, but they shared few cultural commonalties and developed a mutual distrust (George 1978; Johnson 1988). Today the distinction between descendants of Bahamian blacks and those from elsewhere in the United States is for the most part socially and politically irrelevant. It has been replaced, however, with tension such as that between established resident blacks in Miami and the Haitian newcomers (Stepick et al. 1990, 46).

Jews also compose a significant proportion of the population in Miami and have suffered discrimination and persecution similar to that experienced by blacks and other ethnic minorities. Throughout the first half of the twentieth century it was not uncommon to see signs reading "No Jews or Dogs" posted outside many of the hotels in Miami Beach (Sheskin 1991, 163). Today Jewish residents own many of those same hotels in Miami Beach and constitute a large and powerful force in the political and economic life of metropolitan Miami. When it comes to ethnic categorization, however, the Jewish population has been largely subsumed under the heading "Anglo" or, more appropriately, "non-Latin white."

Miami, like many other cities, has changed dramatically over the last one hundred years. Throughout this time ethnicity was and continues to be a salient form of social stratification and group identification. The reasons for this are complex, and they cannot be analyzed in isolation from the changing character of power and politics in Miami. This chapter analyzes Miami politics over the last thirty years. The late 1950s is an appropriate starting point because of the particular social, political, and economic factors that began to take shape at that time, factors that continue to define the tenor of life in contemporary metropolitan Miami.

MAGIC FOR WHOM? MIAMI FROM 1950 TO 1960

By the 1950s, sunny beaches, warm temperatures, and a tropical allure had earned Miami its reputation as a "Magic City." Tourists flocked from the northern United States as well as Canada and South America to soak up the sights and sounds of Miami. As the decade wore on, however, it became increasingly clear that in addition to sun, surf, and tourists, Miami was home to a sizable population of blacks, who were frustrated at not being afforded the same opportunity as their white counterparts to reap the benefits of the Magic City (Chapman 1991; Parks 1981).

Prior to the 1960s the demographic makeup of Miami was similar to that of other southern cities in the United States. In 1950, 13.1 percent of the population of Dade County was black and an estimated 4 percent was Latin. As mentioned above, the black population included a significant number of immigrants and descendants of immigrants from the Bahamas. The small Latin population at the time consisted primarily of Cubans, most of whom had fled to Miami after the Cuban revolution of 1933 (Boswell and Curtis 1991, 145). Among the remaining white population, approximately 54,000 were of Jewish origin (Sheskin 1991).

percentage please

Following the Jim Crow habit of the rest of the South, Miami was a very racially segregated city. As Joan Didion points out, "Miami blacks did not swim at Dade County beaches. When Miami blacks paid taxes at the Dade County Courthouse they did so at a separate window, and when Miami blacks shopped at Burdines, where they were allowed to buy although not to try on clothes, they did so without using the elevators" (Didion 1987, 47). The majority of blacks were forced to live in small, overcrowded slums. One such area was the downtown district of Overtown, known at the time as "Colored Town." Despite the deplorable living conditions—most residents inhabited dilapidated shacks with no electricity, bathing facilities, or hot water—by the 1940s this area had evolved into an important center of black culture in South Florida (Mohl 1988, 215). The Overtown of the 1940s and 1950s was said to be reminiscent of Harlem in the 1920s. This analogy remains prominent in black discourse today, as former residents frequently make reference to Overtown as "a viable community in which people had common causes and related to each other. There was economic development, businesses, furniture stores, a soda water bottling company. The professionals, doctors, lawyers, others, were there. It was a focal point for black people. Segregation, of course, contributed to that, but segregation caused it to be a community where people had a real sense of community" (Hampton and Fayer 1990, 650).

All of Miami at this time, including Overtown, was reaping the benefits of a booming tourist industry.[3] After World War II, Miami developed into the premier winter vacation resort for the eastern United States, and it became the destination of an increasing number of northern retirees. The tourism industry was at a peak in the 1950s, when television personalities such as Jackie Gleason and Arthur Godfrey touted the magic of Miami. Huge, new luxury hotels began to spring up, and visitors arrived en masse. The tourist trade generated the bulk of Miami's jobs, primarily in service industries such as hotels, restaurants, and entertainment. And a growing market for resort wear helped to rejuvenate the local garment industry (Levine 1985, 53). In addition to an expanded and diversified service sector, Miami experienced a construction boom during the postwar era. Dade County's population increased by 90 percent between 1940 and 1950 and again between 1950 and 1960. During the 1950s alone more than fifty thousand new residents settled in Miami each year. The building industry flourished as the influx of people stimulated the construction of new homes and businesses (Levine 1985, 53; Stepick 1989).

Miami was growing rapidly, and the changes were taking place in a metropolitan area that was still quite young relative to many other large cities in the United States. This youth is frequently cited to explain different aspects of social, political, and economic life in Miami. Some cite the fact that the city was not incorporated until July 1896 as a reason why the Miami of the 1950s lacked a cohesive and well-organized power elite: "Prior to 1960, Miami was an American city but not a typical one. It was newer, less traditional than other urban centers. It was neither fully southern nor northern. It had a large transient population and a large proportion of inhabitants who were first-generation migrants. As a result, it lacked a consolidated socio-political structure and a coherent elite" (Stepick et al. 1990, 34).

Writing about the Miami milieu of the late 1950s, political scientist

Edward Sofen said that "Miami is almost wholly devoid of strongly organized political factions and of strongly organized labor or minority groups.
It is generally lacking in organized and consistent community leadership"
(1961, 20). In addition to the city's youth, the absence of any perceived
threat from minority groups, labor, or political machines apparently created an environment in which the power holders had little reason to mobilize openly their political or economic strength (Sofen 1961).

Despite the amorphous nature of power in Miami, it was, without question, wielded almost exclusively by white men. Some observers call attention to the significant but unacknowledged role played by blacks in the
founding of the city in 1896. Of Miami's 367 founding fathers, 162 were
black, and the first name that appears on the city charter is that of a black
man. But these same observers are quick to point out that this event
marked both the beginning and the end of meaningful participation by
blacks in Miami's political system for years to come (Stack and Warren
1992).

Ironically, these particular factors—youth, inexperience, and the disenfranchisement of minority groups—did not prevent Greater Miami from
establishing one of the most innovative forms of metropolitan government
in the nation in the fifties. On 21 May 1957 Dade County voters approved
a home rule charter that established a metropolitan form of county government and ushered in revolutionary changes in the daily operation and
structure of local government. Miami's metropolitan experience, since
known as Metro, remained in place until the 1990s, outlasting similar government structures in metropolitan areas throughout the United States.[4]

Prior to the 1960s there was no obvious power struggle between whites
and blacks in the political realm; nor was there any indication that minorities could pose a threat to the existing social or political structures in
Miami. The city was not, however, without its share of racial strife, nor had
it been for many years. Racial hatred and incidents of white terrorism
against blacks were common throughout the city's history (George 1979;
Porter and Dunn 1984). In 1940, 1950 and 1960 Miami had the highest
degree of residential segregation by race of one hundred U.S. large cities
(Taeuber and Taeuber 1965, 40). As racial patterns in certain neighborhoods began to change, Miami became the site of frequent protest marches

by whites, cross burnings by the Ku Klux Klan, and dynamiting of apartments rented to blacks in formerly all-white complexes. The Ku Klux Klan officially arrived in Miami in 1921 and, according to historian Raymond Mohl, "acted with impunity throughout the depression decade and remained dangerously active well into the 1950s" (1991, 129). Certainly this was due in part to tacit approval by local law enforcement officials. Various sources indicate that blacks in Miami suffered decades of unjust treatment at the hands of local police officers. By the late 1950s, relations between the two groups had reached a dangerous level of mutual distrust (George 1979; Porter and Dunn 1984).

Despite great resistance from whites, persistent terrorism on the part of the Klan, and what amounted to a "ubiquitous pattern of police harassment of blacks," by midcentury blacks in Dade County had achieved several significant civil rights gains. During the 1940s Miami swore in the first black judge in the South since Reconstruction and the first permanent black police officers in the South. The protest by black soldiers who waded defiantly into the water at an all-white beach in Miami marked a significant and early beginning to the civil rights demonstrations that would sweep the nation in subsequent years. And in 1959 Miami also became the site of the first racially integrated public school in the state of Florida (Buchanan 1977).

Accompanied by debilitating setbacks in other arenas, many of these gains proved to be only superficial in nature. Some of the programs that were intended to improve the situation of blacks had the opposite consequence. Federal housing reform launched during the New Deal era became a tool with which the local elite in Miami could clear the downtown area for further expansion of the business district and relocate blacks to a housing project six miles from the city core. This area eventually grew into the sprawling black ghetto now known as Liberty City (Mohl 1991, 124). Similarly, highway urban renewal programs of the fifties and sixties helped to fund the construction of interstate highways that sliced through the black neighborhoods of downtown and destroyed the homes of thousands of Overtown families (Chapman 1991, 41; Mohl 1988, 220).

As the 1950s came to a close, not only blacks but many of Miami's other residents had ample reason to question the city's "magic." The tourism industry was in decline as jet service to the Caribbean forced Miami to compete for much-needed tourist dollars. The construction boom had begun to taper off, and the once thriving middle-class section of town, along Flagler Street and southwest Eighth Street, was becoming a depressed area cluttered by vacant shops (Boswell and Curtis 1991, 146). A former president of Florida International University referred to Miami at the end of the decade as "essentially a deteriorating city" (Levine 1985, 60).

THE CUBAN INFLUX: ECONOMIC MIRACLE OR MAYHEM?

The 1960s ushered in a decade of social and political turbulence throughout the United States. In addition to the urban race riots that plagued cities across the nation, Miami was to feel the effects of an equally turbulent set of events taking place ninety miles south, on the island of Cuba. According to one group of knowledgeable observers, "The history of Miami since the 1960s has been affected thoroughly by one particular phenomenon, immigration. In a sense, much that has happened in Dade County since the waves of immigration started to arrive has been in reaction to or a result of immigration" (Stepick et al. 1990, 21).

Although few would deny the very real impact immigration has had on Miami, the precise nature of that impact is debated. Claims that emerged in Miami during the late 1960s and 1970s lay the foundation for two competing discourses that would characterize public debate in Miami for years to come. One interpretation saw the arrival of the Cuban refugees in Miami as an economic miracle bestowed upon a city in decline. The other characterized the immigrant influx as an unwelcome invasion, and the cause of great social, political, and economic disruption.

By the late 1950s longtime Cuban dictator Fulgencio Batista had clearly lost the support of the Cuban people, as well as that of the United States. Except to a few loyalists, along with those who had benefited from an increasingly corrupt regime, his overthrow by Fidel Castro in December 1959 was a welcome relief. Anticipating the turmoil, many of the Cuban elite had transferred their wealth—and in some cases themselves and their families—to Miami before the revolution began. They were soon followed by a trickle of disgruntled Cuban compatriots who became disenchanted with the new government in Cuba. By 1965 that trickle had become a steady flow as thousands of Cubans were airlifted from the island and flown to Miami aboard "freedom flights" twice daily (Boswell and Curtis 1984).

An estimated twenty thousand Cubans resided in Miami prior to the 1959 revolution. Over the next two decades more than five hundred thousand more arrived in the city. Despite efforts of the federal government to resettle these "entrants" throughout the United States, a remarkable number returned to Miami within a matter of years. One survey, conducted in 1978, found that 40 percent of Dade County's Cubans had returned to the area after living in another U.S. city (Boswell and Curtis 1984, 66). Studies have shown that this concentration of Cubans presents an interesting exception to the general pattern of geographic dispersion exemplified by other Hispanic nationality groups (McHugh 1989, 429).

The dramatic shift in Dade County's population during the sixties and seventies was not simply the result of Cuban immigration. Other Hispanic immigrant groups continued to arrive in Miami, as did black immigrants from Caribbean nations such as Haiti and Jamaica. As these groups came, others left (see fig. 1). The percentage of white Americans in Dade County

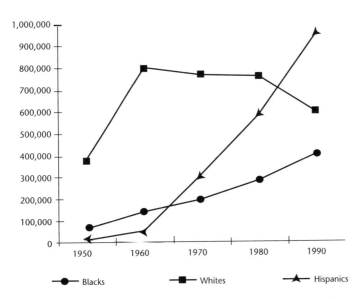

Figure 1. Ethnic profile of Dade County: numbers of whites, blacks, and Hispanics, 1950–1990.

relative to other groups began to decline in 1960, and the absolute number of whites has decreased since 1970. In addition to the out-migration of non-Latin whites, Dade County also experienced some degree of non-Latin black flight. The numbers were not as great, however, and the loss of black population was largely offset by net international immigration from the Caribbean. In 1963, for example, the first boatload of Haitians arrived in South Florida, followed by a second in December 1972 and a steadier flow thereafter (Boswell and Curtis 1991, 141–45).

It is highly unlikely that any city or, for that matter, state or nation could have absorbed such a massive influx of immigrants without experiencing some degree of social, political, or economic dislocation. This was certainly a concern expressed by Dade County residents and local officials alike when the first Cuban refugees began arriving in the early 1960s. Black leaders immediately feared that the refugee crisis would threaten the very fragile political gains recently accrued to blacks as a result of the civil rights movement. Miami residents in general—black and white, employed and unemployed—were dismayed that the already depressed Dade County economy would now be forced to support an additional burden.[5] In response to this local outcry, and to a situation that had significant implications for U.S. foreign policy at the time, the federal government pumped generous sums of money into Miami to assist with the processing, settlement, and, in some cases, relocation of the newcomers (Pedraza-Bailey 1985). In this regard, U.S. policy toward the Cuban refugees both reflected and reinforced a national consensus that these immigrants were the victims of a brutal communist dictatorship and, as such, deserved not only our sincerest sympathy but also our most generous support.

Despite these efforts, certain individuals and groups in Miami continued to voice discontent with the immigrant presence throughout the 1970s. At the same time there emerged a compelling and contradictory discourse that reflected the fact that Miami's economy was not sinking deeper into depression but had actually improved and was faring better than the economies of many other U.S. cities. In fact a series of developments that occurred during the 1970s is credited with transforming a "honky-tonk tourist town, akin to Las Vegas and Atlantic City, into a cultural and commercial hub of the Americas" (Levine 1985, 47). It was at the end of this decade that Miami officially earned the title "capital of Latin America."[6]

The popular phrase "Latin connection" referred to the entry of Latin products and people into the United States through Miami and to the expansion southward from Miami of U.S. commercial and financial interests seeking to exploit the vast markets of Latin America and the Caribbean. Cuban immigrants are widely credited with bringing this international trade and finance to Miami. Not only did the relationships between the Cuban exiles in the United States and those that had settled elsewhere in Central and South America facilitate transnational business networks but the Cuban presence in Miami also created a Hispanic flavor that made the city increasingly attractive to Latin businesses and travelers. By the early 1970s, Miami's fledgling tourist industry had been resuscitated by an influx of foreign visitors. Noting the great change brought on by the Hispanicization of Miami's image, one observer remarked: "Of course, tourists still come to Miami, but most of them now speak Spanish and fly *north* to get there" (Levine 1985, 47).

The Cuban émigrés clearly facilitated Miami's link with the international economy, but their residence in the Miami area also helped rejuvenate the city itself. The refugees initially settled in a concentrated area southwest of the city's central business district. Within a short period of time they began to open small family businesses in the vacated shops along Flagler Street and southwest Eighth Street. In December 1971 the newly formed Latin Chamber of Commerce had a membership list of 678 organizations; in July 1972 that number exceeded 1,000 (Stevenson 1975, 8). This is the area that developed into the bustling center of Latin social, political, and economic life in Miami, now widely known as Little Havana.

In some respects the 1970s fulfilled its promise as a "decade of progress." In addition to Miami's new status as a center of international trade and finance, the city passed a very ambitious bond issue, Florida International University opened its doors in 1972, the arts flourished, and Miami's new professional football team, the Miami Dolphins, won two consecutive Super Bowls (Chapman 1991, 41). But just as the "magic" of Miami was not universal in the forties and fifties, the "progress" of the seventies did not equally benefit all groups living in Dade County. Relative to the extraordinary success of the Cuban exiles, blacks in Miami continued to suffer economic deprivation. The black unemployment rate was twice that of whites, and through the 1970s blacks constituted a disproportionately high percentage of those individuals in Dade County living below the poverty line (Stepick et al. 1990, 43). With regard to the relative deprivation of blacks, some analysts have said that the emphasis should be placed on the word *relative*. Certain measures indicate, for example, that although the economic status of blacks in Miami did not match that of Hispanics during the 1970s, they fared better than blacks in other parts of Florida and the United States. Similarly, in terms of employment in professional and administrative occupations and median income, black growth outpaced that of both Hispanics and non-Latin whites (Stepick et al. 1990, 39).

Blacks in Miami had made significant political gains by the 1970s as well. The first black was elected to the Miami City Commission in 1967. In the decade that followed her seat was filled by two black clergymen, both of whom were active in the civil rights movement (Mohl 1991, 131). Dade County also selected its first black superintendent of schools during the 1970s.[7] Hispanics also were becoming a potent political force in Miami by the mid-1970s. In June 1972 a massive voter registration drive registered hundreds of Cuban Americans. On 6 July 1972 the first Cuban exile was appointed to the Miami City Commission. A very large number of eligible Hispanics began to exercise their right to vote, and the election of the Puerto Rican Maurice Ferre as mayor of Miami in 1973 was viewed as evidence of this new Latin political clout (Buchanan 1977).

Despite these gains by both blacks and Hispanics, power in Miami continued to be held by the civic and business elite, and that elite continued to be predominantly non-Latin white. The leadership in Miami that in 1960 had been characterized as a "relatively narrow and ineffective traditional elite, akin to an old-boy network" had reached its zenith by the 1970s as a "still narrowly-based but effective, organized, corporate, modern elite" (Stepick et al. 1990, 59). This transformation was partly evinced by the formation of the evocatively named Non-Group, an informal leadership group established in 1971 by the leaders of big business in Dade County. Perhaps the most influential member of this group, and a key figure in civic leadership in Miami for many years, was Alvah Chapman. Chapman's position as chief executive officer of Knight-Ridder, the parent corporation of the *Miami Herald,* also solidified the position of the media as an important powerbroker in Miami politics. The Non-Group and a reorganized Greater Miami Chamber of Commerce were extremely influential in bringing about major infrastructural development in Miami during the 1970s, including the construction of Metrorail (Stepick et al. 1990, 57). Although this leadership group was made up of an Anglo elite, the very fact that they represented the predominant business interests in Dade County made a potential alliance with an emerging Cuban entrepreneurial class likely.

As suggested earlier, some resentment toward the Cubans' influx was evident from the beginning, but for the most part ethnic relations in Miami remained calm throughout the 1970s. Blacks, whites, and Hispanics tended to exist in separate worlds. And as one observer noted, "Nothing of substance in Miami's race relations changed during the 1970s" (Mohl 1991, 133). The world in which blacks existed in Miami was a deprived one, and the lack of substantive change meant that the deprivation persisted. Already sour relations with the police deteriorated further. In 1968 two white police officers routinely arrested a black youth for carrying a concealed weapon. On their way to the police station they stopped to dangle him naked from an expressway one hundred feet above the Miami River. When the incident became public, it was also revealed that Chief of Police Walter Headly had dismissed as "silly" the request that one of the officers involved be transferred due to anti-black conduct (Porter and Dunn 1984, 14).

On 7 August 1968 mounting discontent among Miami's black community erupted in angry rioting, while the Republican party held its national convention just across Biscayne Bay in Miami Beach. No immediate connection was drawn between the Republican convention and the Liberty City disturbances, but some analysts noted that several black leaders and influential political groups viewed the convention and surrounding media attention as an opportunity to organize rallies in the black community. One of those rallies evolved into Miami's first official race riot when a white man with a "George Wallace for President" bumper sticker on his pickup truck drove by (Porter and Dunn 1984, 15).

The disturbance during the summer of 1968 was followed in June 1970 by the "rotten meat riot." This upheaval began as a black protest against the sale of spoiled meat by a local white grocer. It was evident, however, that the bitter hostility displayed by blacks during that hot week in June had its origins in something much more complex than rotten food. *Newsweek* suggested a deeper cause "dating all the way back to the lofty promises made to Miami Negroes to placate them after a riot during the 1968 Republican Convention. Jobs, garbage collection, and equitable housing codes were all pledged by the city fathers and all went unredeemed" ("Meat Riot" 1970).

Between June 1970 and January 1979 Dade County experienced thirteen outbursts of racial violence (Didion 1987, 44). In each case the precipitating factors were distinct, but common to all the incidents were a sense of despair among blacks with regard to their social and economic plight and a complete lack of trust in a political and legal system that was unwilling or unable to curb the persistent injustice. It is significant that prior to the 1980s these racial disturbances were almost never discussed in connection with the Cuban immigrants—not by blacks, who lived the despair, or by whites, who hoped that if the problems were ignored they might disappear.

The complaints from blacks were consistent—lack of jobs, poor housing, low pay, and high rent. One Liberty City resident who was interviewed after the riots explained: "We've got a lot of problems. What you people don't realize is that this is a deep problem within each of us. What happened today is merely a culmination of a lot of little wrongs that we have suffered at the hands of the white man" (Wyche 1968). The response of the white community in Miami ranged from making promises that seldom were kept to blaming the social upheaval on "outside agitators." After the 1968 riot, Mayor Steve Clark claimed to have "conclusive evidence" that the rebellion had been a result of outside agitation. Chief of Police Walter Headly echoed the claim: "Fifteen people were imported into this area to start this thing in Liberty City. They did, and after they got it going, they immediately left and went to St. Petersburg. I don't know who paid their way. We know they were an out-of-town group and we're still working trying to identify them" ("Chief Headly" 1968). A Dade County grand jury eventually concluded that there was no evidence to support this claim (Kennedy 1968).

While Liberty City periodically smoldered from the sparks of black rebellion, Miami's Cuban community, just miles away, was engaged in a battle all its own. Throughout the 1970s the Cuban immigrants were concerned with liberating their homeland from the grip of Castro's communist regime. To this end, a multitude of paramilitary exile organizations spent long hours in the Everglades training diligently to invade the island. The struggle—*la lucha*—was against not only Castro but also "his allies, and his agents, and all those who could conceivably be believed to have aided or encouraged him" (Didion 1987, 18). This anti-Castro furor brought *la lucha* to the streets of Miami, not to mention Washington and New York, in an explosive way.[8]

Bombings and assassinations became commonplace in Miami during the 1970s as anti-Castro terrorists attempted to silence anyone who advocated anything resembling dialogue with Castro. During one twelve-month period terrorists bombed more than twenty "targets" in Miami (Allman 1987, 331). The journalist Luciano Nives, who made the unfortunate mistake of suggesting that Castro might be brought down "politically," was assassinated in February 1975. In 1976, after criticizing the bombings and assassinations that were taking place within Miami's exile community, the radio broadcaster Emilio Milan had both his legs blown off by a car bomb. Violence and the threat of violence also forced various publishing offices and radio stations to close their doors and relocate elsewhere in the United States (Americas Watch 1992; Didion 1987, 99–107).

As one observer pointed out, "No Cubans in Havana were endangered by these antics, but Cubans in Miami were not so fortunate. Periodically the city would be swept by terrorism as local 'freedom fighters' turned on local 'Communists'" (Allman 1987, 331). Certainly not all Cuban exiles were consumed with *la lucha* to the point of engaging in acts of brutal terrorism. The violence that did occur was largely a reflection of disagreements among the Cuban exiles over how to best deal with Fidel. These disagreements eventually spawned a variety of different exile organizations, each with a distinct outlook on appropriate policy approaches toward Castro's Cuba. In spite of this division, throughout the 1970s the majority of

Cubans in Miami remained united by their common exile experience and by the hope that their stay in the United States was only a temporary one (Allman 1987, 383; Stevenson 1975, 43).

Neither the agony nor the inconvenience of exile prevented large numbers of Cubans in Miami from excelling economically. It was in this arena that Anglo and Hispanic interests tended to coincide, at least initially. As a result, the relations between these two groups were relatively smooth throughout the 1970s, but the level of resentment remained and perhaps even deepened among certain elements of the Anglo population. By the 1970s, for example, non-Latin white flight from Miami was well under way. This trend is frequently viewed as evidence of the growing frustration among Anglos over the "Latinization" of Miami.

During this time period the predominant discourse was one, not of resentment, but of praise. The pragmatic marriage of "Latin hustle and Anglo muscle" was credited with lifting Miami out of its economic doldrums. Then, in 1973, either as an act of appreciation or merely as a recognition of reality, the county commission passed a resolution officially declaring Dade County to be bilingual and bicultural (Castro 1992). This move symbolized dramatically the clout of Miami's Latin community and eventually served to mobilize the simmering pockets of nativist resentment throughout the county. Miamians' attitudes toward the refugee influx varied throughout the 1970s from that of the bank president who proclaimed, "Send us a thousand more" ("Those Amazing" 1966, 148), to the angry Anglo employed by the license bureau who complained, "The Cubans here are really a pain. They can't speak English, and we've had to hire people who speak Spanish just to deal with them. I plan to leave Miami just because of them" (cited in Stevenson 1975, 106). In retrospect, obvious elements of social tension present in Miami during the 1970s could have been interpreted as warning signs, but relations between the various ethnic groups were not blatantly explosive and few anticipated the turmoil to come.

PARADISE LOST: MIAMI IN THE 1980S

A variety of factors converged in 1980 to earn that year and the entire decade of the 1980s the reputation as Miami's "darkest days" (Parks 1981).

Long-term demographic, economic, and political trends collided in an explosive fashion with several contemporary and unanticipated social upheavals. One result was that the city's all-important image took a brutal beating. The once "Magic City" became better known nationally and internationally as "Paradise Lost." According to T. D. Allman,

In 1980, Miami's image changed, and not for the better when it was struck by a triple disaster that might have crippled a less resilient place. First, Liberty City and many of its other black neighborhoods exploded into some of the most frenzied civil disorders ever seen in this country. Then Miami fell prey to a veritable foreign invasion as more than 100,000 people fleeing Castro's Cuba poured into the city. Finally, scores of Haitian boat people drowned in its waters off south Florida, and in full view of visiting tourists, their bodies washed ashore on the beaches. (10)

As Allman suggests, such a series of events might have permanently disabled many cities, but Miami did survive the 1980s, in some regards better than other U.S. metropolitan areas.

The 1980 census counted 581,030 Hispanics in Dade County (U.S. Bureau of the Census 1980). This total was calculated just prior to the Mariel boatlift; therefore, it did not include the 125,000 Cuban refugees who arrived in Miami during April 1980. The census figures also could not accurately reflect the number of immigrants residing illegally in the metropolitan Miami area. When Congress passed the 1986 Immigration Reform and Control Act (IRCA), with an amnesty provision for those undocumented aliens who could show proof of having been in the United States since before 1980, close to three thousand persons in Miami filed for legalization (U.S. Department of Justice 1990).

Even if we accept that the census estimates are probably conservative, the 1980 data still indicate dramatic shifts in the demographic characteristics of Dade County. In 1950, 10 percent of the Dade County population was classified as foreign-born; by 1980 that figure had reached 35.5 percent for the county and 54 percent for the city of Miami. This percentage of foreign-born residents was twice that of Los Angeles and more than twice that of New York, qualifying Miami as the most immigrant-intensive city in the United States (Mohl 1986, 52). By 1980 Miami also had become one of only sixteen metropolitan areas in the nation with a black population of more than three hundred thousand. Blacks made up 17.3 percent of Dade

County's population in 1980, up from 15 percent in 1970. Since the 1950s the rate of increase of the black population in Miami has surpassed that of the black population in the country as a whole, and between 1970 and 1980 it was exceeded only by that of blacks in Atlanta (Stepick et al. 1990, 27).

The arrival of Haitians in very large numbers during the 1970s and 1980s contributed to both the relative and the absolute growth of Dade County's black population. The Haitian "boat people" began to settle near downtown Miami; "by mid 1978, it was becoming increasingly clear that Miami had a problem—a very serious problem. Hundreds and eventually thousands of undocumented Haitians were slipping illegally into the country and into Miami's Little Haiti" (Stepick et al. 1990, 26). The flow of Haitians into Miami reached a peak between 1978 and 1981. As was the case with illegal Hispanic immigrants, an accurate count of the number of Haitians in Dade County was difficult to come by. One report estimated that approximately seventy thousand Haitians were living in the Greater Miami area by the mid-eighties (Stepick et al. 1990, 25). Meanwhile, the non-Latin white population in Miami continued to decline, dropping by almost a third between 1980 and 1990. Most of this reduction was due to "non-Hispanic white flight" to other parts of the United States (Boswell and Curtis 1991, 145). In 1983 there were seventy-four thousand fewer non-Latin white students in Dade County public schools than in 1969 ("Non-Latin White" 1983).

Miami's transition to an international city, which had begun in the 1970s, intensified during the 1980s. Hundreds of multinational corporations, employing thousands of personnel, established regional headquarters in Miami. Citicorp and Chase Manhattan, along with more than fifty new foreign banks, opened branches in Miami. International trade and finance attracted these businesses; passing through the Port of Miami, Miami International Airport, and other terminals was an estimated $7.5 billion worth of Latin exports and imports. At this point more foreign visitors were arriving at Miami International than at any other American airport except for John F. Kennedy Airport in New York City. This international commerce provided employment for more than seventy thousand people in the Greater Miami area; particularly indicative of the economic restructuring taking place in Miami was the fact that tourism now generated only 10 percent of the city's jobs (Levine 1985, 61).

Latin investors and visitors poured billions of dollars into the Miami economy each year. At one point during 1980 one-half of all property sold in the Miami area was sold to foreigners. The disadvantage of such close ties with Latin America was that when countries throughout that region experienced severe economic downturns in the early 1980s Miami also suffered. Tourism declined, real estate purchases by foreigners dropped, and several corporations were forced to close down. "When the debt crisis exploded and the countries plunged into recession, South Florida was hard hit," said the Miami economist Manuel Lasaga, managing director of the International Management Assistance Corporation. "We will look at the '80s as a lost decade" (Bussey 1992b).

The economic recession of the early 1980s was global in scope, and its impact reverberated throughout Latin America, the United States, and the world. Despite this, Miami's economy weathered the crisis relatively well. The unemployment rate for Dade County remained lower than the national average, for which the rise of the Cuban enclave economy was considered partially responsible. One analyst, comparing the economic crisis of the 1980s with the killer hurricane of 1926, concluded: "Although it swept away a few *tiendas* and several corporate offices, the recession of the early 1980s left Miami's modern assets virtually intact. The city's geographic locale, its financial markets and service industries, its bicultural ambience, its lively cadre of Cuban traders—all of these remain" (Levine 1985, 67).

Dade County's economy appeared to remain stable, but there was some indication that the social and political structures were less resilient. The 1980s saw the Anglo elite in Miami challenged on a variety of fronts as Cubans began to extend their economic success into the political realm. "The 1980s," according to a Ford Foundation report, "was a period of transition, as the mainstream elite encountered the existence of other centers of power and resistance from new players. The response was to selectively incorporate players from the newcomer Cuban community, as well as a smaller number from the resident black minority" (Stepick et al. 1990, 59).

In 1988 Hispanics constituted 34 percent of all registered voters in Dade County and were a powerful and effective voting block. Several formal and informal political contests during the 1980s attested to the growing strength of the Latin community and to the increasing concern among Anglos about the potential challenge this immigrant group now posed. One of the most visible political struggles between these two groups involved a special election in 1989 to replace veteran U.S. Congressman Claude Pepper. The election boiled down to a contest between a Cuban American Republican woman and a Jewish American Democratic male. The final victory went to Republican Ileana Ros-Lehtinen, who won with 98 percent of the Hispanic vote. The campaign, like many during the 1980s, was an ethnically divisive one, and voting closely followed ethnic lines (Stack and Warren 1992).

The Anglo elite in Dade County recognized the political and economic ascendance of the Latin community and began limited attempts to incorporate key minority figures into the established power structure. By 1989, in addition to selecting a Cuban American president of the Greater Miami Chamber of Commerce, the Non-Group had added six Cuban Americans to its membership list. Similarly, one of the largest Anglo-owned banks in metropolitan Miami had appointed a Cuban American as vice-chairman (Stepick et al. 1990, 62).

The changing nature of relations between the *Miami Herald* and the Cuban community during this time period is also significant, because in Dade County the *Herald* is considered to be a primary component of the local power structure. Several of the individuals interviewed for this study offered unsolicited commentary on the role of the local media and emphasized the need to view Miami politics as the politics of a "one paper town." When asked to name the biggest problem now facing Miami, one black leader and veteran Miami politician said, "We have one daily newspaper deciding the fate of the community. It [the *Miami Herald*] is so blatant and so one-sided" (interview, 22 October 1992).

Whether in recognition and acceptance of the Latin presence in Dade County or simply because it was a marketing necessity, the *Herald* added a Spanish-language version to its daily publication in 1976. In 1987 *El Herald* was reorganized and renamed *El Nuevo Herald* in an attempt to grant greater autonomy to the Spanish counterpart. The company also invited a specialist from Florida International University to enlighten *Herald* staff members on Cuban culture and sent a staff member to the university's seminar entitled "Cuban Miami: A Guide for Non-Cubans" (Didion 1987, 55; interview, 17 September 1992). Although this may have been a genuine attempt on behalf of the *Herald* and Knight-Ridder to reach out to the Latin community, also at stake was the business success of the corporation itself, for the *Miami Herald*'s readership had begun to decline. Pointing to the fact that Miami's economic base had become dependent upon Spanish-speakers, one group of analysts concluded: "As far as we can tell, this is the only time in U.S. history that a majority group, dominant newspaper has been forced to publish another language edition in order to recapture their market" (Stepick et al. 1990, 87).

If the *Herald* was reaching out, the gestures were perceived as purely token by Miami's Latin community. Throughout the 1980s the relationship between the two worsened as Cuban Americans increasingly held the newspaper responsible for fostering an anti-immigrant, anti-Cuban mentality in Dade County. The *Miami Herald*'s aggressive campaign against the Mariel boatlift was viewed as badly tarnishing the image of these newest refugees and of the Cuban community as a whole. But even prior to Mariel, Cuban Americans had accused the *Herald* of castigating the exile community: "All our achievements have been accomplished with a national press coverage that has often portrayed us as extremists. This has been the most unfair and prejudiced perception we have experienced in America. The *Miami Herald* bears tremendous responsibility for this injustice. . . . The *Miami Herald* is aggressive in its ignorance of our people" (quoted in Portes and Stepick 1993, 138–39).

The 1980s brought another significant challenge to the established elite in Miami, in the form of a political alliance between blacks and Hispanics who were displeased with the structure of local government. In 1986 several prominent leaders within both communities filed suit against Dade County for violation of the federal Voting Rights Act. The plaintiffs charged that the county's at-large voting system diluted the voting strength of local minorities. Former mayor Maurice Ferre, one of the plaintiffs, charged: "For thirty years Metro-Dade has been irresponsible in dealing with minorities. This [the suit] is the result" (Filkins 1992c).

Despite dramatic shifts in the ethnic composition of Dade County's population, the county commission continued to be dominated by non-Latin whites. Because of the nature of Dade's metropolitan government, this governing body maintained substantial control over a variety of decisions affecting Miami and the twenty-seven other municipalities in the county's jurisdiction. The situation of the Dade County School Board was similar: it too was considered to be a very influential decision-making body, and it too was made up primarily of non-Latin white members. Despite what the plaintiffs argued was substantial voter turnout in favor of particular minority candidates, both blacks and Hispanics alleged that the at-large system prevented them from electing their preferred candidate.[9]

Sorting through the various dimensions and shifting character of power and politics in Miami during the 1980s requires some caution. The apparent alliance between blacks and Hispanics as plaintiffs in the Voting Rights Act lawsuit eventually fell apart when the two groups determined that their interests in this matter did not necessarily coincide (interview, 24 September 1992). The Cuban community in Miami was clearly a growing force, but the extent to which they posed a threat to the hegemony of the established non-Latin white powerbrokers remained questionable. Also questionable was the extent to which the Anglo elite were actually incorporating the newcomers or coopting a significant few. Irrespective of subtle maneuvering and negotiation in the political realm, social relations in Miami took a sharp turn for the worse during the 1980s. The decade was characterized, not by these subtle questions, but by various blatant displays of resistance and counterresistance by different social groups.

The furor that overtook Liberty City on 18 May 1980 dramatically foreshadowed the dynamics that would dominate social relations in Miami throughout the 1980s. Miami experienced three major race riots during the 1980s, each precipitated by the death of black men at the hands of white police officers. On 17 December 1979 Arthur McDuffie, a black insurance agent, was beaten by a group of at least six white police officers after a high-speed motorcycle chase. He died days later from severe head injuries. On 17 May 1980 an all-white jury in Tampa found each of the defendants not guilty. The Liberty City riots began that evening (Porter and Dunn 1984).

Two years later, on 28 December 1982, a twenty-year-old black male was shot and killed by a Hispanic police officer while playing a video game near downtown Miami. Overtown immediately erupted into a full-scale riot. In 1984 an all-white jury found the police officer, Luis Alvarez, not guilty. In January 1989 violence spread throughout Overtown, Liberty City, and Coconut Grove after a Hispanic police officer fired a single shot at a motorcycle speeding in his direction. The driver died from the bullet, and his passenger died from the subsequent crash—both were black men. On 7 December 1989 a jury of two blacks, one Hispanic, and three non-Latin whites found officer William Lozano guilty.

What changed during the 1980s was not police-community relations; these had never been good. Instead, what the decade brought was more immediate, violent, and widespread outrage among blacks in response to incidents perceived as severely unjust. The 1980s also brought an increasing tendency to portray social conflict in Miami in ethnic terms. Police officers in Dade County had been accused of brutality against blacks for decades, but as time passed observers were quick to note that "this time the policeman doing the shooting was a Cuban" (Rieff 1987a, 178). Similarly, all-white juries had been returning dubious verdicts for many years, but as the ethnic composition of jury pools diversified, so did the politics of jury selection. Blacks in Dade County had also rioted on several occasions since the 1960s, but in the 1980s reports on the causes and consequences of civil disturbances in the black community focused less on jobs, housing, or inequality and more on the immigrant influx and relations among the various ethnic groups now residing in Miami.

Although the Anglo community in Miami did not riot in the streets during the 1980s, they did express a growing dissatisfaction with many of the changes sweeping through their communities. In 1980 a group of disgruntled non-Latin white residents organized a petition drive to place on the ballot a referendum that would prohibit "the expenditure of any county funds for the purpose of utilizing any language other than English or any culture other than that of the United States." The "anti-bilingualism ordinance" passed with 71 percent of the non-Latin white vote and 44 percent of the black vote. This marked, according to some, "the first shot in the 'language wars' of the 1980s that would be fought in a number of states in addition to Florida" (Boswell and Curtis 1991, 156).

In 1988 this same group of residents, the Citizens of Dade United, worked diligently in a statewide effort to declare English the official language in Florida. If the widespread support for these measures left any doubt about the local mood, a 1980 public opinion survey in Miami did not: 61 percent of the non-Latin whites and 58 percent of blacks disagreed with the statement, "The Latin influence has helped this country's economy and made it a more enjoyable place to live" ("Public Opinion" 1980). Three years later another public opinion survey in Dade County reported that 42 percent of non-Latin whites surveyed and 49 percent of blacks agreed with the statement, "There are too many Cuban Americans in Dade County." Interestingly, however, 42 percent of Cuban Americans also agreed with the statement ("Local Attitudes" 1983).

Various issues and events converged during the 1980s to place the Cuban community in Miami on the defensive. Explanations for the riots frequently cited the economic hardships blacks in Miami allegedly had suffered as a result of Hispanic immigration. The language issue was indicative of an increasingly aggressive posture among Dade County's Anglo community, as were bumper stickers such as those that read, "Will the Last American Leaving Miami Please Bring the Flag!" The Mariel boatlift further aggravated tensions, and the negative publicity focused on this group of refugees threatened to stigmatize Miami's Cuban community as a whole.

Cuban American leaders reacted quickly, drawing on their acquired social, political, and economic capital to mobilize what they viewed as a necessary counteroffensive. It was during the 1980s that the Cuban American National Foundation (CANF) was formed to act as a powerful lobbying group for the Cuban American community and Facts About Cuban Exiles (FACE) was organized to combat anti-Cuban stereotypes. Similarly, the anti-bilingual referendum served to renew the activism of the Spanish American League Against Discrimination (SALAD), initially organized in 1974 to study discrimination in the public school system. As prominent SALAD member and former county manager Sergio Pereira stated, "We think we've been taken in because our English is flawless, because we dress nice. Well the ordinance proved that we [Cubans] have not really been accepted yet, that there is still a lot of work for us to do. Like I tell my friends in Key Biscayne—just because you belong to the yacht club doesn't mean you belong to the system" (Balmaseda 1981, 1C).

The Cubans in Miami were not the only ones struggling to protect their image during the 1980s. Miami's reputation as the "American Riviera," a reputation that had served the city well, appeared forever changed: "Suddenly, so far as many people in other parts of the country were concerned, and for many people in south Florida, too, it was clear what Miami was— the place where the American dream had turned into a nightmare" (Allman 1987, 11).

CITY OF THE FUTURE: MIAMI IN THE 1990s

Leaders from each of the city's ethnic groups are anxious to dispel the myth of Miami as a dangerous city, prone to persistent social chaos. They prefer instead to portray Miami as a young and vibrant city that has con- *perhaps* fronted and survived numerous problems with which the rest of the country is only beginning to grapple. T. D. Allman's (1987) depiction of Miami as the "city of the future" is echoed frequently in discussions with the city's elite. One very active Cuban American community leader explained that he preferred to view the 1980s as a "decade of awareness, cultural awareness" instead of as a "Paradise Lost" (interview, 30 September 1992). Similarly, when the *Herald*'s publisher, David Lawrence, invited Ross Perot to hold his convention in Miami, he wrote:

Dear Mr. Perot: If you're looking for something different and something significant, Mr. Perot, come to Greater Miami. Come see the face of the future of America. . . . What is happening here today previews our nation entering the next century. The challenges that the next president will face nationwide—economic stagnation, immigration, an increasingly diverse population, racial unrest, health care, the homeless, the quality of education—all are faced here today. If we in Greater Miami can meet our challenges, and we can, then we could serve as an example for the rest of this country. (Lawrence 1992a)

Miami's near obsession with image was particularly evident as the city prepared to host the 1994 Summit of the Americas. Arthur Teele Jr., chairman of the Dade County Commission, explained: "Very few communities ever have an opportunity to redefine their image. . . . For too long, the negative connotation of 'Miami Vice' has plagued our city." In reference to the many presummit business conferences, the deployment of more than two thousand volunteers at information booths, and the expenditure of $15 million in landscaping and road improvements, Teele explained: "We want Miami to look like the Garden of Eden before the apple." In announcing why Miami was picked as the site of the summit, President Clinton himself praised the city's efforts "to build a genuine multicultural, multiracial society that would be at the crossroads of the Americas and, therefore, at the forefront of the future" (Navarro 1994b).

The extent to which Miami constitutes a bellwether of social, political, and economic trends nationwide remains to be seen, as does the extent to which the city has successfully overcome its many challenges. Meanwhile, with the exception of a major race riot, the actors, events, and issues that characterized life in Miami during the 1980s persisted into the following decade. The non-Latin white population in Dade County continued to decline, constituting only 30 percent of the county's total population in 1990. The percentage of blacks was 19 percent, and the Hispanic population had grown to make up 49 percent of the county's population (U.S. Bureau of the Census 1990). The population of foreign-born residents in Dade County not only increased but also diversified. The percentage of Dade County's Hispanics who were of Cuban origin had declined from 83 percent in 1970 to 66 percent in 1990. Nicaraguans, an estimated 150,000 of whom arrived in Miami during the 1980s, had become Dade's second largest Hispanic nationality group by 1990 (Boswell and Curtis 1991, 148).

Large numbers of other Hispanic immigrants continued to arrive from countries throughout South America, and the political and economic situations in both Cuba and Haiti during the early 1990s seemed to guarantee that the flow of refugees from both countries would not soon cease. In 1991 the U.S. Coast Guard picked up 2,203 Cuban rafters who were attempting to cross the Florida Straits, and by October 1992 the number of Cubans rescued had already passed the previous year's record (Weston 1992). By the end of 1992, media headlines were warning of the hundreds of boats being built in Haiti as Haitians readied themselves for a mass exodus following President Clinton's inauguration.[10] In 1993, 3,656 Cuban rafters were rescued at sea, and by July 1994 the previous year's record had already been surpassed, with a total of 4,059 refugees picked up by the U.S. Coast Guard in the Florida Straits (Fiagome 1994b).

The economic effects of the 1980 recession continued to ripple through Miami in the 1990s, but so, too, did the benefits of globalization. In 1992 Ricardo Petrella, director of the Forecasting and Assessment of Science and Technology Division of the European Community, listed Miami as one of twenty metropolitan areas that forms a "high-tech archipelago of affluent, hyper developed city-regions" in the world system (Petrella 1992). Foreign trade in Miami increased 13 percent in 1991, to $21.6 billion. This far outpaced the nation's growth, with exports from South Florida rising three times as fast as overall U.S. exports in 1991 (Bussey 1992c; Lamensdorf 1992). At the same time, however, the closure of Pan Am World Airways, Eastern Airlines, the SouthEast Bank, and Jordan Marsh had a devastating impact on employment in Dade County. And the city of Miami was reported to have the fourth highest poverty rate of large cities in the United States and one of the worst homeless problems in the nation (Goldfarb 1992; Kirby 1992).

On the political front, the 1990s saw the Non-Group—still primarily representative of Anglo business interests in Dade County—joined by Miami's New Group and La Mesa Rotunda (Roundtable). The New Group, formed in 1991 to improve the political and economic standing of Dade's blacks, was described as "much like the old-guard Non Group that the New Miami Group fashioned its name after" (Due 1992). Similarly, La Mesa Rotunda represented the business and civic interests of the Latin community in Dade County. Whether either of the two latter groups represented the same level of influence or power as did the first is questionable, but the traditional distribution of power and prestige in Miami was changing. Those challenging the status quo scored what was considered to be a significant victory when federal court judge Donald Graham ruled in favor of the plaintiffs in the *Meeks* v. *Dade County* Voting Rights case.

On 14 August 1992 Dade County's thirty-year-old metropolitan form of government was declared unconstitutional, and aspiring leaders from various groups readied themselves for a new era in Miami politics. Through the early 1990s the county commission continued to be dominated by Dade's shrinking white population. Blacks and Hispanics made up 70 percent of the population but held only one seat each on the nine-member commission. In April 1993 elections were held under the new system of single-member districts. Hispanic candidates captured six of the thirteen seats, blacks won four, and the remaining three went to non-Latin whites. One black activist triumphantly declared: "In South Florida as in South Africa, minority rule is over" (Filkins 1992a).

Relations between the Cuban community in Miami and the *Miami Herald,* which was still widely perceived to be an organ of the Anglo establishment, had worsened. The CANF and other exile organizations continued to accuse the *Herald* of "unjust harassment," "distortions," and "disinformation," and in January 1991 they launched a bitter campaign against the newspaper that included prominent advertisements on city busses that read, in Spanish, "Yo no creo en el Herald" [I don't believe the *Herald*] (Rohter 1991). In one particularly vitriolic episode on Spanish-language radio CANF president Jorge Mas Canosa stated: "The *Miami Herald* is the most powerful institution in the state of Florida. And these are unscrupulous people, people who chop off heads, destroy people, families, put people in jail . . . create an atmosphere to harm certain people" (Lawrence 1992b).

In 1993, four years since Miami's most recent major riot, few were willing to state that ethnic relations had improved. When asked whether ethnic hostility in Miami had increased, decreased, or stayed the same since the early 1980s, only nine of the sixty people interviewed for this study believed that tensions among Dade County's various ethnic and racial groups had decreased *(see fig. 2).* In spite of what appeared to be relative calm in the streets, the incident that had sparked the last upheaval had yet to be settled. A Dade County jury had found Officer William Lozano guilty of manslaughter in December 1989. In June 1991 an appellate court had ordered a new trial based on evidence that the jury had been unable to render a fair verdict for fear of inciting a riot. The location of the trial had been moved several times as other cities in Florida had attempted to avoid the type of controversy that led to violent explosion in Los Angeles in 1992 and had wreaked havoc in Miami on numerous occasions (Hamalludin 1992; Steinback 1992).[11] When asked about the potential for violence in Miami should Lozano be acquitted, one high-ranking black Miami police officer responded: "There are people stock-piling weapons as we speak" (interview, 28 September 1992). Similarly, after hearing UCLA Professor

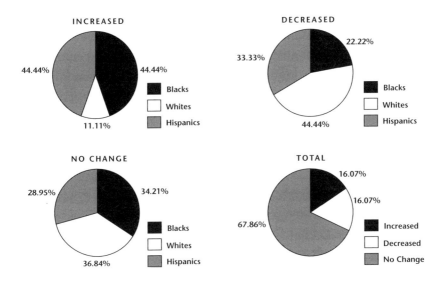

Figure 2. Summary of responses to interview question #3: Since 1980, has ethnic hostility in Miami increased, decreased, or stayed the same?

James Johnson deliver a speech entitled "Los Angeles: The Implications for Miami," Florida International University professor and prominent African American community leader Marvin Dunn responded, "I feel saddened by this discussion. You could substitute Miami for L.A. and Cubans for Koreans." He went on to predict that in Miami "we will have yet another trial by fire" (Hancock 1992b).[12]

Although some individuals warned of a potential for further violence in Dade County, other leaders, particularly within the black community, insisted that the pattern of black protest in Miami had changed. The Reverend J. C. Wise, of the African American Council of Christian Clergy, said that "Miami has matured. We have come to realize that rioting does not solve our problems. Neither does looting, nor burning our homes, nor people losing their lives. We have demonstrated that there is a better way and that is the silent riot" (St. Paul 1992). The Reverend Wise's statement refers to the black boycott of Miami's tourism industry, or the "Quiet Riot," organized in response to the official snubbing of South African leader Nelson Mandela during his visit to Miami in June 1990. The Cuban community was outraged by Mandela's friendly association with the Castro regime.

When elected officials in Dade County, many of whom were Cuban American, refused to formally welcome the South African leader, blacks in Miami responded with equal rage.

The snub of Mandela and the subsequent boycott were widely perceived as another in a long line of confrontations that pitted Latin immigrants against Miami's disenfranchised black community. However accurate this perception may be at one level, it overlooks other significant social and political dimensions of the conflict. Cuban Americans insisted, for example, that the issue was not a racial issue but an ideological one: they respected Mandela as the leader of an important struggle for human rights but were strongly opposed to his association with Castro and the communist regime in Cuba. With regard to the city's decision to rescind a proclamation welcoming Mandela, Miami City Commissioner Victor De Yurre explained: "We support every person who is fighting for liberty and rights, but when persons are so wrong in their stances, as is Mandela when he says he supports the ideas of Fidel Castro . . . for our own self respect we have to withdraw our support" ("Mandela Remarks" 1990).

To view the Mandela controversy purely in terms of blacks versus Hispanics also obscures the extent to which the subsequent black tourism boycott quickly developed into a potent political tool for Miami's black community. To the initial demand for an apology to Mandela was quickly added the call for an investigation into a recent incident of police brutality against Haitian immigrants, a review of U.S. immigration, and substantial reforms in Dade's tourism industry to allow increased employment and business opportunities for blacks (Rowe 1990).

These demands indicate not only a shift in the nature of black protest but also an expansion of black ethnic discourse to include issues and concerns not traditionally considered part of the agenda, in particular those concerning Haitians. After a decade of tense relations between African Americans and Haitian immigrants in Dade County, the 1990s brought to the forefront of Miami politics various issues around which the two groups could unite. The snubbing of Mandela was one such issue; the U.S. government's policy toward Haitian refugees was another. In the past black Americans in Miami had joined whites in expressing resentment toward the Haitian influx. By the early 1990s, however, the inherent contradic-

tions and racist implications of U.S. immigration policy grew quite pronounced. The numbers of both Cubans and Haitians crossing the Florida
Strait had increased; but whereas the Cubans were being granted immediate political refugee status and all the benefits it bestows, the Haitians were
being repatriated without a hearing (Marquis 1992). The demands of the
Boycott Miami Now committee reveal an attempt by African Americans to
forge greater solidarity with the Haitian community in Miami, as does the
increased activism of black leaders in Dade County with regard to federal
immigration policy toward Haiti.[13]

THE TRI-ETHNIC FALLACY

Despite the numerous intricacies and complexities of the boycott and
related controversies, the tendency to view social reality in ethnic terms
has become nearly universal in Miami, and the "tri-ethnic" approach to
social, political, and economic analyses of Miami predominates. It had
become clear by the 1990s, however, that the tri-ethnic framework is a
gross simplification of very diverse social groupings. A variety of issues and
events demonstrates that the categories "black," "white," and "Hispanic"
can themselves be meaningless for understanding or predicting human
behavior. As Marvin Dunn explained with regard to Miami's black "community," "There are many shades of black in Miami. There are ethnic, economic, religious, political and regional shades of black. Given this diversity
among blacks in South Florida, there is really no such thing as 'the black
Community' of Dade County. Indeed, except for the commonalty of skin
color, blacks in Dade County may be as different among themselves as they
are from the whites and browns who have enveloped them" (Dunn forthcoming).

In addition to being culturally or even economically different, blacks in
Miami are also divided on significant local political issues. The black leaders who filed suit against the county's at-large electoral system did so on
behalf of the black community as a whole. There were, however, voices of
dissent among other black leaders who did not support the change to single-member districts. One black community leader and former county
commissioner felt that the proposed changes would "make the community
more divided. . . . Miami is unique. It will only cause more problems if you

do this in Miami—more war-like politics. The Cubans will take everything for their communities, and the Anglos will too. There will be nothing left for blacks" (interview, 27 July 1992). Another black community activist and business person opposed to the lawsuit explained: "It will backfire. Blacks are individualistic, more open-minded, and will listen to candidates black or white. Latins will only vote for you if there is not another Latin running" (interview, 19 June 1992).

The boycott had widespread support among blacks in Miami and elsewhere, but there were also many who disagreed with the approach and the principle upon which it was founded. One black business owner and local activist explained: "I have not had a lot of involvement in the boycott; it may have had some impact but should have been handled differently. They should have said 'Buy Black' instead of 'Boycott Miami.'" In a statement that reflected the potential for additional cleavages along gender lines, this same respondent, a black female, also remarked: "I am not a feminist, but men have tremendous egos, and the boycott is being run by men. It is not very representative" (interview, 19 June 1992).

Similar divisions exist among Hispanics. The Hispanic population in Miami is made up òf an array of national-origin groups, socioeconomic classes, races, and religions. Dade County is home, for example, to an estimated 150,000 Nicaraguans—the largest concentration in the United States (Navarro 1994a). Many of these different groups and individuals share little cultural commonalty beyond language, and some openly reject the "Hispanic" label. Take, for example, the popular Cuban American bumper sticker that reads "No Me Digas Hispano, Soy Cubano" [Don't call me Hispanic, I'm Cuban]. Even the Cuban community itself, however, is very fragmented. In Miami there are old Cubans and young Cubans, Cubans who fought in the Sierra Maestra and Cubans who have never been to Cuba. Dade County is home to black Cubans, white Cubans, Catholic Cubans, Jewish Cubans, Cuban Democrats, and Cuban Republicans. Some of the potential social and political implications of this diversity became obvious in the wake of the Mariel boatlift. As one high-ranking Cuban American county official explained, "Tensions got worse in Miami after Mariel. Even within the Cuban community we did not see eye to eye. When that whole thing first started, I was proud to see how we [Cubans] all worked together—the support among families and neighbors; but when we realized what Castro had done, what he had sent us, it all fell apart" (interview, 24 September 1992).

The established Cubans in Miami became some of the harshest critics of the new arrivals, fearing that the "Marielitos" would tarnish their hard-earned reputation as productive members of American society. One Cuban American city official stated: "Mariel destroyed the image of Cubans in the United States and, in passing, destroyed the image of Miami itself for tourism. The marielitos are mostly black and mulattoes of a color that I never saw or believed existed in Cuba. They don't have social networks; they roam the streets desperate to return to Cuba. There will be two hundred more plane kidnappings" (quoted in Portes and Stepick 1993, 21).

The Cuban refugees who arrived in 1980 were different in some respects from earlier groups. They tended to come from slightly lower socioeconomic and educational backgrounds, and 40 percent, or approximately fifty thousand, were black (Dixon 1982). Despite its pervasiveness, however, the image of this group as mental patients, hardened criminals, homosexuals, and "scum" was flawed. Although many had served time in Cuban jails and a small number did end up in U.S. prisons, the majority quickly and quietly adjusted to their new surroundings. By the 1990s the stigma of Mariel was fading rapidly (Boswell and Curtis 1991, 155).

Because the heterogeneity of the non-Latin white population in Miami is widely accepted, the tendency to assume shared cultural or political norms and behaviors among this group is much less pronounced than the tendency to make the same assumption about other groups. The president of the local B'nai B'rith Anti-Defamation League made an interesting point, however, when, after cautioning that "the tri-ethnic formula is totally useless," he went on to illustrate the potential irony of ethnic categorization by asking, "Where but in Miami can a guy with a name like Teitelbaum be classified as an Anglo?" (interview, 6 July 1992).[14]

CONCLUSION

Whether one accepts the validity of the metaphors "Magic City" and "Paradise Lost" or the categories "black," "white" and "Hispanic," the Miami of the 1990s was, without question, different from the Miami of the

1950s. Massive waves of immigration transformed Dade from a county with a population that was only 4 percent Latin in 1950 to one in which 57 percent of the residents spoke a language other than English in the home in 1990 (U.S. Bureau of the Census 1990). Similarly, Dade's economy grew from one that depended primarily on seasonal tourism to a bustling center of international trade and commerce. The political system also changed gradually, and by the 1990s there was evidence of significant gain by groups outside the traditional power elite.

Simultaneous changes were taking place within individual groups. Cubans in Miami evolved from an exile community focused on returning home to a immigrant group intent on adapting to its new surroundings and then to a substantial player in the social, political, and economic establishment. Blacks in Miami, who were described as apathetic prior to the 1960s, appeared to be anything but apathetic during the riots, and by the 1990s they had effectively mobilized a peaceful campaign against the city that forced local leaders to respond. The percentage of black registered voters in Dade County increased steadily after the late 1960s, as did the black voter turnout. In 1990 blacks made up 18.6 percent of registered voters in Dade County, and the 1992 elections witnessed a record turnout of black voters. Analysts theorized that redistricting had been a motivating factor and predicted an end to political apathy in the black community (St. Paul 1992).

Dade County's non-Latin white community has in many respects, changed from a majority voice to a minority one. Some have reluctantly accepted the change or left peacefully, others have waged a fierce battle against what they perceive as an unwelcome invasion, and still others have openly embraced the advantages that come with living in a multicultural, high-tech, global city. Miami's recovery from a "Paradise Lost" is still not complete. Economic woes persist, and few local leaders express optimism about the present level of ethnic tension. If Miami is indeed the "city of the future," much of that future remains uncertain.

This uncertainty was amplified after August 1992, when Dade County became the site of what was termed the worst natural disaster in U.S. history. Hurricane Andrew ripped violently through southern Dade County, causing an estimated $20 billion in damages (Miami Herald 1992). Immediately forecasters began to predict the length and likelihood of economic recovery in Dade County, and demographers recalculated estimated population trends. Among professional analysts and observers alike, the tri-ethnic framework was again to predominate: Would the hurricane increase the rate of white flight from Dade County? How would the ethnic composition of neighboring Broward County be affected as hurricane victims from all ethnic groups migrated north? In what ways did the level of destruction and recovery response vary by the ethnic and racial composition of individual neighborhoods?

As experts debated these questions, the newspapers were filled with both heartwarming stories about neighbors helping neighbors regardless of color or creed and unsettling headlines such as the one that appeared in the *Miami Times* on 10 September 1992, "Hurricane Andrew Did Not Blow Away the Racists in Our Midst." The article was written by the attorney H. T. Smith, who claimed that "Hurricane Andrew destroyed thousands of homes but it didn't put a dent in the pervasive housing discrimination in Greater Miami." Complaints of racial and ethnic discrimination in the aftermath of Andrew became so widespread that the U.S. Justice Department sent attorneys from Washington to field grievances from minorities seeking rental housing (Smith 1992b).

The role of power and politics does not diminish in times of crisis; it may become even more pronounced. Speaking before crowds in Liberty City just days after the storm, Jesse Jackson urged blacks to fight for their share of federal relief funds, cautioning that "those who have the power get their power turned on first" (Martin 1992). Similarly, the ongoing power struggle between Miami's non-Latin white civic and business elite and the ascendant minority leadership surfaced during the formation of a committee to oversee Dade County's rebuilding effort. President Bush appointed Alvah Chapman, former chief executive officer of Knight-Ridder and a founding member of the Non-Group, to head an organization called We Will Rebuild. Local elected officials began to complain not long after Chapman had assembled his team. Arthur Teele, the only black member of the Dade County Commission, stated, "It seems to me the leadership comes from one narrow organization—the Non Group. I see that as almost sinister" (Tanfani and May 1992).

The nature of power and politics in Miami has changed, but ethnic divisions persist. Despite dramatic shifts in the population, the economic base, and the political environment, ethnicity as a form of individual and group identity has not diminished and is perhaps becoming more prominent. The apparent resilience of what is often believed to be a primitive, or *premodern,* form of social attachment in *postmodern* Miami invites further inquiry. What must be examined, however, is how ethnic ties and ethnic tension in Miami are not only the product but also part of the process of social, political, and economic change.

3

Miami vs. LA as post modern cities.

— the power structure is not this static, stiid entity — it is not a coherent whole to be overtaken (Foucault) but one to be re-imagined

THE DISCOURSE OF DISPLACEMENT

Constructing the Threat of an Immigrant Takeover

In Miami, for the first time in American history, a foreign culture and a foreign language have come to dominate a major American city. The Miami Hispanics do not intend to join the English-speaking American culture. On the contrary, they have every intention of widening and expanding their sphere of influence in Dade County and South Florida.

John Ney, *Miami Today*

— they want to intermingle, intermix, not to dominate — they, as foreign immigrants, want to participate in the power structure

— coming in from the outside.

The United States is one of the few countries in the modern world that has not experienced an armed invasion of foreign troops on national soil. At several points in history, however, the threat of invasion has figured prominently in U.S. public discourse. Most commonly feared by Americans is not an invasion of armored tanks but one of human refugees, individuals and groups who come not to overthrow the United States but to avail themselves of what they perceive as a level of economic, political, or social freedom superior to that in the country from which they come.

Despite the symbolic invitation extended by the open arms of the Statue of Liberty, U.S. citizens—the overwhelming majority of whom are themselves immigrants or descendants of immigrants—have a long history of viewing the world's tired, hungry, and poor as at best a burden and at worst a veritable invasion that threatens the moral fabric of U.S. society. A statement issued in 1958 by the son of Irish Catholic immigrants illustrates the point well: "The cold hard truth . . . is that today, as never before, untold millions are storming our gates for admission. Those gates are cracking under the strain. The cold, hard fact is, too . . . that this nation is the last hope of Western Civilization, and if this oasis of the world shall be overrun, perverted, contaminated, or destroyed, then the last flickering light of humanity will be extinguished" (Bilderback 1989, 223).

Nativist concerns in the United States have included the loss of jobs to immigrant workers, a potential strain on an already overburdened social welfare system, and the penetration of cultural practices, including language, that may challenge the hegemony of the status quo. Neither the threat nor the enemy to which it is attributed has remained constant. In the late 1800s immigrants were accused of subverting American [i.e., Protestant] religious values. In the 1920s many Americans believed that immigration posed a threat of irreparable genetic damage to the native population through the infusion of inferior genes. Today's restrictionist arguments center primarily on economic concerns and the inability of the United States to absorb any more newcomers (Bilderback 1989, 226). In addition to shifts in the nature of the perceived threat posed by immigration, the status and impact of particular immigrant groups is often reinterpreted over time. As Loy Bilderback points out, "In American history, immigrants past are paragons, immigrants present are greenhorns who will just never fit in, and immigrants future may well be a menace to all we hold dear" (223).

An overview of the historical construction and reconstruction of immigration to the United States reveals a variety of problems, crises, enemies, and threats. Not only does the specific content of the public discourse on immigration fluctuate but the claims that provide that content are seldom supported by sound empirical evidence. Their fluidity or shaky empirical grounding notwithstanding, this configuration of problems and threats constitutes a powerful arsenal in the public resistance against an immigrant takeover. This chapter examines the social and political construction of the immigrant threat in Miami. Some analysts have called attention to the role that perception plays in the tense relations between different ethnic groups in Miami, but little attempt has been made to unravel the processes that translate private perceptions into public problems. As the U.S. city with the largest percentage of immigrants, Miami provides an ideal laboratory for exploring these issues. Aside from the xenophobic alarm sounded in John Ney's essay *Miami Today—The U.S. Tomorrow* (1989) he may well be correct in portraying Miami as a bellwether of future social relations throughout the United States and the world (Ney 1989).

Miami did not become a primary point of entry for foreign immigrants into the United States until the Cuban refugees began to arrive in large numbers during the early 1960s. Talk of an "invasion" surfaced almost immediately and has been an element of public discourse in Miami ever since. This discourse defines a social reality in which Cuban immigrants, as well as other newcomers from throughout Latin America and the Caribbean, are responsible for a variety of Miami's social, political, and economic ills. The threat of a takeover in Miami relies heavily upon the claim that Hispanic immigrants have displaced native workers, and particularly African Americans, in Miami's labor market. Labor market analyses, however, do not support the job displacement thesis, and there are competing claims that the net economic impact of immigration on Miami has been positive.

Rather than attempting to settle definitively the job displacement debate, this chapter addresses how the emergence of claims such as job displacement become widely accepted independently of their basis in fact. The approach builds on the theoretical and methodological insights of a body of literature, introduced in chapter 1, that focuses not on the objective makeup of problems themselves but on the role of individual leaders, local officials, politicians, and the media in constructing problems, crises, enemies, and threats. Also explored are the various functions fulfilled by this "claims-making activity," including the creation and maintenance of a public discourse that serves to perpetuate the existing configuration of social, political, and economic power in Miami.

CLAIMS-MAKING ACTIVITY IN MIAMI: 1960 TO 1990

A WEARY WELCOME

Concern over the Cuban "invasion" surfaced among Miami residents as soon as the first refugees began to arrive. On 2 December 1960 the *Miami Herald* published a story headlined "Jobless Citizens Resent Cuban Hiring But Officials Claim No Competition." The head of the commercial division of the Florida State Employment Service, D'Arey O'Meara, claimed to have received vague reports about refugees replacing American workers in factories that were becoming sweatshops. According to O'Meara, "This kind of talk is causing a lot of resentment, but I know of no such instances." The article also reported that the Cuban Refugee Employment Center had received angry telephone calls and letters from many of the 20,500 American citizens who were seeking jobs in an already depressed Greater Miami economy ("Jobless Citizens" 1960).

In an October 1961 interview with the *Miami Herald,* black labor leader Charles Lockhart stated that job displacement by Cubans had been considerable. He admitted having no official statistics but claimed that unemployment among tenants in the area's largest agency for housing blacks had risen 15–20 percent. "This is a real problem, not just an emotional thing with Negroes," he said. "It is a fact that Negro workers are being displaced by Cubans" ("Negroes Resent" 1961). The television documentary "Crisis Amigo" aired the same year, and Miami news commentator Wayne Farris stated that "the huge Cuban labor supply has sharply reduced the job opportunities of Dade's 122,000 Negroes, 70 percent of whom are unskilled. Twenty percent are unemployed and seeking relief" (U.S. Senate 1961, 183).

Media reports indicate that Miamians did experience some initial excitement at being a shore of freedom for asylum-seeking Cubans, but that excitement quickly faded. In 1962 one article reported that "prejudices are developing despite the Cubans' effort to adjust . . . and the community relations experts say Miami is a powder keg with an exposed fuse" ("Miami Cools" 1962, 12). Signs reading "Aquí Se Habla Ingles" [English is spoken here] indicated a growing resentment among local residents, as did quotations such as the one that appeared in the May 1962 issue of *Kiwanis Magazine:* "They [Cubans] leer at girls, spit in the streets, and work for slave wages that depress Miami's already shaky wage scale" ("Miami Cools" 1962, 12).

In 1963 *Ebony Magazine* published an article entitled "Miami's Cuban Refugee Crisis: Invasion of 100,000 Exiles Creates Grave Problems for Hard Pressed Negro Laborers." The article detailed a variety of hardships suffered by blacks as a result of the Cuban influx, including (1) widespread loss of formerly "Negro" jobs; (2) loss of some homes by blacks; (3) eviction of black tenants from homes and apartments; (4) a sharp increase in crime among Miami's blacks; (5) a marked increase in gambling by blacks; and (6) a noticeable reduction in receipts of black-owned businesses (Morrison 1963, 98).

The article quoted the union manager Robert Gladnick, who said that "since the [dress goods] industry expanded, between 1,000 and 1,500 new jobs were created and they all went to Cubans. The arrival of the Cubans definitely stopped the progress of the Negroes in the industry. The Negroes were about to make a breakthrough as sewers when the Cubans came in" (98). Although the article emphasized that "over 12,000 Negroes in the county have lost jobs since the Cuban migration began" and that "anti-Cuban feeling has been rising noticeably during the last twelve months," it pointed to "a surprising lack of bitterness" among blacks and said that "few Negroes can be found who will state categorically that they were displaced from jobs by refugees" (98).

Next to quotations by African American leaders such as newspaperman and local politician C. Gaylord Rolle, who proclaimed that "the coming of the Cubans has accentuated the crisis of Miami's Negro population," were statements by others, such as the Reverend Theodore Gibson, president of the Miami NAACP, who claimed that "Cubans have helped the Negroes of Miami by coming here. There are places where Negroes can now go where they couldn't go before. Cubans have opened certain avenues and opportunities for Negroes" (97).

Cubans were not the only refugees portrayed as "invading" Miami in the early 1960s. In September 1963 a boatload of twenty-five Haitians landed on South Florida's shore only to endure a lengthy and unsuccessful campaign for political asylum. The jobs problem was cited frequently by those opposed to admitting the Haitian refugees. Edward Kerr, of the Florida State Employment Service, explained that there were thousands of unemployed, unskilled workers in the area and that admission of the Haitians in large numbers would make the situation even more critical. Kerr claimed to have no available figures on the number of unemployed unskilled workers, but he said that he believed it was considerable and included a large proportion of blacks. The *Miami News* reported that

"Negroes of the Miami area have already complained bitterly that the huge Cuban refugee influx has cost them jobs" ("Jobs Problem" 1963).

In 1965 widespread concern resurfaced as Miami prepared for a large Cuban influx that would bring an estimated five thousand refugees per month. The *Miami Herald* ran several articles about the anticipated arrival, reporting that the most outspoken concerns were voiced by labor leaders and black civil rights leaders. In an article by Juanita Greene entitled "Miami Fears Effects of Cuban Influx," Edward Stephenson, president of the Dade County Federation of Labor, was quoted as asking, "What will be the impact on employment here? Will our working citizens again find that their jobs are being taken by outsiders willing to work at cut rate wages?" And J. O. Brown, coordinator of the Congress on Racial Equality (CORE), commented, "We just don't have the facilities here to absorb the new refugees. And we don't want to see happen again what happened before—the displacement of our own native citizens in jobs."

The president of the local chapter of the NAACP, Donald Wheeler Jones, expressed similar concerns when he stated, "It is a fair assumption that the greater influx will result in greater economic pressures on the largely unskilled Negro community. This could lead to some difficulties." However, both Brown and Jones acknowledged that they had observed no tension between the black and Cuban communities and did not expect any in the future. The Department of Health, Education and Welfare, which administered the refugee program, reported that unemployment in Greater Miami had actually gone down despite the large Cuban population (Greene 1965a).

During the same week that Greene's article appeared in the *Miami Herald*, the *Miami News* reported: "More Cubans are about to enter our town and, as we experienced in the first influx, there are fears; fears of lost jobs, fears of dropping real estate values. . . . Miamians' fears of the Cuban 'invasion' have been expressed in letters to the editor; and in phone calls to the *Miami News*" ("More Cubans" 1965). One shop operator and native Miamian exclaimed, "What happens when a Cuban refugee gets off the boat? He asks where the welfare office is, that's what. You don't hear them ask where the employment office is." And an Anglo motel operator in Miami complained, "We've already got racial trouble enough. The Cubans can only make it worse. When they do go to work, they take over many jobs the Negroes would have. This builds up the pressure" ("Feeling Grows" 1965).

Much of the tension that was brewing between the newcomers and established residents in Miami could be witnessed in the Dade County school system. By September 1962 there were 18,260 children of Cuban refugees enrolled in Dade's schools. In October 1965 the county faced the possible enrollment of several thousand more Cuban schoolchildren in the months to come. Just prior to local elections in November 1965, school officials reported receiving numerous angry letters and telephone calls from voters who intended to oppose a requested millage because they did not want to spend local money educating Cuban children ("Why School Chief" 1965).

The first planeload of Cuban refugees arriving under the federally arranged airlift program landed in Miami in early December 1965. That same week the *Miami Herald* began a series of articles examining the effect of this influx on the city's economy, its people, and its customs. The articles covered various points of potential conflict between the refugees and the native population but focused most specifically on the issue of jobs and welfare. It detailed the concerns and complaints of local residents as well as the demands by local leaders, government agencies, and church groups that the federal government share the fiscal and administrative burden being placed on Miami as a result of the refugee influx. In one article, *Herald* staff writer Juanita Greene pointed out that "it is generally acknowledged that many Cubans are now working at jobs that would be held by Americans if the refugees had stayed home. But nobody can say how many. Nor is it known how many new jobs the Cuban influx has generated, or how many of the presently unemployed or underemployed Miamians could have qualified for Cuban-held jobs" (Greene 1965b).

The year 1965 marked a peak in the number of Cuban refugees arriving on Miami's shores. It also marked an apparent peak in the outcry among disgruntled residents. As *Fortune* reported in October 1966, "Ripples of dread passed through Miami as each of the successive waves of refugees hit town . . . loud, anguished cries came from the Negro community and some labor organizations because Cubans were going to work for half the prevailing wages" ("Those Amazing" 1966, 146). A variety of individuals and groups worked diligently to ease the tension between residents and new-comers. The Dade County Community Relations Board secured an additional $60,000 for its budget after Chairman and Episcopal Bishop James Duncan warned of "very deep tensions" that "pose a threat of imminent disaster to our community" (Einstein 1965).

Throughout the remainder of the decade, complaints concerning the Cuban influx continued to surface, but the complexities of the displacement debate grew more pronounced. Critics of the airlift maintained that Miami's economy was not strong enough to withstand a new "assault," but some prominent Miami businessmen and bankers began to argue otherwise. Tully Dunlap, of Riverside Bank, stated flatly: "It's time the other side of the story is told. The Cuban is industrious, aggressive and honest. He definitely is an economic asset to Miami." And William Pallot, president of the Inter-National Bank, said, "Frankly, I've not understood the complaints. If the refugees weren't here, there'd be an overabundance of vacant stores and apartments. Miami would probably be suffering economically if not for them" (Birger 1965).

In a 1965 study of Cubans in the United States, the Reverend William Weedman, of the Southern Baptist Theological Seminary, concluded that "some of the ill feelings of Miami Negroes toward Cubans about jobs has subsided, but there's still some underlying resentment left. . . . The main difference between the two groups is that Cubans have ambition, drive, and hope. The Negro many times feels hopeless and lacks ambition and drive" ("Reverend Studies" 1966). And in November 1966 the vice-president of Florida's AFL-CIO, Art Hallgren, stated that although the AFL-CIO had been "very concerned" when the refugees began arriving in Miami, "the Cubans have adjusted very well." He also believed that an exodus of Cubans back to Cuba could have a strongly adverse effect on the local economy ("Concern over Influx" 1966).

"LEST WASHINGTON FORGET"

Many of the claims that have made up Miami's public discourse about immigration over the last thirty years have been directed at Washington. As early as December 1961 several local leaders from Dade County testified in Washington before the U.S. Senate Subcommittee to Investigate Problems Connected with Refugees and Escapees. During the testimony Dade County Commissioner Arthur Patten warned of rising resentment among blacks because of displacement by Cubans: "The reason they [blacks] are out of work is because the Cubans have their jobs. And as these people begin to mingle together, I am afraid there will be trouble in the not too distant future." And H. Daniel Lang, also a Dade County commissioner, cautioned that it was difficult to measure the impact of the refugee influx on native workers but predicted that "unless the supply of jobs increases in the Miami area, since they are already in short supply, the Cuban refugees will displace even more workers because of the skills they have to offer if they continue to flow into the community" (U.S. Senate 1961, 133).

In March 1963 Congressmen Dante Fascell and Claude Pepper held a series of hearings in Miami to address local concerns over the "Cuban problem" in South Florida. A large and vocal crowd of Miamians attended the hearing. They reportedly clapped approvingly when State Attorney Richard Gerstein stated that a "great percentage of traffic offenses are caused by Spanish-speaking people" and that the refugees had had "an impact on the crime situation." The reaction was similar when County Manager Irving McNayr reported that Cubans were crowding "our own citizens" out of public parks and had cost the county almost half a million dollars in direct expenses at Jackson Memorial Hospital and when Metro Commission Chairman Joe Boyd asked with a sense of extreme urgency, "How many more refugees are going to come?" Speaking on behalf of the black population in Miami, community leader Luther L. Brooks stated that between 12,000 and 15,000 blacks had left Dade County because of the depressed economic situation; and James Whitehead, of the Greater Miami Urban League, urged the congressmen to collect authentic figures on "the number of Cubans here, the number working, and the number of Negro workers displaced by Cubans" (Greene 1963).

The fears and concerns expressed in Miami during the "second wave" of Cuban immigration were also being debated in Washington. In a passionate speech before the House of Representatives, Congressman Dante Fascell demanded congressional hearings on the Cuban crisis in Miami, a limit on the number of Cuban refugees, and adequate screenings. He argued,

"There is a limit to how many refugees Miami can take to its heart and absorb into its economic life" ("Fascell Demands" 1965). In the months that followed, Fascell worked diligently to secure congressional approval for a federal program aimed at easing unemployment among blacks and low-income whites displaced by Cuban refugees. He assured his constituents in South Florida that the program "will do much to correct the inequities and loss of job opportunities caused by the influx of Cuban refugees." Congressman H. R. Gross echoed Fascell's concerns that the new influx would "compound poverty and compound unemployment." He encouraged the House Foreign Affairs Committee to "find out why Castro is interested in getting rid of these people" ("Federal Program Aimed" 1965).

Despite the recognition of various benefits bestowed upon Miami as a result of the Cuban influx, Dade County officials continued to complain that Washington was not doing its part to assist South Florida with the absorption of the refugees. In 1967 County Manager Porter Homer explained that "when the first waves of refugees diminished, federal support of health services dwindled. When the new wave began, the federal support continued to shrink. [The result] is a snowballing displacement of native Americans from the preventative health service intended for them to the point that a major downtown clinic is now 94 percent Cuban everyday" ("Metro Asks Health" 1967).

A *Miami Herald* editorial entitled "Lest Washington Forget about Our Refugees" reminded readers that the Cuban refugees continued to arrive—nine hundred per week—and that "the plus signs of the Cuban influx do not balance out the squeeze that the refugees have put on Dade's schools and welfare facilities. This is a continuing problem and Washington should be constantly reminded of its obligation to pay the bills" ("Lest Washington Forget" 1967).

Shortly after the federal report was released, an editorial in the *Miami Herald* forcefully called upon Washington to end the airlift from Cuba. It charged that the freedom flights actually served to recruit refugees, and it challenged readers to consider the following "facts":

Cuban refugees get greater care than underprivileged U.S. citizens.
In transportation alone, the airlift costs nearly one million dollars a year.

The recent study commissioned by the President to determine causes of last August's riot here cited Negro resentment of special treatment for refugees as a contributing factor.

This expensive program goes on at a time when the needs of American cities are critical. . . . The question is one of priorities. The airlift and Cuban Refugees Program should not stand ahead of the pressing needs of American citizens. ("It's Time to Ground" 1969)

A decade later Miami was again consumed with the threat of invasion when a series of events culminated in the Mariel boatlift of 1980.[1] Many of the grievances that emerged in connection with this influx were directed at the federal government. On 29 April 1980 the *Miami Herald* stated: "Carter administration officials seem afraid to anger Cuban-American voters by demanding an end to the influx, but they don't want to legitimize it by mobilizing Federal assistance. . . . Local resources—particularly housing—already are exhausted, and a potentially ugly backlash is building among non-Hispanics." On 27 June 1980 a *Miami Herald* editorial strongly criticized Carter's handling of the crisis: "The President consciously let the threat of mob reaction intimidate him into ignoring the law and allowing his own policies to be trampled. When the President finally ordered the boatlift halted on May 15, he did so because the Cuban-American community itself had become unhappy over the mental patients and criminals that Fidel Castro had included among the Mariel refugees" (quoted in Portes and Stepick 1993, 24, 26).

In November 1984 the Immigration and Naturalization Service announced that more than 120,000 Mariel refugees without criminal records could begin applying for legal residency in the United States. This was part of a U.S.-Cuban agreement under which 3,000 Mariel criminals and mental patients would be returned to Cuba and those who remained could become U.S. citizens with the unrestricted right to send for husbands, wives, parents, and children still on the island. Not only did many South Florida residents adamantly reject the plan but local officials again turned to Washington, asking, "Who will pay?" R. Ray Goode, a major Miami developer and former county manager, explained that more than "the lunatic fringe" was concerned: "The Federal government must recognize that this is by no means a local problem. It came about as the result of federal policies—or nonpolicies—and they [Washington] must subsidize the cost." Agreeing with Goode, Governor Bob Graham complained that he had not been consulted on the decision to legalize the Marielitos and that Washington still owed Florida governments more than $150 million for local services provided during the boatlift. Graham declared: "Immigration policy is a federal responsibility. Washington must pay the cost" ("South Florida's" 1985, 87).

By 1994 demands for Washington to do its part had reached the level of the federal courts. Florida Governor Lawton Chiles had filed a lawsuit against the federal government charging that Washington owed Florida millions of dollars for services provided by the state to undocumented immigrants. "There are illegal aliens in Florida as a result of federal policy, or an absence of federal policy," said Chiles. "And we're saying the federal government should pick up the bill" (Dillin 1994).

REFUGEES AND RIOTS

Miami experienced its first major race riot in the summer of 1968, another in 1970, and thirteen arguably less destructive disturbances prior to 1979. Immediately following the first civil upheaval few statements directly linked the riots to the influx of Cuban refugees. Yet by the 1980s immigration was being cited as a key factor in almost every analysis of the rioting and social tension in Miami.

The riot of 1968 received a great deal of local media attention and prompted President Lyndon Baines Johnson to commission a study to determine its causes. That report, published in early 1969, concluded that the disturbances in Liberty City had originated out of the accumulated deprivations, discriminations, and frustrations of the black community. The report emphasized that the concerns and conditions in Liberty City were similar to those in urban black communities throughout the United States but had been exacerbated by "special local circumstances" in Miami, specifically "the loss of local jobs by blacks over prior several years to Cuban refugees." The 1968 riot demonstrated the level of anger and frustration among blacks in Miami, but the focus of that discontent was less clear. The federal riot report called attention to the loss of black jobs to Cuban refugees, but when asked about the causes and consequences of the riot, many blacks responded differently. One Liberty City resident interviewed by the *Miami News* explained: "Well, I don't know about that 'loss of local jobs.' There weren't all that many jobs to start with" ("Federal Report" 1969).

Some black leaders in Miami cautiously accepted the job-takeover explanation. Robert Simms, executive director of the Community Relations Board in Dade County, explained: "There has been no clash between Negro 'groups' and Cuban 'groups.' But there certainly has been some real concern among individuals who have been replaced, for one reason or another, by Cubans. I know of a Negro man who was a foreman. When the Cubans began coming in, he was given the job of training one of them. The man he trained was then given his job . . . that man went back on a street corner and told other Negroes what had happened. And bad news travels very fast" ("Federal Report" 1969).

The various reports and analyses that appeared in the months and years following the 1968 riot revealed that the black community in Miami had been suffering many of the same social, political, and economic ills that plagued urban areas throughout the United States and that little had changed since the riot. Miami's blacks lived in substandard housing, could not depend on adequate public services such as garbage collection, and were the bitter victims of "urban renewal" and a variety of other broken promises. In January 1969 *New South Magazine* published a report entitled "Violence in Miami: One More Warning." The report painted a dismal picture of the social conditions in Miami's ghettos. It quoted one affluent and influential black agency executive, who stated flatly: "Nothing has happened since the riot; we're right back where we started. It's certain to happen again. Next time I'm going to put down my attache case and pick up a brick" ("One More Warning" 1969).

After the 1968 riot, the *Miami Herald* invited the Black Brothers for Progress, a group formed during the riot to present demands for change to white government and business leaders, to discuss what had precipitated the riot. The consensus that emerged from the discussion was that the problems that had caused Liberty City to explode not only had not been solved but had gotten worse. Police harassment had increased, but opportunities and services had not. The participants in the discussion com plained of overcrowded housing, filth, lack of jobs and recreational facilities, and lack of concern on the part of public officials. At the top of their list of complaints immediately following the riot, as well as six months later, was harassment of young blacks by Miami police officers ("Black Brothers" 1969).

Race relations in Miami received minimal media attention throughout the 1970s, and the most prominent public discourse with regard to immigration sang the praises of Cuban immigrants as an amazingly entrepreneurial and industrious immigrant group. In 1980, however, when Liberty City exploded in one of the most hostile social rebellions in U.S. history, an enormous amount of attention was again focused on Miami's "melting pot," or what came to be more frequently referred to as "a boiling pot" (Mohl 1986, 51).

The McDuffie riots of 1980 occurred only weeks after 125,000 Mariel refugees landed on Florida's shores. The riot was quickly labeled one of the most violent and destructive race riots in U.S. history; and most of the explanations that surfaced to account for the upheaval drew explicit connections between the riots and the large number of refugees that continued to flow into Dade County. Joan Didion, for example, called attention to the fact that while Liberty City burned, 57,000 newly arrived refugees from the Cuban port of Mariel camped under bleachers at the Orange Bowl (Didion 1987, 42).

Governor Robert Graham immediately created the Governor's Dade County Citizens' Committee to explore the causes of the riot and make necessary recommendations. The committee's report, published on 30 October 1980, listed poverty, unemployment, and underemployment as the leading causes of the upheaval. In the explanation that followed, the committee emphasized the "shock waves" that had impacted upon the community with each new arrival of immigrants: "As many blacks see it, the recent influx of Cuban refugees into the Miami area has exacerbated the jobs problem. Not only has ability to speak Spanish become a primary qualification for a vast number of jobs, but also it has resulted in the replacement of blacks by Cubans, Haitians and other Latins in a wide variety of unskilled jobs. This new wave of refugees consequently places additional pressures on an already fragile job market. As a result, the different racial and ethnic groups are pitted against each other in a scramble for the most marginal jobs in our economy" (*Report of the Governor's* 1980, 14).

In a photographic essay in *Ebony Magazine* entitled "Miami: Roots of Rage," the caption under a particularly dismal photograph read: "The burned out buildings of Overtown are symbolic of the destroyed dreams of many black youth unable to find employment, often because jobs for unskilled workers have gone to immigrants from Latin American countries" (Sleet 1980, 138). Just months after the 1980 riots, in an article titled "The Welcome Wears Thin," *Time Magazine* claimed that "Dade County's blacks fear that Cuban and Haitian refugees will crowd them out of jobs. That resentment helped touch off the riots that rocked Miami in May, killing 18 and causing $100 million worth of damage, although there were no documented attacks against the new Cuban refugees" ("The Welcome" 1980, 9). And in 1981, in a story that officially earned Miami the designation "Paradise Lost," *Time Magazine* wrote: "The blacks are upset by both kinds of Cubans. Stuck on the bottom rung of South Florida's economic ladder, they have always resented the more prosperous Cuban minority. With the arrival of the Marielitos, blacks feared that they would lose out in the scramble for the few low-skill jobs available in the region. Even in Liberty City, where 18 people died in last year's riot, the Latin influence is apparent" ("Paradise" 1981, 31).

Two years after the McDuffie riots the *Economist* reported that little had changed in the lives of Miami blacks "since resentment at their predicament exploded into three days of rage in 1980." According to the *Economist*, "Miami is not a good city in which to be black. . . . Miami has no black business class. . . . Miami has no black political establishment. . . . And, unlike blacks in almost every other American city, they cannot even count on a monopoly of the low-paid, low-grade jobs: Miami's blacks always live in danger of losing their jobs to the latest wave of immigrants off the islands prepared to work for peanuts" ("The Forgotten" 1982, 22).

Miami continued to experience civil disturbances throughout the 1980s. In analyses of the riots and unrest, authors, politicians, journalists, civic leaders, and academicians all continued to call attention to the impact of immigration, and particularly the economic impact of immigration on Miami's black community. In her historical discussion of the racial inequalities facing Miami's blacks, Didion explains: "This had been a familiar enough pattern throughout the South, but something else had happened here. Desegregation had not just come hard and late to South Florida, but it had also coincided, as it had not in other parts of the South, with another disruption of the local status quo, the major Cuban influx, which meant that jobs and services which might have helped awaken an inchoate black community went instead to Cubans" (1987, 47). According to Jan Luytjes, of Florida International University, "Prior to the 1960s you had blacks in all the traditional businesses, just like in any other southern city. But here, just as they were ready to come out, the Cubans arrived and exerted a downward pressure on the blacks" (Porter and Dunn 1984, 195).

In their well-known analysis *The Miami Riot of 1980: Crossing the Bounds,* Bruce Porter and Marvin Dunn provide background information on race relations in Miami, discuss the 1980 riot in detail, and conclude with a final chapter entitled "Some Reasons Why." One of the reasons they give, in a section titled "The Cubans," is the devastating job takeover experienced by blacks: "Many of them middle-class and looking as white as the Anglo population, the new arrivals were considered to be members of a minority group by virtue only of their foreign language. Given this status, however, they succeeded not only in diverting attention from Miami blacks during the crucial integration period, but also, by virtue of their greater social acceptability and entrepreneurial skills, in winning the lion's share of public and private money available for minority economic development" (Porter and Dunn 1984, 195).

Several years later David Rieff, author of *Going to Miami,* used evidence from Porter and Dunn's research on the 1980 riot to proclaim: "Indeed, the riot was without question as anti-Cuban as it was anti-Anglo. Cubans had not only replaced blacks in the jobs they had formerly occupied, they were seen as having unfairly been allowed to take over small businesses in Miami as well." Rieff points to a decrease in black ownership of gas stations in Miami from 1960 to 1979 and an increase in Cuban ownership during that same period. He also cites a higher percentage of small business loans to the Hispanic community as an explanation for the economic displacement of blacks (1987a, 177).

By the end of the decade analysts were linking civil unrest among blacks not only to Cuban immigration but also to the influx of other refugees. In his analysis of the 1989 riots Raymond Mohl called attention to the "200 Nicaraguans pouring into Miami everyday" and the "estimated 100,000 additional Nicaraguans predicted to arrive within the next year." He wrote: "It was hard to escape the contradictions: the blacks were burning down their neighborhoods in despair, but the thousands of newly arrived Nicaraguan refugees pinned their hopes for the future on a new life in Miami" (1990, 38).

THE "TAKEOVER" IS COMPLETE

Well, it is finally over! Roberto Suarez's becoming president of the Miami Herald publishing company kills—once and for all—any chance of Miami's ever returning to its former status as an English-speaking American city located in the U.S.! Shortly, it will be time to begin a death watch over the Herald's English editions. To get a letter printed you'll have to say nice things such as how very enjoyable it is to listen to the 120-decibel level of casual Cuban conversation. Well, I don't need a big pile of El Nuevo Heralds to fall on me—it's time to move on. Maybe I'll go back to the U.S. I still remember some English. I'll get by.

Bob Resnick, *Miami Herald*

Resentment toward the "Latinization" of Miami grew particularly pronounced during the 1980s. The complaints being heard were not just about jobs, nor were they being voiced solely by blacks or labor leaders. The above letter to the *Miami Herald* from Miami Beach resident and activist Bob Resnick exemplifies much of the resentment expressed by non-Latin whites. This resentment was expressed through various forms: an increase in white flight out of Dade County, overwhelming support among Anglos for both anti-bilingual and English-only proposals, and the popularity of bumper stickers such as those that read "Will the last American leaving Miami please bring the flag," "I'm a Native—An Endangered Species," and "One Nation, One Language, One Flag."

The Citizens of Dade United, the group that had spearheaded the anti-bilingual campaign in 1980, campaigned diligently in 1988 to have English declared the official language in the state of Florida.[2] The language issue continued to be a point of tension throughout the 1980s and does not appear to have diminished in the 1990s. In 1992 Arthur Teitelbaum, president of the Anti-Defamation League, referred to the language debate as "a continuing poison in the bloodstream of the community" (interview, 6 July 1992). Many other cities and states are dealing with controversies related to bilingual and multilingual populations, but the language debate in Miami is peculiar in a manner accurately captured by Joan Didion:

> This question of language was curious. The sound of spoken Spanish was common in Miami, but it was also common in Los Angeles, and Houston, . . . What was unusual about Spanish in Miami was not that it was so often spoken, but that it was so often heard: in, say, Los Angeles, Spanish remained a language only barely registered by the Anglo population, the language spoken by the people who worked in the car wash and came to trim the trees and cleared the tables in the restaurants. In Miami Spanish was spoken by the people who ate in the restaurants, and the people who owned the cars and trees. (1987, 63)

Increased complaints about spoken Spanish were accompanied by derogatory allegations about other aspects of Cuban culture and the Cuban American community in Miami. This was particularly true during the Mariel crisis, when Castro's portrayal of these refugees as the "scum" of society was picked up and perpetuated by many in Miami.[3] The image of Mariel refugees as criminals, mentally insane, homosexuals, and drug addicts dissipated during the 1980s, but as recently as October 1992 one prominent non-Latin white local official in Dade County referred to the Mariel boatlift as the time when "Castro flushed his toilets on us" (interview, 9 October 1992).

In 1981 *Newsweek* published a story on the public outcry in Miami surrounding the practice of Santería, a Cuban cult religion brought to the island from Africa by Yoruba slaves. The story reported that "as poor immigrants from Haiti and Cuba have settled in Miami, animal sacrifices associated with several Caribbean religious cults have flourished—raising tensions between the immigrants and natives." It quoted a retired Miami detective living on a sailboat on the Miami River as complaining that "not a day goes by without chickens or doves, with their heads cut off and feathers on, floating by" (Reese and Coppola 1981).

Writing for the *New Yorker,* David Rieff explained: "Santeria, the cult religion of Cuba, was cause for lamentations over the coming of the bar-

barians to Dade County. 'You find goat heads in the Cubans' refrigerators,' complained a secretary I met at a party" (Rieff 1987b, 70). And a non-Latin white county employee and native Miamian complained: "My daughter doesn't even like to shop at malls in Miami anymore because it's all Latin designs. . . . At our Publix, the one we've shopped at for years, they are now selling those little Cuban statues" (interview, 16 June 1992).

Various claims were also put forth linking the Hispanic population in Miami to practices of crime and corruption. This was exemplified by a headline in the 20 December 1990 *Miami Times* that read, "Miami Run by a Cuban Mafia." Similarly, in field interviews conducted during 1992 the integrity of the Latin community was called into question on several occasions. One non-Latin white elected official repeated the lament of a colleague who found it increasingly difficult to conduct business in Miami without doing it the "Cuban way" a reference to widespread bribery and corruption. The respondent agreed that "these Hispanics do operate differently. If they support you, they expect something in return" (interview, 27 July 1992). In a related statement about the relative ease with which the Latin community "made it" in Miami, a prominent black civic leader emphasized that the Latin community had never suffered from a lack of financial capital. The respondent then said, with a tone of suspicion: "Wherever that money may be coming from, I don't know, and I don't make it my business to know" (interview, 22 October 1992).

As the refugee influx continued throughout the 1980s, it became clear that Miamians were not only upset by the potential burden placed on the city by the most recent and allegedly less resourceful Marielitos but also resentful of those immigrants that had done well in Miami. Monsignor Bryan Walsh, a prominent community leader and longtime resident of Miami, said: "I wonder who really upsets whites the most, the poor Cuban on welfare or the rich Cuban with three Cadillacs and a Mercedes out buying the county" ("Paradise" 1981, 31).

THE JOB DISPLACEMENT DEBATE

Over the last thirty years a number of individuals and groups in Miami have voiced a variety of grievances. The claim that Hispanic immigrants displaced blacks in Miami's labor market was a particularly prominent concern. This claim, based on very limited empirical support, persisted over time. The curious discrepancy between argument and evidence in Miami mirrors what is occurring more generally throughout the United States and the world. In Europe growing support for far right political parties is fueled by politicians, government officials, and the media, who often attribute worsening economic conditions to the large numbers of immigrants and foreign guest workers residing in those countries. Canada, long considered a safe haven for political and economic refugees worldwide, recently levied a federal "head tax" of $975 per person on prospective immigrants and has seen an increase in anti-immigrant sentiment, as well as a surge in hate crimes against foreigners (Cannon 1995; Thompson 1995). Even South Africa, never before considered a popular destination by migrants, now faces an influx of blacks from neighboring countries who seek opportunities in the postapartheid economy and resentment among native blacks, who feel that these foreigners are competing for scarce jobs ("The Miseries" 1995, 40).

In the United States, nationwide opinion polls report that an increasing number of Americans feel that immigration is a problem that should be more strictly controlled, that too many immigrants are now entering the United States from Latin America, and that immigrants take jobs from U.S. workers (Federation for American Immigration Reform 1990, 1). These nativist concerns about an immigrant takeover have resulted in legislation such as California's Proposition 187, which denied illegal aliens access to social services, including education and health care. Petitions are now circulating in Miami to place similar initiatives on the November 1996 ballot (Navarro 1995a); and the Republican-controlled Congress is considering legislation that would require public hospitals to report illegal aliens who seek medical treatment and would require public schools to turn away students who are in the country illegally (Firestone 1995).

In some cases, as in Miami, limited empirical analysis has been brought to bear on the issue of job displacement by immigrants; in other cases the topic has received significant attention. Irrespective of the amount of empirical analysis focused on labor market substitutability, however, the job displacement controversy remains unresolved. Many of the arguments and counterarguments related to the impact of immigration on the labor market are presented in this section. My intent is not to disprove or debunk the job displacement myth but to illustrate that it is only one, albeit the predominant one, of many discursively constructed realities. My explicit argument is that the hegemony of job displacement as a definition of social reality is rooted, not in the quality or quantity of supporting evidence, but rather in the powerful convergence of the political interests of various social actors.

Nativist resentment toward immigrants, particularly in the United States, is not new. As Loy Bilderback pointed out in 1989, "Sentiment for restricting immigration, like immigration itself, has come in waves, although these waves are not perfectly synchronized with the waves of immigrants" (225). And although nativism among U.S. residents does not correlate directly with the influx of immigrants, a study by Wayne Cornelius, of the Center for U.S.-Mexican Studies, shows that American public opinion does relate to the rise and fall of U.S. unemployment rates (Cornelius 1982). U.S. immigration policy has both reflected and reinforced this ambivalence toward immigrants, and many argue that the history of immigration policy reveals an element of schizophrenia in U.S. national consciousness. Not only has the United States alternately encouraged and discouraged the influx of immigrants but seemingly contradictory goals have been advanced simultaneously within the context of a given policy. One of the most recent battles over immigration policy came to a temporary close with the passage of the 1986 Immigration Reform and Control Act. One key component of IRCA emphasized increased enforcement of immigration law through tighter control over U.S. borders and the imposition of sanctions on employers who hired illegal aliens. The other key component was an amnesty provision that legalized all immigrants who had come to the United States illegally prior to 1982. The Immigration and Naturalization Service (INS) is thus charged with guarding against the influx of "bad foreigners" and protecting and assisting with the transition of "good foreigners" into the mainstream of American society (Bilderback 1989, 227).

The debate surrounding the passage of IRCA reveals not only ambiguities in the U.S. approach toward immigration policy but also the constructive capacity of the public debate itself. In the early 1980s there were a number of hearings on the topic of immigration. And as Loy Bilderback stated, "It is impossible to now recapture the spirit of recklessness that characterized the allegations of danger to the Republic and general evil said to accompany the illegal immigration and the rapidly growing 'hidden population' it was said to feed" (1989, 232). Members of Congress used phrases such a "hemorrhage of people" and referred to the border between the United States and Mexico as a Maginot line. Governor Lamm of Colorado warned of the "immigration time bomb" (Lamm and Imhoff 1985); and former CIA director William Colby claimed that immigration posed "a greater threat than the Soviet Union" (Ehrlich, Bilderback, and Ehrlich 1979, 190).

During the course of the debates that led up to the passage of IRCA the purported number of illegal aliens residing in the United States crept progressively upward from the Social Security Administration's 3.9 million estimate to the INS's "12 million or more" (Keely 1979). Certainly the tone of the entire discussion was influenced profoundly by the appointment of a former Marine commander to head the INS. Through a number of speaking engagements, press conferences, and public pronouncements General Chapman instilled fear in the American public and Congress with a well-honed message: "A hitherto unknown menace has arisen and now threatens each one of us individually, as well as the American Way of life" (Bilderback 1989, 227).

Despite the rhetoric and hysteria surrounding immigration politics, the debate has not been entirely void of cautious or concentrated attempts at empirical analysis. On 5 October 1978 Congress addressed the immigration controversy by establishing a Select Commission on Immigration and Refugee Policy. The commission issued its final report in 1981. With regard to the impact of immigration on the United States, the report identified four areas of primary concern: social services, job displacement, wage depression, and American law and society. The discussion of American law and society was the most conducive to rhetorical ramblings, but concern over the impact of immigration on social services was disposed of relatively quickly: "Interpretations . . . vary, although most studies indicate that undocumented/illegal aliens do not place a substantial burden on social services" (Select Commission 1981, 38).

Job displacement and wage depression posed greater difficulty for the commission. Very reputable and prestigious economists offered conflicting testimony. Some stated that illegal immigrants were causing unemployment among the legal population of workers (North and Houston 1976). Others argued that illegal immigrants actually created more jobs (Piore 1979). The commission concluded that a definitive response to the question of job displacement remained elusive but that the most recent and comprehensive research suggested that immigrants did not profoundly affect the earnings or employment of the native-born population. In 1989, after also reviewing numerous competing and contradictory labor market studies, the U.S. Department of Labor concurred that the overall economic contributions of immigration exceeded its economic liabilities (U.S. Department of Labor 1989, 180).

The conclusions of task forces, government agencies, and special commissions have done little to settle ongoing debates among labor economists. Econometricians, for example, devote substantial energy to attempts to estimate the impact of immigration on native workers' wages. Borjas (1982) found that male immigrants did not affect black male earnings but had a small negative effect on the earnings of white men; and Greenwood and McDowell (1988) concluded that the aggregate effect of an increase in the supply of immigrants on earnings of native workers was small. In a later article, Borjas analyzed the extent of labor market competition between blacks, Hispanics, and whites in the United States. He concluded that black workers and Hispanic workers were complements but that black and white workers might be substitutes (1983). Grossman (1982) found that immigration caused marginal job displacement of domestic workers. Similar research on illegal Mexican workers found that they had no significant effect on black workers and were complements to other workers (Bean, Lowell, and Taylor 1988).

Several studies have emphasized the way immigrants stimulate employment demand through human capital, or increased demand for infrastructural development, and have called for higher levels of immigration. Muth (1971) concluded that one additional migrant results in about one additional job. Ben Wattenberg and Karl Zinsmeister, of the American Enterprise Institute, have advocated an increase in the number of immigrants, emphasizing the education, skills, and even investment capability of immigrants, which help enrich the United States (*Congressional Record* 1990). In the *Economic Consequences of Immigration* (1989), Julian Simon documents the net positive benefits of immigration; and the economist George Borjas contends, in *Friends or Strangers: The Impact of Immigrants on the U.S. Economy* (1990), that overall employment rates are not affected by even a 10 percent increase in immigrant labor.

The debate continued well into the nineties. In 1994 the Alexis de Tocqueville Institute of Washington released a study claiming that immigration does not cause unemployment and may actually increase the total number of jobs in the United States. The institute studied the six states having the highest levels of immigration since 1900, including Florida, and found no correlation between increased immigration and unemployment. In fact Florida's unemployment rates were consistently the same as or lower than the national average. Opponents, such as the Cornell University economist Vernon Briggs, were quick to challenge the report. Briggs stated: "We have 27 million functionally illiterate adults in the U.S., . . . we have tremendous unemployment in that sector, and illegals are taking those jobs" (Erlich 1994).

The Department of Labor acknowledges that the bulk of this literature warrants an important caveat. Many of the findings were averaged across multiple labor markets, and many were based on 1970 and 1980 decennial census data, which do not reflect changes in immigrant composition or the dynamics of a changing economy. Borjas and Tienda (1987) argue that because of the tendency of the foreign born to concentrate in selected areas and the diversity of the industrial mix in those regions, immigration may have a disproportionate effect in certain areas. The Department of Labor report suggests that further disaggregation along various ethnic, racial, industry, and age lines is in order.

In places such as the United States, Canada, and Europe immigration politics and policy continue to be analyzed, evaluated, and debated regularly in academic journals, at conferences, and within various government agencies. But even when "hard" data such as income, employment, and occupation are incorporated into the debate, the findings are inconclusive at best. While some labor economists might argue that immigrants are "taking a bigger piece of the pie," others maintain that they are instead "making the pie bigger." Meanwhile, people around the world continue to move across state borders at an unprecedented rate, and as immigrant populations expand, particularly in urban areas such as Miami, these academic debates seem far removed from the ethnic and racial tensions in the daily lives of the local residents.

THE MIAMI CASE

The limited available labor market research on Miami has primarily examined the existence and impact of a Cuban enclave economy (Portes and Bach 1985; Wilson and Portes 1980). Enclave theory, which gained popularity in the 1980s as an alternative to both the assimilationist theory and the segmented labor markets approach, has been used frequently to explain the unusual entrepreneurial success of the Cuban community in Miami. Wilson and Martin (1982) employed the concept of the ethnic enclave in a comparative analysis of Cuban and black businesses in Miami. They found that businesses in the more advantaged Cuban enclave were characterized by high interdependence and low dependence on majority industry. The black enclave was weakly interdependent and more dependent on majority industry. They also concluded that economic success in the Cuban community had not occurred through taking over or driving out black competition; rather, the "Cuban community has obtained its success primarily from production of ethnic goods, textiles, cigars, and food, and from the Latin connection, the development of which coincides with the growth phase of the Cuban enclave" (156).

In an attempt to quantify the impact of the Cuban influx on less skilled workers in Miami, the Princeton economist David Card used Current Population Survey data from 1979 to 1985 to examine the effect of the Mariel boatlift on the Miami labor market. He concludes that "the Mariel influx appears to have had virtually no effect on the wages or unemployment rates of less-skilled workers" (1990, 245). Robert Cruz (1991) used Miami as a case study for examining the empirical link between the growth of production in a central city and the distribution of income among its residents. He found that although employment within the city of Miami grew from 1970 to 1980, the per capita income of city residents declined, and black families were the most severely injured by this trend. Cruz cautions, however, that despite the widespread perception that Hispanic immigrants had taken jobs from black residents, "no objective evidence of this conclusion has been put forward. . . . Indeed, . . . significant gains in the number and proportion of blacks employed in higher paying, white collar jobs occurred between 1970 and 1980. Hence, the reasons for the lack of participation of blacks in the City's economic progress may lie more with occupational distribution rather than with a loss of jobs to immigrant groups" (6).

A close examination of the data on ethnic employment by industry in Miami reveals that although the Cuban presence expanded rapidly in various segments of the labor market, this took place primarily at the expense of native whites (Portes and Stepick 1993). There is certainly no denying that the Cuban influx had a powerful impact on the local economy in Dade County; however, as Portes and Stepick point out, "There was no one-to-one substitution of blacks by Cubans in the labor market, nor a direct exploitation of one minority by the other. There was, however, a new urban economy in which the immigrants raced past other groups, leaving the native minority behind" (43).

Not only do existing labor market analyses indicate a discontinuity between the rhetoric and the reality but many of the claims put forth reveal the confusion and ambiguity that characterize the job displacement debate. In their discussion of possible explanations for the 1980 riots Porter and Dunn (1984) refer to the Cuban influx and the devastating job takeover experienced by blacks. They point out that from 1972 to 1977 the number of Hispanic businesses in Miami rose by 70 percent whereas the number of black businesses increased by only 40 percent. They provide additional data to demonstrate the disparity in loans given to the two groups by the U.S. Small Business Administration. Between 1968 and 1979 Hispanics received 47 percent of the total loan money in Miami; whites received 46.5 percent; and blacks received only 6.4 percent. Although this information is indicative of the disadvantaged status of blacks in Miami, it is not proof of a Hispanic job takeover.

Porter and Dunn acknowledge that "the surge of Cuban economic activity should not be surprising . . . the working class element that joined in the exodus tended to share the historic willingness of other immigrant groups to take on the lower order of jobs—the jobs that were often spurned by black Americans who felt they deserved something better" (196). Clearly, if Cuban immigrants took jobs spurned by black Americans, there was no "job takeover." These types of inconsistent images and conflicting themes permeate the immigration debate in Miami and elsewhere and produce contradictory portrayals such as the following one quoted by Bilderback: "Aliens were lazy, bloated welfare bums who worked so hard and for such modest wages that they crowded upstanding red-blooded Americans out of the workplace" (1989, 227).

The lack of empirical evidence to support the claim that Hispanic immigrants have displaced blacks in the Dade County labor market suggests that the job displacement issue was not placed on the public agenda in Miami because of the problem's intrinsic gravity. Nor is job displacement the only commonly held perception in and about Miami that is not well grounded in empirical "reality." Even before the first Mariel refugee set foot in Miami it was widely believed that this group of Cubans was very different from those who had come before them. Harsh and vocal outcries came from residents, local officials, politicians, and the media, who believed these refugees to be criminals, mental patients, homosexuals, AIDS victims—in Castro's own words, the "scum" of Cuban society.

For many, the tarnished image of Mariel remains, but since 1980 various claimants have argued that this group of refugees differed little from earlier arrivals. Some studies indicate, for example, that only 15 percent of the Cuban refugees who arrived during the Mariel boatlift had actually served time in a Cuban prison; and it bears keeping in mind that a prison sentence in Cuba may result from an offense as relatively minor as speaking critically of the Castro regime. Although reports that the Mariel refugees came from lower socioeconomic backgrounds and that a larger number were classified by INS officials as "black" are well known, less widely acknowledged are the studies indicating that this group of Cubans has adjusted to life in Miami in much the same way as did their predecessors (Hufker and Cavender 1990; Portes and Clark 1987).

AN IDEA WHOSE TIME HAD COME

Some perceptions in Miami are perpetuated by claims with little basis in empirical "fact." Other grievances go unnoticed or fail to gain widespread attention from the public at large. Leaders within the black community in Miami did express concern over the massive influx of Cuban refugees. They also complained, however, of poor housing conditions, inadequate public services, police brutality, and a general neglect by city and county government. Why, then, did the issue of a Hispanic job takeover achieve prominence on the public agenda in Miami, and how has it been perpetuated over time?

The work of various political scientists, policy analysts, and social problem theorists provides important insights into how and why some issues or problems become the focus of concern within a given polity but others do not. In his path-breaking work *Agendas, Alternatives, and Public Policies* (1984) John Kingdon examines the factors underlying the common phrase "It was an idea whose time had come." He asks, "How does an idea's time come?" An examination of how an idea's time comes takes into consideration the context in which a particular issue emerges, the role of various contexts in shaping and defining the issue or idea, and the biases inherent in any political system that either facilitate or obstruct the emergence of certain ideas. This and other works move beyond the assumption that issues or problems are rooted in an objective reality to focus on how a perceived reality is socially and politically constructed and how that construction determines why some concerns become public problems and others do not.

RISING EXPECTATIONS, RELATIVE DEPRIVATIONS, AND RIOTS

The emergence and legitimation of the job displacement claim must be viewed in the context of a changing social, political, and economic environment in Miami over the last thirty years. When the job displacement claim initially surfaced in the early 1960s, in many instances it was put forth by leaders of Miami's black community. The concern expressed by these individuals seemed to reflect an insecurity with regard to the status of blacks in Miami, which represented only a small and fragile improvement resulting from the civil rights movement. The hard-won victories in the long struggle for civil rights had increased the expectations of blacks in Dade County and throughout the United States. The possibility that Cuban immigration would weaken these fragile advancements, detract much needed attention from a still desperate plight, or in any way impede the future social, political, or economic progress of blacks in Dade County was viewed as a major threat. Many of the grievances issued during the 1960s by various leaders, from Martin Luther King Jr. to local union organizers, had as much to do with problems that might arise as they did with hardships that had already been incurred as a result of the Cuban influx.

The plight of blacks in Miami remained bleak throughout the 1970s; blacks consistently constituted a disproportionate share of Dade County's poor. There are some indications, however, that the economic situation of many blacks in the metropolitan Miami area actually improved even as the Cuban immigrants continued to arrive. But although blacks in Miami may have fared well compared with blacks in other metropolitan areas, Cubans fared better. And as scholars of relative deprivation suggest, people often tend to measure their success relatively, not absolutely (Hochschild 1981, 81).

Blacks in Miami perceived not only that Hispanics had achieved superior economic success but also that Hispanic' success was due in part to favorable treatment by both local and national government and business officials. Some blacks viewed the very influx of Cuban immigrants as a political strategy calculated and controlled by the non-Latin white power structure. One black activist who heads a prominent civic organization in Dade County spoke at length about the "divide and conquer" strategy of the "white supremacist power elite" in Miami. "After acquitting McDuffie," he explained, "they [the white power elite] brought in 150,000 more Cubans" (interview, 18 June 1992). In a similar discussion about the disenfranchisement of the black community in Dade County a prominent black business person in Miami explained, "They [the Anglo establishment] destroyed Overtown. They scattered people all around then brought all the Cubans in" (interview, 8 July 1992).

By 1980 the environment in Miami had changed dramatically. Not only had the Cuban refugee population doubled in size but it had evolved from an exile community into a locally as well as nationally powerful social, political, and economic force. The native population in Dade County, both non-Latin whites and blacks, experienced the "Latinization" of Miami at the same time that they experienced the effects of a nationwide recession. The influx of Cubans continued, but these poorer and darker "Marielitos" were joined by large numbers of immigrants from Haiti and other islands in the Caribbean.

The agenda-setting theorist John Kingdon has argued that "problems are often not self evident. . . , but may need a little push to get the attention of the public" (1984, 100). This "push" is provided in part by "triggering devices" or "focusing events," unforeseen or unanticipated events, such as natural catastrophes, spontaneous human riots, technological and ecological change, that influence the shape and content of issues (Cobb and Elder 1972; Kingdon 1984). The combination of events that took place in Miami during the 1980s would legitimately constitute a "shove" rather than just "a little push." The Mariel boatlift and the Liberty City riots occurred within a few weeks of each other. These events also coincided, or collided, with an increase in Haitian immigration and with a growing mood of nativism among local residents in Dade County. This was the context in which job displacement and the immigrant takeover became an accepted definition of social reality in Miami.

ISSUE CREATION

In addition to focusing events, various actors, or "initiators," play an important role in placing issues on the public agenda. The convergence of events in 1980 attracted a great deal of local, national, and international attention, and their severity demanded a response. That response poured forth from public officials at all levels of government, politicians, the media, academicians, and authors of popular literature. As social tensions appeared to worsen throughout the decade, these individuals and groups continued to offer explanations.

In many instances the individuals or organizations making claims explicitly acknowledged the conjectural nature of their statements. *Ebony Magazine* explained, for example, that "few Negroes can be found who will state categorically that they were displaced from jobs by refugees" (Morrison 1963, 98). This caveat certainly does not diminish the level of frustration that may have been present among local residents, but it does point to the need for understanding the processes that translate private concerns into public issues. According to social problem theorists Spector and Kitsuse, for example, "A condition may be experienced in a vague and undefined way by some groups. They may even voice complaints about it, but not effectively. Then the trouble may be picked up and seen as a classic instance of exploitation, discrimination, or corruption by a political party, labor union, professional radical, or service organization. Such groups may give coherence or a rationale to the complaint" (1987, 145).

The argument advanced here is that the process of providing coherence or rationale for a complaint is an inherently political one. In any polity, individuals and groups are engaged in a constant struggle to advance their particular grievances and concerns onto the public agenda. An important part of this struggle often entails attempts to expand the scope and visibility of a particular issue in order to reach a wider public (Cobb and Elder 1972). Political leaders, public officials, and the media are all involved in defining, redefining, and expanding issues or problems and may have any number of reasons for doing so. Political figures play an instrumental role in fomenting concern with certain problems and putting a damper on concern with others. Ross and Staines point out that by raising a public issue, officials can point to rivals who take an unpopular position or can take a popular position themselves. They may also use public issues to distract attention from embarrassing issues. Public officials are also believed to have a political interest in blaming individuals rather than attributing problems to broader systemic conditions because they must justify and maintain their own positions of authority. As a result, problems tend to be interpreted not as the fault of authorities or the responsibility of the system but rather as the result of aberrant behavior on the part of some members of society (Ross and Staines 1971, 22).

Much has also been written about the pivotal role played by the media in defining problems and expanding issues. Edelman, for example, refers to the blurring or absence of any realistic detail in the news that might weaken or question the symbolic meanings people read into it: "It is no accident of history or culture that our newspapers and T.V. present little news, overdramatize . . . and that most citizens have only a foggy knowledge of public affairs though often an intensely felt one. The public wants symbols, not news" (1964, 9).

Molotch and Lester define news reporting as an activity that not only reacts to events but creates them as well. The media can, for example, influence the legitimacy of an issue through pointed inclusion or exclusion of critical factual information (Molotch and Lester 1974). Cobb and Elder also attribute an important degree of influence to the media when they acknowledge that "once the media take an interest in a controversy they will often play an important role in reinforcing or altering the prevailing definition of the conflict" (1972, 143).[4]

Finally, as Murray Edelman explains, political opinions have various functions for the individual, functions that need not meet the check of reality and may in fact be best served by ignoring reality. One of those functions is *externalization*. Edelman contends, for example, that during a time of depression or anxiety a group may come to believe that Jewish, or communist, or Catholic conspiracies in the government explain their business failures or their inability to realize other ambitions. These opinions will continue to be held and even strengthened as long as they work, and whether or not they are consistent with what is happening in the world (Edelman 1964, 8).

Many of the complaints about job displacement in Miami during the early 1960s came from government employees, politicians, and civic leaders in Dade County. These officials complained forcefully that Miami was being swamped with refugees and that Washington was not shouldering its share of the burden. The claim of potential civil unrest as a result of the Cuban influx was a tool local officials used to pressure the federal government to provide greater financial and administrative assistance with the refugee crisis. To lend credence to the threat, claimants emphasized the competition between blacks and Cubans and the fears of an immigrant takeover.

Civil unrest did occur in Miami. During the late 1960s and early 1970s Miami's black ghettoes erupted in fury on several occasions. There is little indication, however, that this frustration was directed at Cuban immigrants or that those involved in the unrest considered immigration to be the cause of their plight. Nor is there much evidence that local officials or the media publicly drew a direct connection between the riots and the refugees prior to 1980. During the 1980s, however, talk of a foreign invasion resurfaced with a vengeance. It was accompanied by the charge that immigrants were taking jobs from U.S. workers.

In the 1980s, as in the 1960s, black leaders were among those expressing grievances about the impact of immigration on Dade County. Although they voiced a variety of other concerns as well, emphasis on the Hispanic job takeover served to provide coherence to a diffuse but powerful sense of dissatisfaction among blacks in Miami. The focus on immigration and a takeover of jobs also became, during the 1980s, a means by which black leaders could attach their grievances to more general concerns of the public at large—or "expand" the scope of their problems to a wider audience (Cobb and Elder 1972). Of all the grievances discussed in connection with the riots the Cuban takeover was clearly the most visible. It was also the claim that had the the greatest capacity to gain the attention of large numbers of people—black and white—in the metropolitan Miami area.

Although the media printed headlines about a foreign invasion, and many public figures warned of brewing tensions as a result of the devastating job takeover, other voices within the black community were consistently more moderate in their appeal. In 1962 a member of the Dade County Urban League denied any evidence of job displacement and explained, "Cubans are going after jobs that Negroes never had in the first place, so how can we claim they're taking employment away from our people?" ("To Miami" 1962, 92).

In interviews conducted in May–November 1992 with members of Miami's black community several individuals claimed that Cubans had displaced blacks in the local labor market. Others, however, stated otherwise. Johnnie McMillian, president of the local NAACP, pointed out that "blacks never had the jobs anyway, because if we'd had them, I doubt they could have taken them" (interview, 3 September 1992). When asked about the Cuban job takeover, one high-ranking black city official responded, "I hate to fault a group of people for our lacking . . . a lot of them have been employed, and you have to admire them for that" (interview, 9 July 1992). Another civic leader within the black community explained the situation as follows: "Right when the Cubans came, blacks had decided they didn't want those waiter jobs, or jobs as hotel maids. The Cubans would do anything for very little money. Blacks thought [the Cubans] took jobs" (interview, 10 September 1992).

Black leaders in Miami were by no means the only ones to voice concerns about the impact of immigration on Dade County. The non-Latin white leadership in Miami—local officials, politicians, scholars, citizens groups, and the media—all engaged in claims-making activity that defined a particular social reality in Miami. In the aftermath of one of the most violent and destructive race riots in U.S. history, as Miami's reputation as the "American Riviera" quickly degenerated into that of "Paradise Lost," image-conscious officials in Dade County struggled to shift responsibility for the social upheaval away from systemic factors.

The recognition and perpetuation of the job displacement claim also allowed the predominantly non-Latin white leadership in Miami to deflect to an outside group much of the anger and frustration of the black community that historically had been directed at a social, political, and economic system dominated by an Anglo power elite. For various elected officials and public figures, it was politically more feasible to emphasize the impact of immigration on the city than to address the longstanding grievances of an extremely disenfranchised black community, grievances that included, but were in no way limited to, labor market competition from immigrants.

Various politicians in Miami seized the opportunity to manipulate the immigrant presence and the threat of a takeover for their own personal political gain. Maurice Ferre's 1985 mayoral campaign popularized reference to a "Cuban takeover" ("Ads Exploited" 1985), and in 1989 Gerald Richmond proclaimed the Eighteenth Congressional District to be an "American seat" (Moreno and Rae 1992). Many Dade County residents vented their frustration toward the "ungrateful immigrants" through claims that portrayed the Cubans in Miami as not "playing by the rules." These opinions and perceptions may have allowed both blacks and whites in Miami to "externalize" their anxiety regarding their own personal hardships. Finally, many analysts and interview respondents emphasized the very critical role the media, and particularly the *Miami Herald*, has played in dramatizing events, manipulating symbols, and creating or perpetuating perceptions that foster divisiveness among different racial and ethnic groups in the metropolitan Miami area.

MOBILIZATION OF BIAS

The creation and redefinition of the issues that public discourse in Miami comprises are not arbitrary; they closely reflect the tug and pull of vested interests and community politics. As stated in the introduction, Joseph Gusfield's discussion of the role of power and influence in the social construction of reality emphasizes that "the public arena is not a field on which all can play on equal terms; some have greater access than others and greater power and ability to shape the definition of public issues" (1981, 8). Cobb and Elder concur, pointing out that the public agenda is formed through the normal struggle of social forces; "at any point in time, it will reflect the existing balance of those forces, or the mobilization of bias within a community" (1972, 161).

Numerous factors serve to sustain and perpetuate this bias, but of particular relevance are the constraints imposed by "systems of limited participation." A system of limited participation, or "stable unrepresentation," is one in which large numbers of citizens remain outside the political arena (Gamson 1968, 19). Although the study of politics in the United States has been dominated by scholars such as Robert Dahl, who describes the American political system as one in which "all the active and legitimate groups in the population can make themselves heard at some crucial stage in the process of decision making" (1956, 137), many scholars have forcefully challenged the assumptions of Dahl and other pluralists, pointing out that the problem lies precisely in what is implied by *active* and *legitimate*. As Charles Jones suggests, *active* implicitly assumes some level of structure, leadership, support, and resources, and *legitimate* implies consistency with some particular standards of social acceptability (1984, 61). In *The Semisovereign People*, E. E. Schattschneider similarly rejected the notion of the American system as a mosaic of politically active interests groups, arguing that the limited range of organized groups that does exist clearly has "an upper-class bias" (1960, 140).

The biased nature of the political system in Miami was forcefully and successfully challenged in a six-year legal battle over the county's at-large voting structure. In 1992 a federal judge ruled in favor of a group of black and Hispanic plaintiffs who charged that the county's at-large system violated the Voting Rights Act by diluting minority voting strength. The plaintiffs' frustration appears justified in light of the fact that as late as 1992 blacks and Hispanics each held one seat on a nine-member commission even though collectively they constituted 70 percent of the county's population.[5] In an insightful analysis of the system of local government in Miami and its unresponsiveness to blacks, John Stack and Christopher Warren identify what they call the "Miami Syndrome." The label is meant to convey "high levels of black frustration in a stagnant political system combined with a crisis of rising expectations that is often expressed in rioting and other acts of non-traditional political protest" (Stack and Warren 1992, 293).

The mobilization of bias, as well as the bias of mobilization, is sustained not only by limiting the number of individuals or groups that play an "active" or "legitimate" role in the political system but also by restricting the range of issues and alternatives that can gain access to the public agenda. Bachrach and Baratz refer to this as the process of "non-decision making," by which demands for change in the existing allocation of benefits and privileges in the community can be suffocated before they are even voiced (1970, 44). Miami has a long history of racial tension that far antedates the influx of Cuban immigrants. Blacks have complained for many years, sometimes violently, about numerous injustices they perceive to have been perpetuated against them by the white majority. These grievances have largely been ignored. The immigration "problem," on the other hand, has received a great deal of attention. By focusing on the Hispanic takeover, the power structure in Miami avoids acknowledging charges of racism, widespread discrimination, police brutality, poor housing conditions, inadequate public services, and a lack of political representation that continue to be advanced by the black community.

What is particularly interesting about the problem of job displacement and the immigrant takeover in Miami is that it not only gains prominence over other claims but also is a definition of reality that puts two minority groups in competition with each other, discouraging a potential alliance

- How does this discourse play out
vis a vis transnationalism?
very true   **THE DISCOURSE OF DISPLACEMENT**   **97**

between the disenfranchised black population in Dade County and the Hispanic newcomers. Both black and Hispanic interviewees in Dade County alluded to subtle but conscious attempts by the non-Latin white leadership in Miami to "divide and conquer" these two minority groups. Some respondents offered specific examples, such as the "tendency of Anglos to pander to the Cubans, while ignoring blacks" (interview, 7 July 1992). One very prominent Cuban American civic leader and community activist explained: "I have black leaders, friends of mine, who tell me they go to meetings with Anglos who say 'Hey, look we're getting pressure from these Cubans.' Then they [Anglos] say to us 'Hey, if those blacks would just work as hard as you Hispanics do'" (interview, 30 September 1992).

When asked, "Between which two ethnic groups in Miami is the level of hostility the greatest?" one black leader and former elected official answered, "Blacks and Hispanics, but you know whites would just stand back and watch everything burn" (interview, 22 October 1992). A black director of a prominent local civil rights organization answered, "The worst relations are between whites and blacks, the tension with Hispanics is about them getting more resources than us. Hispanics don't really have the power, and black people recognize that. This white power structure better wake up" (interview, 3 September 1992).

It is difficult to empirically validate or invalidate the "divide and conquer" claim; however, the history of the emergence and legitimation of the job displacement "problem" in Miami provides some support for this thesis. It is also interesting to note that of those respondents in Dade County who agreed with the statement that Hispanic immigrants had taken jobs from blacks in the Miami labor market, 65 percent were non-Latin whites (see fig. 3).

CONCLUSION

Miami . . . is the clearest example of cultural aggression and takeover, which are the most disturbing long-range threats implicit in heavy immigration from Latin America and Asia. Miami is now notorious as the drug-importing capitol of the United States, with most of the kingpins having come to this country illegally from South America; and also for the highest crime rate in the country, a statistic directly traceable to the drug runners and to the criminals sent from Cuba in the Mariel boatlift. But these problems, while superficially more dramatic and terrifying, are not as significant for the future as the cultural threat.

John Ney, Miami Today

It is widely perceived that Miami has fallen prey to a foreign invasion and that this invasion severely threatens the very fabric of the city and perhaps the future of the country. This perceived threat can be seen in the large number of grievances expressed by different individuals and groups in Miami over the past thirty years. Complaints refer to the loss of jobs, the prevalence of spoken Spanish, the encroachment of a corrupt and undemocratic civic culture, and the practice of bizarre religious rituals. Drawing on these concerns and at the same time reinforcing them, public officials, local leaders, and the media have defined and redefined a series of problems, crises, enemies, and threats.

This definitional process does not take place in a vacuum; it occurs

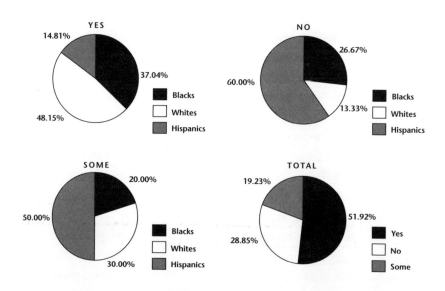

Figure 3. Summary of responses to interview question #8: Have Hispanic immigrants taken jobs from blacks in Dade County?

within a given social, political, and economic context that itself is not static. It is this context that provides the raw material with which public discourse is constructed. The claims-making activity of leaders, politicians, journalists, and scholars, the redefinition and expansion of issues, and the manipulation of potent symbols formed the public discourse on displacement and constructed the threat of an immigrant takeover. This social definition of reality, although not well grounded in empirical data, has served the political purposes of various individuals and groups. Local officials have emphasized the immigrant threat in order to secure support and cooperation from the federal government. Civil rights leaders have lobbied so that the immigrant influx would not detract attention from the plight of black Americans. When the 1980s earned Miami its reputation as "Paradise Lost," image-conscious city officials were quick to hold immigration responsible for the city's demise. The media and other observers capitalized on the drama, offering simplified and often distorted portrayals of very complex issues. And various politicians used the immigrant presence and the threat of a takeover for their own personal political gain.

It is important to emphasize that blacks in Miami have expressed, and continue to express, discontent about a number of perceived injustices with which they cope daily. Few of these concerns have become issues of importance to the community at large, however. The Hispanic takeover, on the other hand, has risen from its place among myriad crises, concerns, and issues to a place of prominence on Miami's public agenda. This phenomenon supports Cobb and Elder's thesis that "through the manipulation of bias and prevailing values, status quo powers may stifle, reinterpret, or otherwise diffuse an issue, and thus prevent it from gaining agenda status" (1972, 12).

This phenomenon also illustrates how a system of limited participation and processes of non–decision making, serve to mobilize biases inherent in a given social, political, and economic system. The job displacement thesis and the threat of an immigrant takeover are social constructions that serve the interests of both blacks and Anglos in Dade County, place these long-time foes in a tacit alliance against the Hispanic newcomers, and discourage the potential for a potent political alliance between blacks and Hispanics in Dade County. Immigrants thus become a convenient scapegoat for a variety of issues that may be only marginally related to their influx.

There is some indication that the prevailing public discourse about immigrants and immigration may be shifting in the 1990s. As large numbers of non-Latin whites continue to move out of Dade County, many that remain increasingly engage in a public discourse that portrays immigration and the immigrants as a benefit to Miami rather than a curse.[6] This discourse expresses more than just an appreciation for the infusion of human and financial capital that was so welcomed by Miami's business elite during the l960s. Editorials such as the one in the 24 March 1991 *Miami Herald* extolling Americans to "Get on the Ball . . . Learn Another Language" represent a growing acceptance of cultural diversity in Dade County and an attempt to portray Miami as a "city of the future" (Lawrence 1991). Whether this view is genuine or an attempt on behalf of the Anglo elite to maintain its position of dominance by coopting potential opposition remains to be seen.[7]

Blacks continue to voice complaints about the Hispanic presence as well as about other aspects of social, political, and economic life in Miami. The outlook of many blacks in Miami, however, is a positive one, in terms of both the Hispanic presence and the future of the city. One black business official said of future relations between blacks and Hispanics in Dade County: "There are lots of prospects for blacks and Hispanics. We get along better than with whites. We share more cultural traits" (interview, 8 July 1992). Speaking about Miami's future, another black businessman and former county employee explained, "Blacks are patient, observant. We've waited many years and watched—it's about to pay off. It's fine with us if all Anglos go to Boca [Raton], we have a great opportunity here in Miami" (interview, 7 July 1992).

Finally, any alteration in the public discourse on immigration in Miami must be viewed in light of a very powerful and persuasive counterdiscourse on the part of Hispanics in Miami, and particularly the Cuban American community. Chapter 4 details the social and political construction of a discourse that portrays Cuban immigrants as an asset to Miami and to the United States as a whole. Taken together, chapters 3 and 4 indi-

cate that constructed definitions of perceived reality in Miami both reflect
and legitimize the prevailing balance of power between various groups.
The definitions are not only socially constructed but also politically contested; and as the balance of social and political forces in a community
shift, so too do the public discourses through which that balance is sustained.

"Last one going, take the flag"
complexities - the borders are
shrinking (growing?) - there is no
panic

4

THE SUCCESS OF THE CUBAN SUCCESS STORY
Cuban American Ethnicity and the Politics of Identity

Only twenty-odd years ago, most of you in the audience who are Cubans were struggling with the difficult and urgent problems that daily confront those who escape tyrants and pursue freedom, who are compelled to settle in a foreign land. The Cubans who came here solved those pressing problems of survival, and more, instead of remaining a burden on the communities in which they settled, Cuban refugees who have come to the United States have made major, indeed extraordinary contributions to the vitality and the growth, not only of Miami, not only of Florida, but of the United States, and indeed of the Americas. Cubans, as everyone knows, are a great American success story.[1]

[handwritten margin note: implies that they were never a burden.]

[handwritten note after "success story": = how nice]

U.N. Ambassador Jeane Kirkpatrick's speech before the Cuban American National Foundation in Miami is just one example of the public pronouncements, articles, editorials, and books that have, over the last thirty years, bestowed countless praises on Cuban immigrants in the United States. Federal government officials have complimented the Cuban émigrés on their loyalty to the cherished principles of freedom and democracy. Business people, politicians, and the media have applauded the entrepreneurial spirit and drive of the Cuban community in Miami. And Cuban immigrants themselves continue to speak proudly of the many obstacles they have overcome in the process of adapting to a new, sometimes hostile environment.

Scholars of diverse backgrounds also have been fascinated by the unusual achievements of these émigrés, and they have put forth a number of theories and concepts that attempt to explain the Cuban community's relatively smooth political, economic, and social adaptation in the United States. Lisandro Perez (1986) examined the role of Cuban family structure and cooperation within the household as determinants of economic success. Lourdes Arguelles (1982) and Silvia Pedraza-Bailey (1985) emphasized the involvement of the federal government in assisting and resettling the refugees. Numerous works have highlighted the Cuban contribution to economic growth and development in Miami (see, e.g., Jorge and Moncarz 1987); and others have compared the achievements of Cubans with similar success or lack of success among other ethnic groups in the United States, including other Hispanics (Pedraza-Bailey 1985; Portes and Bach 1985; Wilson and Martin 1982). The bulk of this literature, however, focuses on the Cuban enclave economy as a unique form of social and economic adaptation to the host society and the primary explanation for Cubans' economic success in Miami (Portes and Jensen 1989; Portes and Manning 1986; Wilson and Portes 1980). Many scholars are still debating both the origins and the implications of the Cuban enclave in Miami (Forment 1989; Jensen and Portes 1992; Sanders and Nee 1992).

Much of the public discourse on Cuban immigration, whether it emanates from the immigrants themselves or from the society at large, paints a portrait of Cubans in the United States as an economically powerful, politically united, and culturally homogeneous ethnic group. Neither this image nor many of the assumptions upon which it is based is well grounded in empirical reality. The Cuban population in the United States represents a wide range of socioeconomic, cultural, and political backgrounds, a variety of distinct immigration experiences, and substantial intragroup cleavage and conflict. Furthermore, where there is evidence of a cohesive Cuban American ethnicity, its content is not static, nor have its constituent themes been simply transplanted from the island. Instead, much of what constitutes Cuban American cultural identity has been invented in the context of the exile experience in the United States. The literature on Cuban immigration, including the seminal works mentioned above, has generated interesting and insightful debates about various aspects of the Cuban experience in the United States, and some scholars have questioned the widely held perceptions of Cuban economic success.

Missing from the discussion, however, is a thorough analysis of the social and political construction of the success story itself and of the related issue of a constructed Cuban ethnic identity in the United States.

Ethnicity has only recently come to occupy center stage in social science debate, and it is perhaps not surprising that the bulk of analysis on Cubans in the United States has focused on Cuban economic success rather than on Cuban ethnicity.[2] Ethnicity has been important to these studies primarily in terms of its relationship to the Cuban enclave in Miami. In this regard, however, much of the literature reveals a lack of precision in dealing with ethnicity as an analytical variable. The work of Alejandro Portes, for example, vacillates between, on the one hand, suggesting that Cuban ethnic solidarity provides the basis for an enclave economy and, on the other hand, suggesting that the enclave economy is what fosters and facilitates ethnic ties and ethnic networks among Cubans in the United States.[3] In "The Social Origins of the Cuban Enclave Economy" (1987) Portes analyzes how ethnicity provides solidarity and communal support for entrepreneurial initiative among Cuban immigrants. This view contrasts with Edna Bonacich's portrayal of immigrant entrepreneurs as "middlemen minorities"; in Bonacich's view, immigrant employers, oppressed from above by large capitalist corporations, merely use ethnicity as a way to oppress or exploit co-ethnics for their own economic gain (Bonacich 1987 and 1973). These divergent perspectives illustrate the potential tension between primordialist and instrumentalist explanations of ethnic behavior. Do primordial attachments among Cubans in Miami and the desire to maintain cultural bonds naturally give rise to or facilitate the emergence of an enclave economy? Or is ethnicity simply the most useful means through which to pursue rational economic and political ends? In this regard, Portes is correct to recognize, if only implicitly, that ethnicity constitutes both an independent and and a dependent variable in the enclave equation.

Forment (1989) expanded the parameters of the debate on Cuban immigrants in the United States by exploring how political competition and negotiation among rival groups gave rise to the ethnic enclave in Miami. Forment criticizes Portes and Bach (1985), and Pedraza-Bailey (1985) for focusing solely on the macrocontext, whether that be a global capitalist economy that provided Cubans in the United States with a unique economic niche or an international political context in which Cuban immigrants were the beneficiaries of an ideological struggle between East and West. Forment argues for a relational approach that combines societal and state factors as well as microlevel political processes within the Cuban community itself. Forment's analysis does not deal directly with Cuban ethnic identity or the success of the success story, but his emphasis on discourse and power contributes to the analytical framework advanced here. Just as the rise of the enclave cannot be explained solely by reference to micro- or macrolevel processes, that is, to the individual émigrés or the global economic and political context in which they thrived, Cuban American ethnic identity cannot be explained in purely primordial or instrumental terms. Instead, Cuban American identity, like the enclave, is a product of negotiated processes or "political practice" (Forment 1989, 49).

The present analysis differs from these earlier works in that its goal is not to explain the origins or implications of the Cuban enclave economy or to compare and contrast the economic and political success of Cubans with those of other immigrant groups in the United States. Rather, it examines the social and political construction of the Cuban success story, how this public narrative both reflects and reinforces the changing character of power and politics, and the implications of the interaction between discourse and power for Cuban American ethnic identity in the United States. This analysis draws on the insights of existing studies that recognized that U.S. political and economic interests influenced profoundly the experience of Cuban immigrants, but it argues that the analysis of the Cuban experience is incomplete without an understanding of the role of discourse in constructing an image and identity of Cuban success. The aim of this discursive analysis, however, is not to uncover beneath discourse some objective, empirically verifiable truth. In other words, it does not attempt to validate or invalidate empirically the purported achievements of Cubans in the United States. Rather, its aim is to understand how meaning is given and assigned and how "truth" or knowledge is linked to power (see Foucault 1980, 109–33; and McNay 1992, 27). In this regard, the Cuban American case provides an ideal opportunity to examine how the confluence of history, political economy, and language constructs and reconstructs ethnic identity.

THE STORY OF SUCCESS

The history of Cuban immigration to the United States is frequently discussed in terms of distinct waves of refugees. Authors differ concerning the precise demarcation of the various stages, but there is some general agreement that the influx of Cubans into the United States can be divided into five phases. During the initial wave, from January 1959 to October 1962, an estimated 215,000 Cubans arrived in the United States. Batista and his supporters were the first to leave Cuba, but they were soon followed by an increasing number of landowners, industrialists, managers, and professionals. A second wave, from November 1962 to November 1965, saw approximately 74,000 Cubans leave the island. The reduced number of refugees resulted from the cessation of all direct flights between the island and the United States as a result of the Cuban missile crisis. In 1965, however, Castro did permit 5,000 relatives of Cuban exiles living in the United States to leave through the port of Camarioca. From December 1965 to April 1973 more than 340,000 Cubans, close to one-half the total influx, arrived in the United States as the result of an agreement between Cuba and the United States that launched twice daily airlifts of Cubans from Varadero Beach to Miami. From May 1973 to April 1980 the number of émigrés dwindled to fewer than 3,000 as a result of the unilateral decision by the Cuban government to terminate the airlift. Then from May to September 1980 an estimated 125,000 Cubans arrived in Miami from the port of Mariel *(see fig. 4)*. This influx, which brought more refugees in one month than the total number that arrived during all of 1962, resulted from Castro's decision to allow the departure of thousands of Cubans who were crowded into the Peruvian embassy demanding to leave the country. Castro also used this opportunity to deport hundreds of Cubans he deemed "undesirables" (Fradd 1983; Jorge and Moncarz 1987; Portes and Bach 1985).

Much attention has been focused on the Cubans that have left, or attempted to leave, the island over the past thirty years. Despite a diversity of opinion and a multitude of claims, several key issues and themes charac-

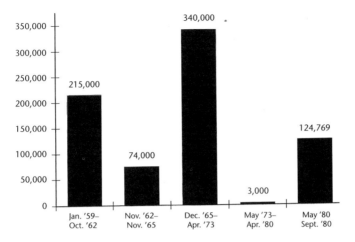

Figure 4. Five waves of Cuban immigration to the United States. Source: Portes and Bach 1985, 85.

terize the public discourse on Cuban immigration to the United States. One such theme defines Cuban émigrés as victims of a communist tyranny and focuses on how these political refugees escaped heroically the iron grip of Castro's regime. Another prominent theme addresses the contributions Cuban immigrants have made to Miami's economy in particular and the American way of life more generally. This narrative of a Cuban economic miracle is enhanced by stories of how the Cuban immigrants have warmly embraced key tenets of U.S. civic culture—individualism, patriotism, and consumerism. Finally, there is a widely held belief that Cuban American success is rooted in the individual characteristics of the immigrants themselves, such as their devotion to hard work, self-sacrifice, and the spirit of capitalist enterprise. Related to this rags-to-riches discourse, as well as to the tales of a "Cuban economic miracle," is a portrayal of Cubans in the United States as "white," like the majority host society, as opposed to "black," like the African American minority. Various claims put forth by non-Latin whites in the United States implicitly and explicitly contrast Cuban refugees with native black Americans and define the Cubans as one of "us," not one of "them." The Cuban exiles themselves recount a more ambiguous tale that, on the one hand, distances them from other minority groups, specifically black Americans and, on the other hand, absolves them from any responsibility for this minority group's disadvantaged plight.

This story of success, along with its constitutive themes, has been promoted and constructed by politicians, government officials, churches, the media, and the Cuban émigrés themselves. The predominance of particular themes has shifted over time, and each has met with varying degrees of resistance from competing themes. Yet the emergent imagery of Cubans in the United States was one of a politically united and economically successful ethnic group. As the present analysis illustrates, this imagery, although it does not necessarily reflect an objective, empirical reality, has served well the foreign and domestic policy interests of the United States and simultaneously helped to transform Cuban exiles from a refugee population in South Florida to a powerful political and economic force in Miami, Washington, and the world.

VICTIMS OF TYRANNY

When the United States officially broke diplomatic ties with the Cuban government in 1961 the plight of hundreds of émigrés already living in Miami was known to few outside of South Florida. As relations between the two governments worsened, the focus on the Cuban refugees grew more intense. The commentary of government officials, church leaders, and the popular press indicated a strong willingness to promote and facilitate the incorporation of the refugees into the United States. In January 1961 Tracy Voorhees, the Eisenhower administration's representative on the exile issue, pointed out that breaking U.S. diplomatic relations with Cuba could help solve Miami's refugee problem: "This should set off a wave of sympathy all over the United States for the refugees. Up to now, the people outside Miami have never heard of them" ("Rift with Cuba" 1961). Perhaps the boldest indication of the U.S. government's commitment to the Cubans was the Kennedy administration's establishment in 1961 of a Cuban Refugee Program to oversee the processing and resettlement of the Cuban immigrants. Upon their arrival, the Cuban Refugee Emergency Center in Miami provided the exiles with food, clothing, medical care, social services, and assistance with housing, relocation, education, and job placement. In addition to a monthly stipend, special federal loans were made available for Cubans who wished to attend universities or start new businesses (Mohl 1990, 49). The Cuban Refugee Program even-

tually became one of the most ambitious and longest-running refugee
assistance packages in U.S. history, with an estimated total cost exceeding
$2 billion (Arguelles 1982, 30; Pedraza-Bailey 1985). *This is what should make the Black*

The federal government not only provided financial assistance to the
refugees but also made a concerted effort to persuade the American public to welcome the Cubans with open arms. The Cuban Refugee Center
printed and widely disseminated information about the tragic plight of
the Cuban refugees and encouraged U.S. citizens to "help the worthy
Cubans help themselves." Various federal officials, such as Secretary of
Health, Education and Welfare Abraham Ribicoff, made frequent pronouncements encouraging every citizen "to help your country aid the
cause of freedom everywhere by supporting the refugees" ("Our Refugees"
1962). The media also played a key role in shaping the public's response
to the Cuban plight. Statements such as the *Saturday Evening Post*'s 1962
editorial "Our Refugees from Castroland" detailed how communism's
"inhumanity to man" was causing an estimated eighteen hundred refugees to flee Cuba weekly. The editorial stated that "in a very real sense this
is a national rather than a local problem. It is the first time that refugees
from Communism have escaped directly into the United States. We bear
a special responsibility to help the Cuban people" ("Our Refugees" 1962,
14).

When U.S. citizens asked about the huge sums of money being spent on
refugee assistance, officials were quick to defend the moral principles upon
which the program had been established. In 1964 J. Arthur Lazell, director
of the Cuban Emergency Relief Center, explained: "This is one of the
largest and most generous refugee programs any nation has ever organized. There are several reasons for this. One is the fact that the Communists for the first time have established themselves close to our shores and
we have been touched by the plight of its victims. We have felt a need to
demonstrate the freedom that we profess and opened our hearts to these
dispossessed" ("Refugee Program" 1964).

In addition to the federally sponsored programs, a variety of private
organizations and particularly the Catholic Church worked diligently to
assist the Cuban refugees. These organizations emphasized the plight of the
Cubans fleeing tyranny and the moral responsibility of all U.S. citizens to

respond charitably. In October 1965, just prior to the start of the twice-daily "freedom flights," Monsignor John J. Fitzpatrick pronounced the Catholic Church ready to receive the expected influx of refugees, and Bishop Coleman Carroll stated, "I am confident that our Catholic people in this area will cooperate in this project with the wholehearted spirit of fraternal charity which has characterized their attitude since our shores became a haven for refugees" ("Bishop Asks" 1965).

Many of the claims being put forth about communism in Cuba were issued by those refugees who had just fled the island. Most of the Cubans in Miami seem to have considered themselves, not immigrants in search of a higher standard of living, but exiles seeking only temporary refuge in the United States until they could return to their homeland. Spanish periodicals and Spanish-language radio stations in Miami fortified the dream of one day returning to the island and reinforced the image of Cubans as the victims of tyranny. They engaged in constant denunciations of Castro, dogmatically preached the evils of communism, editorialized longingly about Cuba before Castro, and sponsored contests to guess when Fidel would fall. The refugees themselves participated in mock elections for the next president of Cuba, and many proudly displayed bumper stickers proclaiming to be "El Primero en Regresar" [The first to return].

Numerous paramilitary organizations grew up amidst this energy and activity, with generous support from the U.S. government. A link between the Cuban exiles and the CIA was established early on in preparation for the Bay of Pigs invasion but continued well beyond the failed military maneuver. The CIA and the exiles shared a commitment to overthrow Castro, and it was through the activities of both groups that *la causa,* or *la lucha,* the struggle, came to symbolize the fight against tyranny in Cuba and to serve as a rallying cry around which to politically mobilize large numbers of Cubans in the United States (Arguelles 1982; Forment 1989).

Issues relating to Castro, communism, and *la causa* served to incite fervor among a substantial proportion of the Cuban American community for many years and resulted in numerous incidents of vocal political protest by even the most mainstream members of the refugee population. During the 1960s the Cuban exiles staged various marches to protest the treatment of anti-Castro leaders accused of terrorist activity. In May 1967 hundreds of

Cubans marched on the Dade County jail to demand the release of Felipe Rivero, a Cuban exile charged with conspiring to bomb the Canadian pavilion at Montreal's Expo '67. They held hunger strikes and, in what became a fairly common form of protest, doused the symbolic John F. Kennedy Torch of Friendship in downtown Miami. Left at the site was a poster that read, "This torch cannot represent freedom while freedom fighters are in prison" (Davis 1967). In 1971 Cubans in Miami organized a huge demonstration to protest Nixon's decision to begin negotiations with China. Large placards read "Nixon: Cuba Is Not Negotiable" and "No Coexistence . . . We Want Liberty" (Stevenson 1975, 48–49). This type of protest continued throughout the 1970s and 1980s, and whether the controversy was a visit by Jane Fonda, a march on contra aide, or the war in Angola, Cubans in Miami came out in force to remind Miami, the United States, and the world of the evils of communism and the threat of tyranny (Didion 1987; Warren, Stack, and Corbett 1986).

The U.S. government also continued, both covertly and overtly, to provide a supportive voice and a sympathetic ear to the Cubans in Miami. U.S. presidents praised the bravery and sacrifice of the Cuban exiles, and both President Kennedy and President Reagan promised that the flag carried by Brigade 2506 during the Bay of Pigs invasion would one day be returned to a free Havana (Didion 1987, 15). The U.S. discourse on communist tyranny subsided with the end of the Reagan era, but Cuba continues to be a controversial political topic even in the post–Cold War world. During the 1992 elections presidential candidates George Bush and Bill Clinton struggled to be credited with supporting the Cuban Democracy Act, also known as the Torricelli bill. The surrounding debate drew heavily on an image of the Cuban people as victims of communist repression and demonstrated that the discourse on tyranny was still alive and well in the 1990s. Supporters of the bill, both Republicans and Democrats, both presidential hopefuls and members of Congress, spoke about the need to increase pressure on Castro's dictatorship so that the Cuban people could benefit from the world culture of democracy that was sweeping the globe (Marquis and Anderson 1992). Jose Cardenas, editor of *Cuba Survey,* praised the passage of the Cuban Democracy Act. "Such a move," he said, "places the United States on the right side of history, and should demonstrate to the rest of the world—and most definitely the Cuban people—that the United States will not sacrifice its principles and its commitment to a free and democratic Cuba for the sake of whatever short-term economic gains can be wrung out of the dispirited island of Cuba" (1992).

Some Cuban exiles still continue their struggle against Castro via the Everglades and the Florida Straits. In October 1992 four men belonging to a Miami-based paramilitary organization, Commandos L, attacked a tourist beach resort hotel on Cuba's northern shore. There were no casualties, but the Comandos L leader Tony Cuesta vowed that "these activities will continue until Cuba is liberated" (Chardy 1992). Another recently formed paramilitary group from Miami had its fishing boat, loaded with weapons and a thousand rounds of ammunition, seized off the coast of Cuba in February 1993. The group's leader, Gonzalez Rosquete, held a news conference at which he announced, "The Partido Unidad Nacional Democratica and Armas del Pueblo formally declare war on Castro-Communism" (Chardy and Reyes 1993). For the most part, however, the battle against communism in Cuba is increasingly waged within the context of the American political system. While the U.S. Congress debated the Torricelli bill in Washington, Dade County Commissioner Alex Penelas introduced a similar resolution in Miami that would prohibit Dade County from awarding a contract to any U.S. corporation whose foreign subsidiaries traded with the island nation. Speaking in support of the Penelas resolution, Fernando Rojas, of the Cuban American National Foundation, stated: "There is no reason why Dade County's taxpayers, many of whom are victims of Castro's tyranny, should benefit companies that insist on trading with Castro and providing him the resources to violate the human rights of the Cuban people" (Filkins 1992b).

A series of newspaper articles, editorials, and television documentaries in 1992 reflected the continued commitment of Cuban immigrants to a "free and democratic Cuba" and attested to the political and economic clout that they were now able to mobilize in pursuit of that goal. When the CANF perceived that the *Miami Herald*'s coverage of the Cuban situation was biased, it waged a nasty battle against the powerful newspaper. The foundation accused the *Herald* of being a tool of the Castro government and conducting "a systematic campaign against Cuban Americans, their institutions, values, ethics and ideals" (Lawrence 1992b). The CANF also completed detailed plans for the future of a free and democratic Cuba, including a constitution, legal codes, property rules, a register of Cuban government property, and a sector-by-sector economic analysis of the island. In addition, an estimated fifteen hundred Cuban Americans have reportedly been trained as an independent Peace Corps, video tapes explaining to the Cuban people "what the future can hold for them" are being smuggled into the island daily, and once Fidel falls, a chartered boat full of investors, stockbrokers, and bankers will sail into Cuba on what CANF president Jorge Mas Canosa calls "a ship of hope" (Slevin 1992b). Mas Canosa himself explains that "we are committed to finding pathways to the liberty of Cuba." He describes Cuban exiles as "simple people who are searching for freedom and happiness for our fatherland . . . a united people divided by one man, Fidel Castro." Mas Canosa also maintains that the future reunification of Cuba will take place "in an environment of harmony, understanding, love and brotherhood among all Cubans" (Slevin 1992a, 1A).

"SEND US 1,000 MORE"

Public discourse about Cuban immigration to the United States emphasized not only the tyranny from which these refugees fled but also the benefit they provided to the United States upon their arrival. Business people, government officials, and the media praised the Cubans, recognizing their entrepreneurial spirit, their loyalty to family and community, and their commitment to hard work, education, and self-advancement. As early as 1962, *Business Week* published an article entitled "To Miami, Refugees Spell Prosperity." The article referred to the Cuban refugees as a "disguised blessing": "The fact is that the 150,000 Cubans who have fled the Castro regime in the past 34 months—most of them with only the clothes on their backs—have turned upside down the economic and social life of Miami." Business and civic leaders in Miami agreed that the refugees had greatly stimulated commerce in Miami and even speculated about the negative impact their return might have on the local economy. Miami Mayor

Robert High frequently proclaimed that these refugees were "a definite asset to our community. They've saved downtown Miami" ("To Miami" 1962, 94).

When fears were expressed about the impact of the refugee influx on Miami's economy, some local officials, such as Monsignor Bryan Walsh, were quick to point out that "we know from previous experience that [their coming] has had a good effect on the area." Bank presidents in Miami issued similar statements. William Pallot, president of Miami's Inter National Bank, said: "With proper government assistance, I believe this area can stand more [refugees] and they will help Miami to eventually achieve its destiny as the great gateway to Latin America." The president of Riverside Bank in Miami concurred: "I have the greatest respect for them and I think they've enriched our community beyond measure" (Birger 1965). Howard Palmatier, director of the Cuban Refugee Program, exclaimed: "It seems to me remarkable that when you consider that these refugees arrived here with nothing but their skills and abilities, that eighty-three percent are fully self-supporting and only seventeen percent require federal assistance" ("How the Immigrants" 1971, 88).

In 1967 the University of Miami's Research Institute for Cuba and the Caribbean published the results of a major study entitled "The Cuban Immigration 1959–1966 and Its Impact on Miami–Dade County, Florida." The report emphasized that any problems associated with this unprecedented migration "have proved largely transitory" and "have been far outweighed by benefits" (Research Institute for Cuba and the Caribbean 1967, xii). The report urged recognition of the exiles as "opportunities" rather than "problems" and essentially confirmed that "downtown Miami was saved by the Cuban exodus as well as other sections of the city, which were on the way to becoming blighted areas. Cubans created new businesses and employment. The displacement of Negroes by Cubans and an assumption that Cubans depressed wages ... were not borne out by facts" ("Refugees Called" 1967).

Praises of this sort were common in the national as well as the local media. In October 1966 *Fortune* published a story entitled "Those Amazing Cuban Émigrés—Send Us 1,000 More." And in 1971 *Business Week* reported that "in the 10 years since Cubans began fleeing to the United States from Castro, they have made faster progress in their adopted country than has any other group of immigrants in this century. Almost overnight they have emerged from the deprived, refugee state and moved into the middle class, skipping lightly over—or never even touching—the lowest rung of the economic ladder" ("How the Immigrants" 1971). During the same year, *Life Magazine* wrote: "It was just ten years ago that the prosperous Cubans . . . began flooding to Miami, refugees from Castro's communism. Most arrived penniless, and took any jobs available. . . . Today many of these same men are bankers, businessmen, manufacturers. At a rate unprecedented among America's major immigrant groups, the 350,000 Cubans in the Miami area have transformed themselves into a thriving, prosperous community" ("Making It" 1971).

The refugees were praised not only for stimulating the local economy but also for the ease and willingness with which they adapted to their new environment. In 1965 the *Miami News* published a report on the rapid and successful Americanization of the Cuban exiles. After quoting an exile who claimed, "I can no longer stand the taste of *cafe con leche* [coffee with milk]," the article went on to explain: "Radios that once blasted into the night are muted, and television is replacing noisy games of dominoes. Lawns, allowed to grow ankle-deep in weeds, 'because mañana we return,' are now proudly kept neatly trimmed" ("Exiles Saying" 1965).

Similar statements were made throughout the 1970s, and in 1983 the Strategic Research Corporation reported that two-thirds of all Latins in the Miami area were using credit cards by 1978 and that the average Miami Cuban was dining out in American-style fast-food restaurants 105 times a year, Kentucky Fried Chicken being a reported favorite (Allman 1987, 335). The accolades continued during the 1980s as authors recounted the amazing story of Cuban success. George Gilder wrote: "They were then unemployed, unpromising, and unsettled, living in accommodations comprehensively in violation of codes, but they were already at work, seething with the spirit of enterprise, figuring out how to transfigure Southwest Eighth Street into Calle Ocho, the main drag of a new Little Havana" (Gilder 1985, 70). Gilder's 1984 book, *The Spirit of Enterprise,* devotes an entire chapter to the Cuban success story; and Miami's Cubans also figure prominently in his 1992 sequel, *Recapturing the Spirit of Enterprise.*

FROM RAGS TO RICHES (BUT NEVER RACIST)

Despite the promise and praise of a Cuban economic miracle, Miami's public image took a turn for the worse during the 1980s. The attention of the media, government officials, and the civic and business elite was focused less on "those amazing Cuban émigrés" and more on the riots, the crime, the drug trafficking, and the urban decay that were fast earning Miami its reputation as a "Paradise Lost." It was in this context that Cuban immigrants began to organize themselves in an effort to promote a favorable image of the Cuban contribution to Miami and to the United States. Although evidence of Cubans emphasizing their contribution to the United States can be traced to the late 1960s, a rags-to-riches discourse among the émigrés in Miami, one that drew on tales of hardship and personal sacrifice, became particularly prominent in the 1980s. Criticism was being heaped on Miami from various sources, but Cuban leaders continued to portray their adopted home as a land of opportunity and to highlight the benefits of Cuban immigration.

At a 1984 conference of the Cuban American Planning Council, Luis Botifoll, a prominent Cuban American civic and business leader and president of the Republic National Bank, delivered what has since become a widely publicized speech entitled "How Miami's New Image Was Created." He opened as follows: "The growth achieved by Miami constitutes a factor which has no precedent in the history of this nation. That growth occurred within what has been called 'The Great Cuban Miracle.' Because of this, I believe that those who left the island in 1959 and those who only recently arrived with the same faith and hope must feel proud not only of what they have achieved for themselves, but also of what they have accomplished for the entire community" (Botifoll 1988, 1).

In the 1990s Cubans in Miami remain quick to recount their stories of struggle and success, emphasizing, as did one Cuban American community leader, that "You must remember Cubans are political refugees, not economic. The United States is accustomed to assimilation—to the melting pot. Cubans have a lot of pride, and we have refused to let go of our culture" (interview, 20 May 1992). Many Cubans also react adamantly to charges that they have somehow been responsible for the city's social ills, and this reaction frequently includes references to racial tension in Miami. When asked in interviews, "Have immigrants taken jobs from blacks in Miami's labor market?" most Cuban Americans (45 percent of those interviewed) strongly disagreed that job displacement had occurred. One Cuban American respondent argued, "There is an impression that we came to take jobs, to impose our culture, but that's not true. We took parking jobs—my first job was in a sewing factory. Those jobs were there, and if people that had the language didn't take them, how can you say we took their jobs?" (interview, 24 September 1992).

Others felt that immigrants may have affected the economic advancement of the black community in Miami but quickly added that if this was the case, it was the result of a willingness among Cuban refugees to work extremely hard at whatever jobs were available and the absence of a similar motivation on the part of blacks. One Cuban American county official who immigrated in the 1960s explained: "When I came to the United States, going on welfare was unheard of. I scrubbed floors. . . . Some blacks may have been cut off, lost some opportunities to incoming Cubans, but today they are still the poorest and immigration can't account for all of this" (interview, 16 June 1992).

With regard to the issue of race several Cuban respondents made a clear distinction between what they viewed as extreme color consciousness in U.S. society and the color-blind context of social relations in Cuba. Osvaldo Soto, a prominent Cuban American businessman and chairman of the Spanish American League Against Discrimination (SALAD), explained: "I came here for the first time for a visit in 1941; I was ten. I was shocked to see signs in hotels that said 'No Dogs or Jews' or 'No Dogs and Blacks.' I sat in the back of a bus, and a lady told me not to sit there, it was for niggers. The problems at that time were not only with blacks, but Jews also. There was much discrimination. We cannot really be the reason. Slavery was here long before we came in the '60s; discrimination had been going on against blacks for a long time" (interview, 20 July 1992). A top Cuban American official with the Greater Miami Chamber of Commerce volunteered the following: "Remember, in Cuba we did not make our blacks ride at the back of the bus" (interview, 11 March 1992). And a former Cuban American county manager explained, "Cubans are not racist. I'm color-blind and did not become aware of these issues until I came here" (interview, 8 June 1992).

This discourse on the absence of racial prejudice among Cubans surfaced in other contexts as well. In 1984 the *Diario Las Americas*, a widely read Latin newspaper in Miami, published an editorial entitled "Cubanos y Americanos Negros." The author explained, "When we say Cubans we are including everyone, regardless of color, because that is how it was in Cuba, how it is between us in exile, and how it will always be. . . . Cubans do not have prejudices, nor do we consider differences, let alone practice discrimination toward black Americans" (Perna 1984).

Five years later, during the controversy surrounding the Lozano trial, the *Diario Las Americas* published a similar editorial by Raquel Regalado, the programming director for a Cuban radio station in Miami, "Radio Mambi." After arguing that Officer Lozano was a victim of racial tension in Miami, Regalado explained: "In our countries we do not have the racial problems that confront us now, we do not have experience with this type of situation . . . the authorities have always wanted to place Hispanics against blacks in place of improving racial tension. To me it is not important if my neighbor is black or yellow, but that he be a decent person" (Regalado 1990).

The Cuban success story has experienced some competition from alternative discourses that often conflict with the image of the immigrants as an unqualified blessing for Miami and the United States. Yet, Cuban Americans themselves, as well as others, continue to express pride in their accomplishments and praise for a political system that affords great opportunity to those who are willing to strive for the American dream. Armando Codina, the first Cuban American to become chairman of the Greater Miami Chamber of Commerce, recently remarked that "America is a land of opportunity. Many native-born Americans take their freedom for granted and find so much fault with the system here that they lose sight of the tremendous advantages. To those of us who came from Cuba, this was— and is—the promised land" (Russell 1992). Codina is also well known for his frequent public references to the luxury boat he purchased in the United States and proudly christened "What A Country" (interview, 7 July 1992).

COMPETING IMAGES AND CONTESTED CLAIMS

Over decades this claims-making activity by government officials, business executives, community leaders, the media, and Cubans themselves has constructed a public image of Cuban success. That image is sustained by a variety of perceptions, portrayals, and myths. Myths exist with regard to who left the island, why they left, how they left, and the events and circumstances that shaped their lives upon arrival in the United States. Even the island itself has taken on a mythical quality as Cubans in Miami reconstruct the history of a Cuba that fewer and fewer can actually remember and increasing numbers have never known. As one Cuban professional living in New York explained, "In Miami, Cubans live, or try to live, in *la Cuba de ayer*—the Cuba of yesterday. It is a mythical country we have fabricated, where nostalgia and myths abound" (Rieff 1987b, 73).

This section refers back to the success story and challenges the myth of sociocultural homogeneity and political cohesiveness among Cubans in Miami, as well as the assumptions about ethnicity that underlie and emerge from these myths. The challenge is not posed with the intent of replacing one false or inaccurate story with a truer or more objectively verifiable one. Rather, various arguments and claims that compete with or contradict the dominant imagery are highlighted in order to demonstrate that the Cuban success story is one among many potential definitions of social reality.

Despite a tendency to view the 1980 Mariel boatlift as a point of drastic alteration in the composition of the Cuban population in the United States, significant social, political, economic, religious, and racial diversity existed among the émigrés from the beginning. Boswell and Curtis pointed out that Cubans "emigrated to the United States from virtually all regions of the island, stretching from the province of Pinar del Rio in the west to Oriente province in the east; they came from the rural areas, the cities, and the suburbs." The Cuban exodus was not limited to the rich and educated; it encompassed "the full spectrum of socioeconomic classes and ethnic groups that existed in Cuba prior to the Castro revolution" (1984, 46). Some analysts have argued that even among the earliest arrivals the "elite" were outnumbered by laborers, clerks, farmers, and fishermen. Doctors, for example, according to some figures, constituted only 1 percent of arrivals during the initial stages of the influx. The proportion of immigrants classified as managers or professionals is said to have dropped significantly when the United States began twice-daily airlifts of Cuban refugees in 1965 (Allman 1987, 306; Boswell and Curtis 1984).

The émigrés' diversity extended to political background and ideological persuasion as well. Early émigrés, who were defenders of the Batista regime, were later joined by former comrades of Fidel Castro; and by 1980 many of the Cubans in Cuba who had defended the island against the Cubans in Miami during the Bay of Pigs invasion were also departing for South Florida's shores. Despite the widely held perception of Cubans in the United States as politically conservative, this is not simply a reflection of, or a carry-over from, the island. As Jorge and Moncarz explained, "Prior to the Castro regime coming to power in Cuba, conservatism was by no means the hallmark of Cuban domestic politics. In fact, the platform of all Cuban political parties had been markedly progressive following the Revolution of 1933" (1987, 30). And Maria de los Angeles Torres said that "even the 1960s generation of exiles was not uniformly conservative. They ranged from batistianos to disenchanted socialists" (1988, 392). It was this "profound political difference" among Cuban exiles that led Charles Forment (1989) to conclude that the Cuban ethnic enclave was a product of political competition and negotiation between rival groups. Among those Cubans arriving in the years 1959–64 alone, Forment identifies three distinct groups—Batistianists, conservatives, and liberals—each representing a distinct political position. A recent survey by Rodolfo de la Garza also indicated that despite the widespread perception of Cuban Americans as politically conservative, they actually share similar attitudes with other Hispanic groups regarded as more liberal, and many of those shared attitudes contradict the conservative line. Ninety-five percent of Cuban Americans believe, for example, that the national government has a primary responsibility to solve problems, and 45 percent believe strongly that the government should guarantee jobs and housing to those in need (Falcoff 1995, 36).

Another popular perception is that Cubans are political refugees fleeing persecution by a communist regime. Yet the changing content, circumstances, and context of Cuban emigration since 1959 suggest that the reasons for leaving were almost as varied as the population that left. Amaro and Portes explained that during the period 1965–73 "increasingly, the emigration ceases to be a political act and becomes an economic act." They said that later arrivals more closely resembled "classical immigrants," who were "pulled" by economic opportunity in the United States rather than "pushed" by the Cuban revolution (1972, 13). According to Boswell and Curtis, "It would be incorrect to assume that all Cubans have come to America strictly to escape . . . Castro." They identify "powerful migrational 'pull' forces," such as "the lure of economic opportunity" and "the quest for family reunification," that prompted many Cubans to leave (1984, 38). As author T. D. Allman points out, "Like all American immigrants, the Cubans came here for a mixture of reasons: freedom, there is no doubt about it, is a powerful magnet; but equally irresistible—to downtrodden people all over the world—is the glittering allure of America's wealth" (1987, 306). *Again, easy to see why there's such a dichotomous exp. between Miami's Cuban + Black's*

Cuban émigrés represent not only different economic backgrounds, different political persuasions, and different reasons for departing but also different ethnic, racial, and religious backgrounds. There are living in Miami an estimated twelve thousand Jewish Cubans, five thousand Chinese Cubans, and a growing number of black Cubans; and race is perhaps the least understood element of diversity among Cubans and among Latin Americans in general.[4] Despite claims of color-blindness by Cubans in the United States as well as by the Castro regime, Cuba was and continues to be a society in which race matters. Since Castro came to power in 1959 it has been difficult to gather reliable demographic, political, or economic data on Cuba, and many scholars agree that the data that are available from pre-Castro Cuba vastly underestimate the physical and cultural presence of the "Negro" (Fagen 1969, 21).[5]

Most analyses of pre-Castro Cuba point to class as the most salient form of social stratification on the island. Other evidence suggests, however, that these class divisions corresponded closely to color, darker-skinned Cubans being disproportionately represented at the lower rungs of the socioeconomic ladder (Helg 1990). Fagen contends that compared with other developing societies during the 1950s Cuba was relatively free of sociocultural cleavages. But he goes on to say that "there was, however, widespread social and economic discrimination based on custom and personal prejudice, and the man of dark skin was in general greatly disadvantaged in pre-revolutionary Cuba" (1969, 21).

A seminal work by Maurice Zeitlin provides similar insights into social relations on the island. Zeitlin quotes from a 1962 interview with a Cuban campesino: "Look, chico, this is many times better than we had before the revolution when our women slept on the floor in the midst of roaches and rats. . . . Negroes had to go to a different beach, they couldn't even buy refreshments in some places in the same store with white American tourists, who came here only to take pictures of pleasure and not of the misery we were living in. We have no running water yet, or gas, or electricity that we can count on; we still carry our water home in pails, but at least now we are alive" (1967, 76).

Despite evidence of discontent among blacks in Cuba prior to the revolution and Castro's claims to have eradicated all social distinctions based on race, class, and gender, black Cubans clearly have been among those leaving the island over the past thirty years. This was obvious during the Mariel boatlift, when an estimated 40 percent of the arrivals were classified as "black," but the exodus of black Cubans from the island dates back to the early 1960s. In June 1963 the International Fraternal Union announced its formation as an association of Cuban blacks in exile with the stated goals of war against Castro and equal rights ("Negro Exiles" 1963). When asked about the estimated number of blacks arriving on the airlift in 1966, the director of Catholic Welfare Services, the largest private resettlement agency in Miami, answered: "The first two weeks of the airlift hardly any arrived. But in the last ten days or two weeks, there have been more coming out than we have seen over the past three years"(Bohning 1966).

Some analysts view the larger number of blacks in the most recent waves of Cuban immigration as an indication of persistent racial prejudice in Cuba (see, e.g., Casal 1980, 20). Others argue that those leaving Cuba today are from the poorer classes and that blacks comprise a large proportion of the Cuban poor (Fox 1971, 21). Carlos Moore, an Afro-Cuban author and ethnologist, argues that the exiles in Miami are wrong to assume that the predominantly black population of Cuba wants their help. "There is a fear among the blacks [in Cuba] that any attempt to change the government violently will lead to an American intervention and an attempt to empower the white Cubans" (Hancock 1990; Moore 1988). The debate over the relevance of race in Cuba continues, but irrespective of the extent to which the revolution has eradicated racial prejudice and discrimination, most analysts and observers agree that the thirty-year embargo by the United States has had a substantial impact on emigration from the island, including that of blacks. The impact in Miami is that many longtime exiles now acknowledge that the increased influx of black Cubans has forcefully challenged their beliefs about the demographic composition of the island. One Cuban American businessman remarked: "We had invented a Cuba in which everyone was white. When the marielitos came, we were forcibly reminded that Cuba is not a white island but largely a black one" (Rieff 1987b, 66).

Another myth that has emerged from the discussion and debate surrounding Cuban immigration to the United States portrays Cuban émigrés as "fleeing" or "escaping" the island. This terminology, which dominates much of the discourse on Cuban emigration, conjures up images of millions of refugees risking their lives daily in daring escapes and treacherous journeys to freedom. There is no doubt that there have been numerous such cases, but as T. D. Allman points out: "In the whole twenty years between 1960 and 1980, only about 16,000 Cubans actually 'fled' Cuba, in the sense of eluding Castro's military patrols and escaping the island, at the risk of their own lives, in small boats or by 'other extremely dangerous means'" (1987, 302). Although the reports of refugees leaving Cuba on rickety rafts are very real and very tragic, larger numbers of Cubans were airlifted by the U.S. government, transported by relatives in chartered boats, or spotted by Brothers to the Rescue, a group of predominantly Cuban American volunteer pilots who conduct surveillance over the Florida Strait, alert the U.S. Coast Guard of any sightings, and follow up on the safe transport and processing of any Cuban refugees rescued at sea (Weston 1992).

Mythology surrounds not only the exodus of Cubans from the island but also their experiences in exile in the United States. The notion of a

Cuban "community" in Miami is widespread even though the same divisions that existed among Cubans on the island resurfaced when they arrived in the United States. Most Cuban immigrants made a concerted effort to recreate their lives as they had been in Cuba. Of the 126 townships that existed in pre-Castro Cuba, 114 were represented by *municipios* in Miami. These *municipios* performed a variety of social and political functions and essentially constituted a form of municipal government in exile (Levine 1985, 56). A similar situation occurred with regard to social clubs and organizations that existed in pre-Castro Cuba. In her discussion of the wide variation in social class origin among Cubans in the United States, Silvia Pedraza-Bailey states that "the former social distinctions were perpetrated and reenacted in exile, often with little bearing to their life in America. Those who had belonged to the five most exclusive yacht and country clubs in Havana founded another in Miami, in nostalgia dubbed 'The Big Five.' Cubans of working-class origin remain outsiders to these attempts to recreate once enviable social positions: a golden past that was not theirs, but which with increased distance in time, seems to grow only more golden" (1985, 18).

Evidence of differences and disagreements among exiles arriving in Miami surfaced almost immediately. In December 1960 the *Miami Herald* did a story on the political and economic gaps that divided the Cuban immigrants: "There is no 'Cuban refugee community' as such. There are hundreds of separate refugee units and their dislike for each other is exceeded only by their hatred of Castro" ("Wide Political Gaps" 1960). These differences persisted over the years in conflicts between different exile organizations over how to deal with Fidel Castro. The terrorist activity of some Cuban exile organizations did not remain focused on the island but was perpetrated against Cubans living in the United States as well. Any individual or organization that expressed an unpopular opinion toward Castro or Cubans could become the target of a violent attack by one of several militant exile groups. This type of activity was most prevalent during the 1970s, but there is some indication that extremism persists. In 1992 Americas Watch, a division of an international human rights monitoring organization, issued the report "Dangerous Dialogue: Attacks on Freedom of Expression in Miami's Cuban Exile Community." The report covered the various exile organizations operating in Miami and their differing postures with regard to dialogue or interaction with Castro. Americas Watch also discussed recent incidents of terrorism and intimidation by different exile organizations, including the 1988 bombing of the Cuban Art Museum in Miami after museum officials exhibited works by painters living in Cuba (Americas Watch 1992).

Controversy among Cuban exiles continues, but it is contained primarily within the realm of public debate and more conventional forms of political activity. Evidence of persistent fragmentation within the Cuban American community surfaced recently during debates over the Torricelli bill. Once the bill was signed into law, Jorge Mas Canosa, who had lobbied hard for its passage, exclaimed: "I'm very, very happy. It's a historic day for Cuba. I think the countdown for the end of Castro's days in power has really begun." Ramon Cernuda, a prominent civic figure in Miami and a spokesperson for several well-known Cuban human rights dissidents, had quite a different reaction: "We do not accept the Torricelli bill as a legitimate law. It seeks to starve the people of Cuba in the name of human rights and democratic values" (Chardy and Corzo 1992). Differing opinions and outlooks among Cuban Americans in Dade County were also evident during the 1992 congressional elections. A Cuban American Democrat ran against the extremely popular Republican Congresswoman Ileana Ros-Lehtinen in what Miami political strategist Armando Villareal said "politically" was "the first serious challenge the exile community has had" (Defede 1992, 26). Although Democrat Magda Montiel-Davis's platform, which was for dialogue with Castro and pro-choice, was unsuccessful, it was viewed as a historic turning point in Cuban American politics. Clifford Krauss, of the *New York Times,* described the race as "historically and culturally important": "To have a Cuban American who is offering a different way to bring democracy to Cuba and who is bringing up other issues like abortion—and to have her heard—shows a new maturity for the community" (Defede 1992, 20).[6]

The image of Cubans in Miami as a united community is fraught with inconsistencies, but so too is the story of their economic success. Several analysts have challenged the accuracy of the Cuban success story, calling attention to the predominantly working-class character of the Cuban community in the United States. Using survey research and data from the U.S. census, economist Raul Moncarz (1978) found that 76 percent of Cubans living in Florida in 1972 had incomes below the U.S. median family income. His research also indicated that between 1966 and 1974, Cubans in Miami as a group experienced no upward occupational mobility. Moncarz concluded, "The evidence gathered in this study concerning education, geographic, and income mobility seems to indicate that mobility, if any, has been minimal" (171). Lourdes Casal also criticized the Cuban success story: "Other information, gleaned from the 1970 census and the U.S. Budget, documents the darker side of the story. For instance, one out of five metropolitan Cubans lives in an area designated as 'low-income' by the Census Bureau" (1979, 118). The significance of these findings is enhanced by the fact that the research was conducted prior to the arrival of the Mariel refugees in April 1980.

In another "reexamination" of the Cuban success story, the sociologist Lisandro Perez (1986) found that although success among Cubans in the United States has been portrayed at the level of the individual, it is more accurately explained at the level of the family or the household. In other words, instead of emphasizing the entrepreneurial drive of individual Cuban immigrants, we must pay more attention to the impact of economic cooperation within families, particularly to the very high rates of female participation in the U.S. labor force. Antonio Jorge cautioned that even the much heralded Cuban enclave economy did not bring unqualified success. The small family-owned businesses that make up the enclave may have limited long-term gains by luring young family members away from the primary labor market and from school (Torres 1988, 393).

In her article "Working against the Miami Myth," Maria de los Angeles Torres points out that the average family income of Cuban Americans is still well below the U.S. average and that the high school dropout rate among Cuban American students has increased more rapidly than among any other Latino group. She remarks: "The facts show that while many Cubans did make it, many more did not—despite the unprecedented welfare benefits, English-language classes, university and business loans, and covert CIA money that flowed into South Florida" (1988, 393). Even among those Cubans who did make impressive economic, social, and political gains in the United States—and there are many—the emphasis on their individual character traits and willingness to "pull themselves up by the bootstraps" completely overshadows the unprecedented assistance, financial and otherwise, they received upon arrival in the United States.

[handwritten margin note: Not a typical "exile" immigrant group]

Underlying and emerging from these mythologies that make up the success story are certain beliefs and assumptions that obscure the constructed nature of ethnicity in particular and identity more generally. Many of the claims about Cubans in the United States assume, implicitly and explicitly, that these immigrants share a common group identity, an identity that is portrayed in terms of cultural, psychological, and affective ties—read: ethnicity. In other words, the same narratives that make up the story of success simultaneously define Cuban Americans as a socially cohesive, politically united, and economically powerful ethnic group. Their cohesion is attributed to a common cultural ancestry, their political unity to a shared ideology, namely, conservative or anticommunist, and their economic achievement to hard work and a shared spirit of enterprise. In essence, much of what defines the Cuban community in Miami as successful is believed to be a product of their ethnicity. *[handwritten: — What about the lush in.]*

This assumption is problematic for various reasons. The tautological premise that members of an ethnic group share similarities because they are of the same ethnicity leaves unanswered critical questions about the origins, content, and malleability of ethnic identity and ethnic group relations. Although few studies deal directly with the issue of Cuban American ethnic identity, there is a tendency to treat ethnicity as an independent variable, as a way to explain Cuban American social and political behavior, rather than as something to be explained. The counterclaims and competing discourses presented above suggest that Cubans in Miami do not necessarily constitute a cohesive community or necessarily share similar ancestries, experiences, or pasts. A shared ethnic identity is not, then, inherent or somehow natural among Cubans in Miami, and the similarities in attitude or behavior that do exist among the émigrés are not necessarily rooted in a primordial past. In fact, the information presented above indicates that there is no single, constant, and all-encompassing Cuban American ethnic identity, just as there is no single definition of social reality. Therefore, an analysis of Cubans in the United States cannot take as given the

[handwritten margin notes: Boston? Talk about myths... "how ethnicity is used"]

notion of a Cuban American ethnic identity but must ask what provides the content for Cuban American ethnic identity at particular points in time, where it comes from, and how or why it changes over time. The final section of this chapter presents Cuban ethnic identity and the related story of Cuban success as social and political constructs closely related to power and politics but not necessarily in a direct or deterministic fashion.

ETHNICITY, POWER, AND POLITICS

The overview of claims-making activity in and about Miami indicates that the Cuban success story is one social definition of reality that competes with and contradicts various other socially constructed realities. Similarly, the image of Cuban exiles as a cohesive and uniformly conservative ethnic community is one of many possible interpretations of the social, political, and economic behavior of Cubans in the United States. Neither image simply mirrors an objective, empirical reality, yet both display impressive staying power in a complex and highly contested social terrain. By focusing on the actors, issues, and events that constructed the story of Cuban success, this analysis argues that social definitions, including the definition of individual and group identity, are the product of a complex interplay of power and politics over historical time. In this case, the so-called Cuban success story promoted the policies and ideology of the U.S. government, advanced the interests and concerns of Cubans in the United States, and constructed a functional ethnic identity for Cuban immigrants in which political symbols, personal passions, and cultural themes were reinterpreted, reconfigured, and assigned new meaning and significance congruent with contemporary configurations of social, political, and economic power in the United States.

CUBANS, CAPITALISM, AND THE COLD WAR

Many of the claims about Cuban immigration were issued by officials, organizations, and agencies associated with the U.S. federal government. These claims conveyed sympathy for the plight of the Cuban refugees and portrayed the United States as a safe and willing haven for those fleeing persecution. Irrespective of the level of sincerity underlying the claims, this discourse reinforced a number of political objectives of the U.S. government. The positive portrayal of Cuban immigration cannot be understood in isolation from the Cold War ideology that characterized U.S. politics from the 1960s to the 1990s. The Cuban revolution dealt a serious blow to the United States in its ideological struggle with the Soviet Union, and the exodus of Cuban refugees from the island provided the United States with potent material for an ideological counterattack. Widely publicized accounts of Cubans risking their lives to escape tyranny served to discredit the revolution and the ideological principles upon which it was founded, and photographs of Cubans kneeling to kiss the ground in Miami portrayed the United States, and the principles for which it professed to stand, as an option superior to communism. The discourse on Cubans as victims of tyranny also helped to restore U.S. national honor after the severe loss of prestige suffered during the failed Bay of Pigs invasion.

Facilitating the success of the success story served other domestic policy objectives as well. The rapid influx of thousands of refugees into South Florida posed numerous hardships for the state and local governments. The refugee influx might have been interpreted as a policy disaster for the administration in Washington, but federal officials appeased local agencies with an infusion of financial assistance and assured the broader public that these refugees were an asset to American society, stating that all U.S. citizens should be proud to take part in the historic effort to aid victims of communist tyranny. In this way a potential policy failure was reinterpreted as a triumph. The discourse on tyranny and commitment to *la causa* also served to appease, or perhaps coopt, the thousands of Cubans who had arrived in the United States and those who would follow them. After the Bay of Pigs debacle Washington felt compelled to assure the growing population of Cuban refugees of its commitment to restore democracy in Cuba. With time the commitment itself became an important tool for mobilizing a very potent political bloc. Politicians at the local, state, and national levels quickly learned to manipulate the symbols of Castro and communism for their own personal political gain.[7]

Much of the discussion that surrounded Cuban immigration to the United States focused on Castro and communism, but the credentials of the Cuban refugees as productive U.S. citizens was also a common theme. Alongside claims of government officials portraying the refugees as political heroes were statements by business and civic leaders commending the Cuban immigrants for their entrepreneurial genius. These claims told the story of a "Cuban economic miracle," a story that conveyed the same ideals of hard work and self-sacrifice as those comprised in the American civic culture. Miami was in the midst of a severe economic downturn when the Cubans arrived. The once-booming construction industry was lagging, and tourists were bypassing Miami on their way to the Caribbean. The immigrants began to settle along the deserted areas of Flagler Street and southwest Eighth Street, opening small family businesses in the vacated shops. Many local leaders quickly recognized the potential payoff of the refugee influx. The business elite in Miami who were calling for "1,000 more" refugees claimed to benefit from the industriousness and integrity of the Cuban community in Miami. It is likely, however, that they were also benefiting from the massive infusion of federal capital and a ready supply of cheap and devoted labor.

During fiscal year 1961 more than $14 million in direct and indirect aid was funneled into Miami. This figure increased to $70.1 million for fiscal year 1963. Of the $384.5 million spent during the 1960s on behalf of Cuban exiles in the United States, $257.8 million was spent in Dade County ("Cuban Program Boosts" 1969). The refugees used this federal assistance to pay for food, clothing, lodging, and transportation. The positive impact on the retail industry in Miami was almost immediate. In 1962 *Business Week* published an article entitled "To Miami, Refugees Spell Prosperity." The article explained that in an otherwise depressed economic year, department store sales were up 8 percent and automotive sales had increased by 20 percent; one Chevrolet dealer was quoted as saying, "Latin sales constitute 30% of our business" (94). Miami's banking community also welcomed the Cuban refugees with open arms. In 1967 William Pallot, president of the Inter National Bank of Miami, claimed that the bank "measures in thousands" its Cuban patrons. "We helped them, based more on character than anything else, and they have become valued customers." Tully Dunlap, president of the Riverside Bank, said that his bank had prospered on Cuban patronage, experiencing a $5 million deposit increase in 1965 and a $4 million increase in 1966. "They borrow small amounts, use the money well and pay their debts, and expand" (Bedwell 1967).

At the national level, there is some indication that South Florida's economy benefited when large manufacturers, primarily in the garment industry, transferred operations from cities like New York to take advantage of the growing supply of cheap and nonunionized Cuban labor in Miami (Portes and Stepick 1993, 127–28). At the international level, many of Miami's business elite also recognized that Cuban financial and human capital was helping Miami position itself to play a strategic role in an increasingly global economy. Amos Martin, executive vice-president of the Miami Chamber of Commerce, spoke enthusiastically about the refugee contribution in 1967: "Their impact has been great. This is part of our becoming the gateway city to Latin America. The availability of good bilingual help is one of the inducements that brought the Latin American regional headquarters of the Dow Chemical Company to Miami. It also has influenced plans of Mutual of Omaha Insurance to open a regional office here" (Lahey 1967).

The Cuban émigrés were portrayed as "amazing" not only because of their business acumen and strength of character but also because of their ability to adapt quickly to their new surroundings. The transition from dominoes and loud radios to trimmed lawns and television was viewed as positive progress toward Americanization, as was the use of credit cards and the consumption of fast food. Implicit in this discourse about the amazing émigrés is, first, that Americanization—whether it is defined as working hard, watching television, or eating Kentucky Fried Chicken—is good and, second, that since Cuban immigrants were able to achieve success in Miami, so, too, could any other group. The Cuban success story not only perpetuated the myth of the American dream but reinforced a belief that any lack of success was the fault of the particular individual or group, not of the political system or economic structure.

This emphasis on individual character traits and culture as an explanation for economic success has particularly relevant implications for the plight of the African American community in Miami. The Cubans arrived in Miami just as blacks were beginning to make greater demands on the political and economic system. Irrespective of the actual impact Cuban immigrants had on the labor market opportunities of blacks, the refugee crisis clearly detracted attention from the black cause. For those interested in denying blacks access to the system, the Cubans offered an ideal diversion. A statement by a white upper-middle-class woman who was a longtime resident of Miami Beach is suggestive in this regard: "The presence of the Cubans has been a good thing. They drive the Negroes off of Flagler Street. It hasn't been good for the lazy Negroes" (Stevenson 1975, 106). What is seldom recognized is that the comparisons of these two groups, irrespective of the context or reasons offered for their differences, reinforce the image of Cubans as successful and blacks as unsuccessful. The images themselves simultaneously facilitate or hinder the actual achievement of more tangible measures of success. In other words, the economic and political achievements of the Cuban Americans not only gave rise to, but also resulted from, an image of success. In Miami, this image has continued to elude blacks.

FROM EXILES TO ESTABLISHMENT

Tales of extraordinary achievement by Cuban immigrants were told not only by businessmen, bankers, and government officials within the established elite but also by the immigrants themselves. As T. D. Allman writes, "Today wealthy middle-aged Cubans—as they relax beside their suburban swimming pools or aboard their boats in Biscayne Bay—like to reminisce about the bad old days when they first reached Miami. The years spent waiting tables or sacking groceries have become to the Cuban success story what the log cabin and the one-room schoolhouse were to an earlier version of the American Dream" (1987, 318). This rags-to-riches discourse fueled the transition of Cubans in Miami from exiles to immigrants to members of the "established elite." Formulated in reaction to competing claims generated by the host society, the discourse also reflected the unique position of Cuban immigrants in a changing political and economic world system.

In the years immediately following the revolution the attention of Cubans in Miami remained focused on their anticipated return to the homeland. The immigrants' involvement in the American political system was minimal, few of them having become U.S. citizens. In 1971 the *Miami Herald* estimated that only 10–20 percent of Cubans in Miami were U.S. citizens and said that "despite their great numbers here, no Cuban holds political office, not even minor ones. Few are members of Boards, study groups, or citizens commissions. None hold appointive posts. On none of the elected councils or commissions of the twenty-eight units of local governments is there a Cuban. In the race for thirty-one seats for the State Legislature, there was not one Cuban candidate" (Greene 1971).

The mid-1970s marked the beginning of a period of political adaptation for Cubans in the United States, and by the early 1980s the refugees more closely resembled a traditional immigrant group in a variety of ways. Larger numbers of Cubans became U.S. citizens and exercised the rights and privileges that went with citizenship. Voter registration and turnout increased among Cuban Americans, and although Castro and communism remained high priorities for them, their political agenda expanded to include issues of general concern to the community at large. Public opinion polls conducted throughout the 1970s and 1980s also indicated that fewer and fewer Cubans remained committed to returning to the island (Jorge and Moncarz 1987; Portes 1984). By the 1990s, Cuban Americans in Miami had not only entered the mainstream of American life but become an integral part of the established power structure in Dade County. The mayor of Miami was Cuban. Three of five city commissioners were Cuban. The county manager, the chairman of the Greater Miami Chamber of Commerce, the presidents of Florida International University, the Dade County AFL-CIO, the United Way, and several large banks were also Cuban. A frequently cited study by the *Miami Herald* in 1987 identified the eighteen "most powerful private citizens who shape today's Miami"; eight were Cuban Americans ("Miami's Most Powerful" 1988). Regarding their anticipated return to the homeland, a 1995 poll taken in Dade County revealed that 64 percent of Cubans surveyed had no intention of reestablishing themselves in Cuba, 24 percent thought they would, and 12 percent remain undecided (Falcoff 1995, 43).

The transformation of Cuban immigrants from exiles to members of the establishment was both reflected in and fueled by changing ethnic discourse. During the 1960s and 1970s, extreme hatred of Castro and contemplation of strategies to bring about his demise dominated discussions among Cubans in Miami. But by the late 1970s and early 1980s many Miami Cubans had begun to articulate social, political, and economic concerns that focused on improving their quality of life in the United States. These concerns were articulated through the formation of organizations such as SALAD, the CANF, and the Cuban American Planning Council, as well as by the increased number of Cuban Americans seeking political office at the local, state, and national level and the increased political mobilization of Cuban American voters that put them there. In a 1981 interview, SALAD director Eduardo Padron said, "Our concern is not the homeland, but a new land" (Balmaseda 1981). And Cuban-American journalist Liz Balmaseda said this of SALAD: "They wanted a voice in the establishment. They wanted access to power. Democracy doesn't listen to a lot of exile talk, they thought; it listens to Money, Power, Status, Persistence" (1981, 1C). By 1990 most Cuban Americans referred to Miami as home and expressed pride in the "city of the future," which they had helped build. Bank presidents were more likely to tell the story of "pulling themselves up by the bootstraps" in Miami's competitive economy than to boast of their combat experience in Cuba.

The content and the fluidity of ethnic discourse among Cubans in the United States served the interests of the immigrant community in a variety of ways. Castro, communism, and Cuba were powerful symbols that fortified the exile sentiment and gave rise to a sense of commonalty among Cubans in Miami that had not necessarily existed before. The focus on returning home helped ease the psychological burden suffered by many Cubans in their attempt to adapt to a strange and often hostile environment. The manipulation of these symbols by leaders within the community, by the media, and particularly by the Spanish-language radio stations reinforced a bond among the Cubans in Miami and drew heavily on a sense of shared purpose, kinship, and common ancestry, whether real or imagined. It also kept pressure on the U.S. government and focus on *la causa*.

For decades the Cuban community in Miami and the foreign policy apparatus of the U.S. government shared similar concerns about Fidel Castro. This was particularly true in the 1960s and again under the Reagan administration in the early 1980s. Twenty years after Kennedy promised a free Havana to those Cubans gathered in the Orange Bowl, Reagan told a Cuban crowd of comparable size gathered in the Dade County Auditorium that "we will not permit the Soviets and their henchmen in Havana to deprive others of their freedom." He went on to promise that "someday, Cuba itself will be free" (Didion 1987, 160). When the political objectives of the Cubans in Miami and the U.S. government did not seem to coincide, the Cuban exiles were quick to mobilize their opposition. During debates over U.S. aid to the contras in Nicaragua, the Cubans in Miami warned that "the freedom fighters of the eighties" shall not be treated by Reagan as the men of Brigade 2506 had been treated by Kennedy (Didion 1987, 16). References to *la causa* also carried great weight with the Cuban American community even when the issues or debates at hand had little to do with Cuba, Castro, or communism. Politicians, Cuban as well as non-Cuban, knew well that an appeal to anti-Castro credentials had great potential to mobilize Cuban American voters and that any appearance of being soft on communism constituted a death knell.

Castro and communism continue to be potent political themes, but as illustrated above, the nature of Cuban ethnic discourse has gradually shifted away from exile politics. This discursive transition does not simply represent a desire or willingness among Cubans to assimilate into the American mainstream. In other words, an increased focus on the "new land" does not signal a disinterest in the "homeland." Instead, the shift away from exile politics is more accurately interpreted as an alternative discursive strategy consistent with an altered set of social, political, and economic circumstances. These circumstances included a changing political and economic environment, at the local, national, and international levels; a growing realization that neither Castro nor "the exile" was temporary; and an awareness that the welcome extended by the land of opportunity was wearing thin. The elements of the exile discourse that drew heavily on the theme of communist tyranny reflected the critical position of the Cubans in an ongoing struggle between East and West. For years the U.S. obsession with the Cold War provided Cuban Americans privileged access to the U.S. public agenda. During the 1970s, amidst an impressive economic boom in metropolitan Miami, claims about "those amazing Cuban émigrés" by the local business elite resonated well with the emergent rags-to-riches discourse among Cubans Americans. This was a more traditional narrative that resembled that of many other immigrant groups, with its emphasis on hard work, patriotism, and an undying commitment to the promises of the American dream. Yet it was not until various social, political, and economic factors converged to create a less cordial context for Cuban residents in Miami that their identity as immigrants intending to stay, rather than exiles waiting to leave, took firm shape.

By 1980 worldwide recession gripped cities throughout the United States and Latin America, and Miami's international economy was doubly pained. The Anglo population had grown bitter about what they perceived as the Latinization of Miami, a bitterness illustrated, in part, by the passage of the 1980 anti-bilingual referendum.[8] Beginning in April 1980 more than 125,000 Mariel refugees descended on Miami, and less than a month later the city experienced one of the worst race riots in U.S. history. With regard to the Mariel refugees, Cubans in Miami feared, and legitimately so, that the negative publicity surrounding the boatlift would tarnish the image of earlier arrivals and the Cuban American population as a whole (Portes and Stepick 1993, 18–37). In terms of the Liberty City riots, it was illustrated in chapter 3 how quickly Cuban immigrants became convenient scapegoats for politicians, public officials, and the media in their attempts to explain the source of anger and hostility among Miami's black community. Certain changes in U.S. immigration policy during the early 1980s also signaled that the Cubans were losing their status as a privileged immigrant group.

In an insightful analysis of the evolution and outcome of U.S. immigration policies toward Cuba, Jorge Dominguez explained that during the 1980s strategic concerns over controlling the influx of Cuban immigrants began to take precedence over ideological struggles with communism (1992, 86). This trend reached its zenith in 1994, when President Clinton terminated a three-decade-old policy of preferential treatment for Cuban refugees seeking political asylum in the United States (Fiagome 1994c). This decision reflected, in part, a strategic calculation on the part of the Clinton administration that the potential alienation of the Cuban American community in Miami was less costly politically than ignoring the growing anti-immigrant mood of the nation as a whole. As Lisandro Perez, of the Cuban Research Institute at Florida International University, explained, "President Clinton is looking at the big picture and not just Florida. He sends a message that he's cracking down on illegal immigration and that's a message that resonates throughout the heartland" (Decker 1995). The Clinton administration may also have sensed, amidst the growing fragmentation of the exile community and the emergence of new and alternative viewpoints on how to deal with Castro, that the Cuban community does not speak in one voice on these issues and hence the likelihood of political backlash is reduced.[9] Irrespective of the precise political motives involved, the change in immigration policy indicates that the influence of the exile community on politics and policymaking in Washington has weakened. Even the very powerful Jorge Mas Canosa and the CANF were excluded from the political negotiations that produced the final policy decision (Greenhouse 1995).[10]

Cuban American leaders readily admit that these "less cordial" circumstances served to galvanize the Cuban community in Miami (Balmaseda 1981). Through a process Portes and Stepick refer to as "reactive ethnicity," the immigrants consciously altered their ethnic discourse in order to counter the growing hostility of the host society (1993, 30–37).[11] This notion of reactive ethnicity is particularly relevant for explaining the Cuban American discourse on race. Cuban Americans have reacted, and continue to react, defensively to discussions of race and racial conflict. This can be explained, in part, as a response to their ambiguous role in the race and class politics of Miami and the United States. Cubans have been privileged over African Americans and Haitian immigrants in terms of economic assistance and political access; at the same time, they have been made scapegoats for the racial and class barriers that inhibit these other groups. In this regard, the narrative of "rags to riches (but never racist)" is an explicit attempt to defend the economic gains of Cubans in the United States as well deserved and to emphasize that any obstacles standing in the way of similar achievements by other groups either predate or are in no way related to the Cuban presence.

By the 1990s, Miami had achieved official status as one of the "high-tech global cities of the world market" and had solidified its role as "the capital of Latin America" by hosting the 1994 Summit of the Americas. This context both permitted and encouraged Cuban Americans to recount the wonders of Miami's transition from a southern backwater to a "city of the future" and to emphasize the part they had played in the process. In

other words, as part of the establishment in a metropolis of growing hemi-
spheric and global importance, Cuban Americans have a vested interest in
Miami and greater opportunity to sing its praises and to avoid responsibility for its ills. Events during the early 1990s also indicated, however, that
the exile discourse was not dead and that the many divisions and disagreements among Cubans in Miami were not insurmountable. Hundreds of
Cubans from various backgrounds and organizations, including some
prominent exile leaders who rarely spoke to one another, used the summit
and publicity surrounding it to mount a united protest against Clinton's
recent change of U.S. immigration policy. With signs such as those referring to President Clinton and Attorney General Reno's apartheid, some
Cuban Americans made it clear that even though Cubans were an established resident majority in Miami, Cuba was not merely a memory from
their distant past (Navarro 1995a).

In analyzing the causes and consequences of the changing ethnic discourse among Cubans in the United States it is important to keep in mind
the relevance of a phenomenon Nina Glick-Schiller termed *transnationalism. Transnationalism* refers to the processes by which immigrants link their
country of origin and their country of settlement, and *transmigrants,* according to Glick-Schiller, are individuals and groups who "take actions,
make decisions, and feel concerns, and develop identities within social networks that connect them to two or more societies simultaneously" (1992,
185). As transmigrants, Cubans in the United States have seen their ethnic
identity shaped not only by political and economic circumstances in the
United States but also by their own relationships to Cuba. To the extent
that a cohesive Cuban American ethnic identity has been constructed in
opposition to Fidel Castro, that identity will necessarily fragment or, more
likely, shift in a post-Castro period. Certainly the exact form or content of
the emergent identity or identities remains to be seen, but one thing that is
certain is that many Cubans in Miami stand poised to benefit from capitalist exploitation of the island as well as from an identity that will both
reflect and reinforce potential economic ties between the United States and
Cuba.

CONCLUSION

Cuban immigration to Miami has been the subject of much discussion and debate over the past thirty years. The majority of comments, claims, proclamations, and suggestions issued by politicians, government officials, the media, and Cubans themselves, tell a story of a population of immigrants who heroically escaped the iron grip of communism to find freedom in a land of opportunity. Based on their hard work and individual sacrifice these refugees are portrayed as establishing an impressive existence for themselves in their new surroundings and greatly enhancing those surroundings in the process. Each of the themes that gave rise to the story of success competed with different but more marginalized definitions of the Cuban American reality. Whether the issue is the socioeconomic origins of the Cuban refugees, how they came, or their subsequent experiences in exile, various contradictory interpretations call into question the empirical validity of the success story's claims. No one competing claim is necessarily more or less empirically valid than another, nor are any particular claims necessarily further removed from vested interests and power politics than others.[12] It is the very existence of this battle among discourses that makes the need to explain how and why the story of success achieved prominence all the more obvious. Attempts have been made to measure the level of success of Cuban émigrés and to identify its underlying causes, but the convergence of social, political, and economic factors that constructed the story of Cuban success and the related image of Cuban American ethnicity have not been previously explored.

This chapter argues that the Cuban success story has been, and continues to be, intricately linked to the exercise of power and politics in Miami, in Washington, and in the world. The theme of communist tyranny, as articulated in the claims of the media, politicians, and federal government agencies, served a number U.S. policy objectives throughout the Cold War. From the perspective of the Cubans in the United States, emphasizing their narrow escape from tyrannical oppression was a way to ease the burden of exile, to create a sense of common purpose around which to mobilize large numbers of émigrés for political, economic, and social gain, and to keep the attention of the American political system focused on their concerns.

The praises of the business elite in Miami demonstrated the complementarity between a sagging economy and the massive infusion of human and financial capital. Large numbers of Cubans who were willing and eager to pursue the American dream and federal government programs designed to ensure that they achieved it had very positive implications for the Anglo elite in Miami. This discourse also created an image of success among the Cubans in Miami that facilitated tangible economic, social, and political gains at the same time that it reinforced the tenets of American civic culture. Finally, the rags-to-riches tales told by Cubans in Miami eased their incorporation into American society and now protects their position within that society.

Among the many myths that emerged from and sustained these different discourses is that Cubans in the United States are a culturally homogeneous group with common political concerns and economic interests rooted in a shared ethnicity. This widely held perception denies the heterogeneity of the Cuban population in the United States and the fact that what Cuban Americans unquestionably share is that they or their parents came to the United States from Cuba and, at least in most cases, speak Spanish. Beyond this, few assumptions can be made about the identity of Cubans in the United States. Instead, what is clear is that the nature of Cuban American ethnic identity has been remarkably fluid over time. Furthermore, the cultural symbols and themes around which Cuban American identity has been constructed may draw heavily on the island itself, but their contemporary significance is assigned, defined, and reconfigured in a context that is very specific to Miami and the United States.

The processes that invented and reinvented Cuban American ethnicity were not arbitrary or inconsequential. Each of the themes that the Cuban success story comprised drew upon notions of achievement and success that were, and continue to be, deeply rooted in North American culture, such as self-reliance, a commitment to individual liberty, and the spirit of enterprise. The prevalence of other themes fluctuated in accordance with local, national, and international events. Finally, just as the invention of Cuban American ethnic identity has not been arbitrary, it also has not been without political and economic implication. From the beginning the Cuban success story functioned to protect and promote the power and privilege of certain individuals and groups, whether North American capitalists, U.S. politicians, or Cuban elites. In this regard the success of the Cuban success story is that it defined Cuban ethnic identity in terms of success. Although the definition itself is not well grounded in empirical reality, it has corresponded closely to established relations of power and politics. The Cuban American case illustrates the need for scholars of identity to explore not only how cultural identities increasingly serve as a basis of conflict and cooperation in the public sphere but also how the distribution of social, political, and economic resources influences the configuration and reconfiguration of identity itself. The following chapter continues the examination of how definitions of social reality are rooted in power and politics but locates the construction and contestation of images and identities within the context of a global system.

5

MANDELA IN MIAMI
The Globalization of Ethnicity in an American City

Released after twenty-seven years in captivity in a South African prison, Nelson Mandela, leader of the African National Congress (ANC), traveled to the United States to thank the supporters who had remained loyal to the struggle against apartheid and to encourage the U.S. government to maintain economic sanctions against the white regime in South Africa. Mandela's itinerary included stops in New York, Washington D.C., and Atlanta. In each of those cities he was welcomed with great fanfare. Huge crowds turned out to greet him, local leaders showered him with proclamations, and public officials handed him the city key. This was not the case in Miami. Mandela's appearance attracted a crowd comparable in size to those in Atlanta and Washington, but the tenor of the reception was unique. Not one local elected official formally greeted Mr. Mandela, nor was he presented with any proclamation of honor by civic leaders. As in other cities where Mandela stopped, hundreds of loyal and enthusiastic supporters surrounded the place where he spoke, but there were also many angry protesters. According to one estimate, approximately three hundred anticommunists, mostly Cuban Americans, stood on one side of the street waving placards that read: "Arafat, Gadhafi, and Castro are Terrorists," and "Mr. Mandela, do you know how many people your friend Castro has killed just for asking the right to speak as you do here?" Across from this group were three thousand Mandela supporters, mostly black, with placards proclaiming "Miami City Council = Pretoria" and "Mandela, Welcome to Miami, Home of Apartheid" (Portes and Stepick 1993, 176).

142

Miami is notorious for social upheaval. Black neighborhoods have erupted in violence on numerous occasions, and the Cuban community is well known for its vocal and sometimes violent protests. Therefore, the controversy surrounding Mandela's visit was immediately interpreted as another in a long series of conflicts pitting Miami's Latin immigrants against a historically disenfranchised black population. After Mandela's departure the *Miami Herald* reported that "the controversy—the latest rift between Miami's black and Cuban communities—continued to dominate Spanish-language and black oriented radio" ("Blacks Reject" 1990, 1B). Days later, another report stated the following: "When Nelson Mandela came to town, Miami's politicians and activists replayed their parts from past ethnic controversies, like wooden horses on a merry-go-round, unable to escape their ideological harnesses. Again, it was blacks against Hispanics, with precious little middle ground" (Goldfarb 1990).

The response to events surrounding Mandela's visit was typical of a tendency to portray social conflict in Miami as the product of deep-seated tensions between members of different ethnic groups and to place particular emphasis on the presumed tension between Hispanics and blacks. Irrespective of the degree to which these assumptions are accurate, their uncritical acceptance serves to obscure other relevant aspects of ethnicity and ethnic relations in Miami. One such aspect is that much of the conflict between ethnic groups in Miami is purely symbolic in nature. The tensions surrounding Mandela's visit are just one example of the battles in Miami that frequently take place about symbols, are waged through symbols, and offer little more than symbols as rewards.

Another aspect of social relations in Miami that is largely neglected by many analyses and interpretations is the extent to which the symbolic struggle within and between ethnic groups occurs in an increasingly global context. Ethnicity and ethnic conflict in Miami are profoundly influenced by actors, issues, and events far beyond the boundaries of Miami. The city itself has come to be widely recognized as an international city, but little attempt has been made to explore the links between ethnic relations at the local level and various social, political, and economic processes operating at the level of the international system.

AN INTERNATIONAL CITY

References to Miami as the "capital of Latin America" have become increasingly popular in recent years, but the city's destiny was accurately predicted almost one hundred years ago, when founding mother Julia Tuttle stated that "someday Miami will become the great center of South American trade" (Parks 1981, 63). The transformation that has occurred in Miami since the city's incorporation in 1896 exceeds even Tuttle's futuristic imagination.

In the last thirty years alone hundreds of thousands of immigrants have poured into Miami from throughout Latin America and the Caribbean, making it one of the most ethnically diverse cities in the United States. The 1980 census revealed that the foreign-born constituted 54 percent of the population of Miami, twice their percentage in Los Angeles and more than double their percentage in New York (Mohl 1986, 52). More than 50 percent of the population is classified as Hispanic, and although Cubans make up the bulk of that group, there are more than two hundred thousand non-Cuban Latins from Nicaragua, Puerto Rico, Colombia, Venezuela, Panama, Ecuador, Argentina, Mexico, and the Dominican Republic. To this group must be added large numbers of Haitians, Jamaicans, Bahamians, and other immigrants from throughout the West Indies.

Little Havana now shares the headlines with Little Haiti and Little Managua as new immigrants establish centers of social and economic activity in their own neighborhoods. Creole joins Spanish as an "unofficial" language of Miami; and debates about the Chamorro government in Nicaragua and Aristide in Haiti now accompany ongoing speculation about when Castro will fall. As one observer noted, "Miami is probably the only city in the United States with three Christmas parades: X-mas, Three Kings and Kwanza" (interview, 12 June 1992).

These are the elements that contribute to Miami's image as a mecca of cultural diversity, but Miami's status as an international city is founded on more than multilingualism and festive expressions of ethnicity. References to Miami as the "capital of Latin America" not only reflect Miami's demographic characteristics but also recognize the extremely close economic and political ties between South Florida and countries throughout Central and South America and the Caribbean. Miami's metamorphosis from a sleepy tourist town to a bustling center of international trade was fueled by links to the Latin American market, and when Latin America felt the reverberations of the debt crisis, Miami also felt the crunch.

An estimated $6 billion in goods passes through Miami annually, and the city accounts for more than 40 percent of the total trade between the United States and the Caribbean. Although the closest links are to the Caribbean, officials in Miami are actively exploring ways to expand trade with Mexico and to benefit from the potential advantages of a North American Free Trade Agreement (Rosenberg and Hiskey 1992). Similarly, local economic development offices have recently established an Africa division. The division's director, John Hall, explained: "We are now at the research stage, defining opportunities that exist in Africa for Miami in general, and black businesses in particular." He also pointed out that there was an interest in Africa to trade with Latin America, using Miami as a hub (Edwards 1992). By 1994 Miami was being described as "The Americas' Hong Kong . . . a cultural and commercial clearinghouse, a key crossroads in the modern world's trade routes" (Fields 1994). A reported fifty-seven Taiwanese companies are now operating in metropolitan Miami, China's share of goods coming into the Miami free-trade zone tripled between 1988 and 1992, and Hong Kong is listed as the largest supplier of products imported into the Port of Miami. Analysts estimate that 80 percent of the goods coming from Asia are then shipped on to Latin America. In the words of John Braga, director of the Hong Kong Trade Development Council in Miami, "It's like a United Nations of traders here" (Fields 1994).

This internationalization has not bypassed the political realm. Miami has been a location for international political activity since at least the 1800s. Much of Cuban liberator Jose Marti's struggle for Cuban independence from Spain was orchestrated from South Florida; and Latin leaders from Castro to Somoza have also used Miami as a staging ground for various political activities. *Newsweek* recently referred to Miami as "the Casablanca of Latin America—a city of schemers, émigrés and refugees, a safe haven for flight capital and fleeing politicians," and pointed out that

if it is not quite true that the whole city throbs to the beat of offshore drums, there is no question that events in Central America and the Caribbean can have a large impact here. The Sandinista revolution has pushed 70,000 Nicaraguan exiles into South Florida since 1979; the contra movement's U.S. headquarters is just across NW 36th Street from Miami International Airport. Little Haiti has its share of opposition leaders hoping for a new day back home, and two Panamanian dissidents, Roberto Eisenmann and Gilbert Mallol, are biding their time here as well. ("Miami" 1988, 24)

Foreign policy decisions made in Washington and designed to deal with international political issues also affect the local economy in Miami. Some analysts have suggested that the U.S. trade embargo against Cuba facilitated the globalization of Miami's economy by forcing Cuban exiles to exploit international networks in their business dealings rather than pursuing import-export dealings with the island (Allman 1987, 317). In 1992, ten months into the embargo against Haiti, local shippers and exporters in Miami complained, "This embargo is just killing us. The whole river is dead"; and the *Miami Herald* referred to the Haitian embargo as "the classic dilemma of global politics affecting the small players, who insist the policy is not only ineffective but is also unfairly burdening the denizens of the Miami River" (Bussey 1992a).

Today Miami is described as one of few cities in the United States that has its own foreign policy. Between 1982 and 1983 the Miami City Commission passed twenty-eight official resolutions, ordinances, and motions dealing with U.S. foreign policy. The majority of these were purely symbolic expressions of anticommunism, such as the following question put before voters in November 1982: "Should funds of the City of Miami be expended to finance in whole or in part, any multinational commercial or cultural conference or convention where representatives of Communist-Marxist countries have either been scheduled to participate or invited to attend?" (Stack and Warren 1990, 19).

In 1992 presidential candidate Ross Perot invited the mayors of several large U.S. cities to meet with him. Most voiced concerns about crime, poverty, and urban decay. Miami Mayor Xavier Suarez questioned Perot about his plans for dealing with Cuba and the Castro regime. Similarly, while policymakers in Washington debated Congressman Torricelli's bill to tighten the U.S. embargo against Cuba, the Dade County Commission quietly passed a similar version of the federal legislation (Filkins 1992b).

Social relations in Miami are also heavily influenced by external factors. Neither the conflict nor the cooperation between different groups has been confined to the standard issues that normally make up urban agendas throughout the United States. In 1986, when police rushed a crowd of participants at a downtown political rally into county busses in order to protect them from a larger and angrier crowd of protesters across the street, the controversy was not over zoning regulations or abortion rights but over U.S. aid to the Nicaraguan contras (Warren, Stack, and Corbett 1986). Similarly, in 1992, when hundreds of local residents, business owners, and politicians attended a huge political gathering in Miami Beach, the focus was not on urban renewal or an upcoming local election. Instead they were taking part in a community celebration of the twenty-fifth anniversary of the reunification of Jerusalem attended by American Jews, Cuban American Jews, Christians, and Hispanic Christian Friends of Israel, as well as two area mayors, representatives from the state legislature, and the only Cuban American member of the U.S. House of Representatives.

The events surrounding Mandela's visit provide another recent example of the extent to which metropolitan Miami is penetrated by the global arena and an ideal optic through which to examine the interdependence between local ethnic relations and the international system.

MANDELA IN MIAMI

News of Mandela's visit to Miami first appeared in the *Miami Herald* on 28 May 1990. This brief announcement included no information regarding Mandela's itinerary, nor did it mention any plans to celebrate his arrival. This initial announcement was followed shortly thereafter by a report that read, "Mandela's visit to include union speech and little else" ("Mandela's Visit" 1990). The union being referred to was the American Federation of State, County and Municipal Employees (AFSCME). The union's members had been loyal supporters of the anti-apartheid movement for thirty years; they were holding their international convention in Miami Beach, and Mandela had agreed to speak. The conference organizers' tight control over the event became a source of frustration for many individuals in the weeks that followed and a scapegoat for many others for months to come.

Union officials initially prohibited members of the community from attending and then decided to allow invited guests to view Mandela's speech on closed circuit television from an adjacent room. The outraged president of the local NAACP, Johnnie McMillian, responded: "That's like inviting us to dinner and making us eat in the kitchen. The NAACP is appalled. We won't take this sitting down" ("Mandela Speech" 1990). Many weeks later, when Mandela was long gone and the controversy raged on, Dade County Mayor Steve Clark issued a regret—not an apology—for what had happened. He emphasized that "I was not invited to Mr. Mandela's meeting until the very last minute, and then only to sit in an adjacent room and watch him on T.V." ("Dade Has" 1990).

Irrespective of the dealings with conference organizers, official acknowledgment of the South African leader's scheduled arrival was very slow in coming. This did not escape the attention of several black community leaders, who early on expressed concern about how the predominantly Cuban and Anglo politicians in Miami would receive Mandela. After all, it was customary for leaders of Mandela's stature to be welcomed in some official capacity by those individuals elected to represent the community at large. Their concern did not stem from an expectation of sheer racial insensitivity on the part of elected officials, although many critics would and did make that claim; rather, it reflected a historically complex and potentially volatile political reality in Miami.

According to various resolutions passed by the Miami City Council throughout the 1980s, Mandela's association with communism could officially classify him as *persona non grata* in the city of Miami (Stack and Warren 1990, 19). George Knox, an attorney and a much respected leader of the African American community in Miami, interpreted the local government reaction as follows: "Many of them are paranoid about openly embracing Mandela and the message it would send the Cuban community." Another prominent black attorney, H. T. Smith, issued a similar statement: "The political leaders believe that the black community is a nonentity politically, so why should they do what's right when it will possibly cause some political backlash from Cuban and Jewish constituents" ("Local Officials" 1990).

This frustration was not only directed at Cuban and Anglo politicians. Both the one black on the Miami City Commission and the one on the

County Commission also drew sharp criticism for their apparent inaction. The local black activist Billy Hardemon, of People United For Justice, had this to say of the one black city commissioner, Miller Dawkins: "His silence is almost criminal. This is a litmus test in my opinion. They're all political animals and the majority of voters in Miami are Cuban" ("Blacks Reject" 1990). Political mobilization along ethnic lines is a reality in Miami, and the Cuban community has been particularly successful in establishing itself as a formidable voting block. The recent reelection of Commissioner Dawkins is just one notable example of a local campaign funded and supported largely by Cuban American voters ("Suarez, Four" 1990).

Despite the apparent ethnic and racial polarization in Miami and a history of vocal protest on behalf of Cuban exiles, it was not at all certain that Mandela's association with communist regimes would automatically preclude him an official welcome in Miami. In fact, the Miami City Commission had already issued an unofficial proclamation—unofficial because of the persistent refusal of one particularly dogmatic Cuban American commissioner to sign the document ("Suarez, Four" 1990). A variety of events quickly unfolded, however, that served to fuel the flames of social tension for which Miami has become well known.

Just days before going to Miami, Nelson Mandela appeared on national television with Ted Koppel. During that interview Mandela expressed appreciation and gratitude for those supporters who had stood by him throughout his captivity; in this context he spoke kindly of Yasser Arafat, Moamar Gadhafi, and Fidel Castro. Comments that may have done little more than raise eyebrows throughout the rest of the country caused outrage in a city where many view Castro, Gadhafi, and Arafat as the embodiment of pure evil. The Cuban community in Miami was up in arms, and although the response was less visible, Mandela's comments regarding Arafat and Gadhafi also upset Miami's sizable and politically powerful Jewish population.

The next day, Miami Mayor Suarez announced that "in view of the statements made last night, it would be difficult to give him [Mandela] any kind of recognition or key to the city ("Mandela Remarks" 1990). Days later, Suarez and four other Cuban American elected officials issued the following statement: "We, Cuban Americans, find it beyond reasonable comprehension that Mr. Nelson Mandela, a victim of oppression by his own government, not only fails to condemn the Cuban government for its human rights violations, but rather praises virtues of the tyrannical Castro regime" ("Suarez, Four" 1990). The city commission rescinded its proclamation, and Mandela came and left Miami without any formal acknowledgment from the city of Miami, Dade County, or the city of Miami Beach.

After Mandela's departure the tensions persisted—on the airwaves, in the newspapers, and on the street. The anticommunist fervor of the Cuban exile community, which had for the most part been tolerated by the rest of Miami, was now directed at a symbol of great importance to blacks. One Cuban American lobby group ran a half-page advertisement in the *Miami Herald* listing, under the headline "Think Again Mr. Mandela," a series of quotations by the South African leader praising Castro and Cuba ("Think Again" 1990).

While Cubans espoused anti-Castro rhetoric, African Americans proclaimed that "apartheid in South Africa and the black experience in America are two sides of the same coin" ("Many Watch" 1990). The black community was visibly outraged; it considered the snubbing of Mandela to be a direct slap in the face. Patricia Due, one of the founders of the Congress of Racial Equality, complained: "I feel sick. How dare they do this to us? Mr. Mandela is a symbol. He is our link to our motherland. After all the blood, sweat, and tears of black Americans, and people are still trying to tell us who we can hear" (Fichtner 1990). The NAACP stated: "To reject Mandela is to reject us. He is our brother. If they say he's not welcome, they're saying we're not welcome too" ("Blacks Reject" 1990). This sense of powerlessness and injustice is not new to Miami's black community, nor is the expression of that frustration in the form of violent protest. This time, however, the anger and frustration were channeled in a different direction.

A group of professionals led by the attorney H. T. Smith had already issued a demand for an apology to the Mandelas and the community as a whole for the inexcusable treatment of a respected world leader. Members of a black sorority, Delta Theta Sigma, who were attending their national convention in Miami Beach during Mandela's trip, issued a similar statement. When the demands for an apology fell on deaf ears, the group aimed to hit the city of Miami where it hurt the most—the tourism industry. The Boycott Miami Now committee was formed, letters were written, and videotapes were produced urging blacks throughout the United States to take their convention and tourism dollars elsewhere: "to keep the pressure on, and to spend your hard-earned dollars with those who treat you with the respect and dignity which you deserve" ("Two Local" 1990).

The boycott continued for three years after Mandela's visit. Numerous conventions reportedly canceled or changed their plans to meet in Miami as a result of the boycott; and although there is some disagreement about the economic impact, the estimated loss of revenue for the city ranges from $10 million to $50 million. The Visitors and Tourism Bureau did create several minority scholarships for study in Florida International University's hotel management program and agreed that more blacks were needed in the tourism industry.

Most notable, however, was the complex political maneuvering that typically characterizes this racially and ethnically divided city. The day after he rescinded the proclamation to welcome Mandela, Mayor Suarez quickly tried to make peace with members of the black community. The mayor showed up at a meeting called by African American County Commissioner Barbara Carey in support of Mandela, where he received a very chilly reception. Reverend Victor Curry accused Suarez of trying to straddle the divide between blacks and Cubans and remarked: "I think it would have been a good idea if he didn't show up." When Suarez attempted to draft a broad statement that would be acceptable to black, Jewish, and Hispanic leaders, the Reverend Willie Simms, of the Dade County Community Relations Board, an African American, exclaimed: "He should have thought about that before opening his big mouth. He proved what an idiot he is" ("Blacks Reject" 1990).

In the beginning, Metro-Dade Mayor Steve Clark reportedly was out of town and refused to discuss the issue. He later issued a carefully worded statement "regretting" the Mandela incident but not "apologizing." County Commissioner Joe Gersten responded angrily to a reporter, "Don't try to drag me into this." Elected officials throughout the city and the county were coming under increasing attack, and they made every attempt to distance themselves from the controversy ("Dade Has" 1990). For their part, some Cuban American leaders attempted to assure blacks in Miami that their criticism of Mandela had nothing to do with the color of his skin. Asking to appear on WEDR—99 JAMZ, a black-oriented Miami radio station, Armando Gutierrez and other anti-Castro activists proclaimed, "This is not a racial matter. Mr. Mandela is a confessed communist" ("Mandela Backers" 1990). *It's not racial ideology, it's political ideology.*

In 1992 Miami Beach Mayor Seymour Gelber, who is Jewish, became the first public official to apologize when he proclaimed 27 April "Nelson Mandela Day" in the city of Miami Beach. Many individuals and groups applauded his decision as an important first step toward healing deep and unnecessary wounds. The gesture was not, however, without political repercussions. Many Cuban as well as Jewish constituents were outraged, and several of Mayor Gelber's political opponents, including fellow city commissioners, quickly positioned themselves to take advantage of what was still a very emotional issue (interview, 6 July 1992). The Mandela dispute became a major issue between two Miami Beach city commissioners who hoped to succeed Gelber, and one former mayoral candidate began an active campaign to rescind Gelber's Mandela proclamation ("Mayor Gelber" 1992).

That the boycott persisted reflects a variety of factors. There is a tendency among the Anglo leadership to ignore problems in hopes that they will go away or at least cause no more than the minimal level of damage to Miami's already badly tarnished image. There is also an intransigence on the part of many Cubans leaders, who insist that the issue is not about race and stand firmly behind the declaration that any friend of Fidel Castro's is no friend of theirs. One Cuban American candidate for the Dade County Commission stated, "If it's an apology they're [blacks] waiting for, it will not come" (interview, 2 June 1992). And Osvaldo Soto, chairman of SALAD, remarked, "I cannot honor a man who has gone to Cuba to shake the hand of a man who has held my native country under oppression for more than thirty-three years" (Street 1992).

What perhaps contributed most to the longevity of the boycott was the realization by blacks that they had discovered a way to get the attention of the power structure. Although there is a great deal of disagreement about

Finally?

the economic impact of the boycott, few will dispute the fact that the campaign itself provided blacks greater political bargaining power, not to mention increased social and political solidarity.

To the initial demand for an apology were added demands for the following: an investigation into a recent incident of police brutality against Haitian immigrants, a review of U.S. immigration policy, single-member voting districts, and substantial reforms in Dade's tourism industry to allow increased employment and business opportunities (Rowe 1990). And during the September 1992 primaries the Boycott Miami Now committee placed several paid political ads in the local black paper urging voters to "Remember Mandela" and "Riot at the Polls."

Boycott organizers also added force to their claims by referring to the boycott as a "Quiet Riot." As H. T. Smith explained, "Our choices were clear. We could once again resort to the emotion-filled chaotic riots that heap death and destruction on our own community. Or, we could take our struggle to moral high ground. Black Miami could coolly and dispassionately move the battle ground from the ghetto streets to the executive suites. And, in so doing, we could wage a Quiet Riot where not one life is taken, not one person is injured, not one fire is started, not one person is arrested, and not one business in our community is looted" (Smith 1992a).

In praise of Circuit Court Judge Thomas Spencer's decision to move Officer William Lozano's manslaughter trial from the predominantly white area of Orlando to a more racially mixed Tallahassee, the *Miami Times* wrote: "There can be little doubt that Boycott Miami, and the alternative to street violence that it embodies, has been a key factor in this heightened sensitivity. . . . This could be the start of a trend that would transform Miami from the 'riot prone' city its reputation says it is to one where genuine, mutual respect for all races sets the framework for communal harmony" ("Towards Justice" 1992).

The saga continued when, in June 1992, the black-owned and -operated *Miami Times* reported that South African Zulu Chief Buthelezi was in Miami and would attend a private luncheon hosted by the Cuban American president of the *Miami Herald*, Roberto Suarez. The outcry from the black community was almost immediate. One prominent black attorney and civic leader said that Buthelezi was a "documented agent of the South African government." And H. T. Smith, leader of the boycott committee, described Buthelezi as "a collaborator of the Nazi-like apartheid regime." The *Miami Herald* immediately issued a statement saying that the luncheon had been canceled, the Cuban American National Foundation quickly announced that it was stepping in to host the affair, and Buthelezi moved to cancel his scheduled Miami appearances (Crockett and Epstein 1992). In an editorial the following week, the *Miami Times* wrote: "He [Buthelezi] has so far chosen to play the White man's game and allow himself to be used in their gambit to maintain power even after majority rule. But it can at least be hoped that his knowledge now that there are blacks in the Diaspora as far afield as the most southern part of the United States who despise his tactics would persuade him to reverse his course" ("No Joy" 1992).

On 12 May 1993, three years after Mandela's visit to Miami, the Boycott Miami Now campaign came to an end. In an atmosphere of great optimism a group of community leaders presented a twenty-point agreement based on which the boycott had been settled. The stated goals included the establishment of an African American–owned convention-level hotel in Dade County, hospitality management scholarships for black students, and increased purchasing contracts for black-owned businesses. Also included was the formation of Miami Partners for Progress, a group of fifteen boycott and business leaders that would monitor the implementation of this "Blueprint for Change" (Pugh 1993).

The event did not end without a warning from H. T. Smith that "failure to keep the promises we have made will have serious consequences because we believe in the future we will not have the credibility to harness the rage, the frustration and the indignation [of the black community]" and attention being focused, by the media and others, on the "noticeably absent . . . Cuban-American leaders, whose criticism of Mandela triggered the boycott." What was missing from the celebration and from the twenty-point plan was any further mention of the Haitian population in Miami (Pugh 1993).[1]

GLOBAL LINKAGES

Careful analysis of the events surrounding Nelson Mandela's visit reveals a great deal about the nature of social and political relations in Miami. It is clear that tensions persist in Miami and that ethnicity continues to be a predominant factor in group stratification and political mobilization. Also evident are the potency of ethnic symbols and the willingness of individuals and groups to manipulate ethnic identity in the pursuit of political and economic gain. An additional, particularly notable implication of the Mandela controversy is the increasing need to place any analysis of metropolitan Miami within the context of the international system.

The empirical reality of a changing world order has not gone unnoticed by analysts in any discipline, and calling attention to the international system is by no means a novel analytic approach. For some time international relations theorists have questioned the utility of the nation-state as unit of analysis, preferring to focus instead on the interdependence of the international system and the predominance of international regimes, which transcend national borders.[2] A diverse body of literature classified under the heading of international political economy has also devoted a great deal of energy to examining the globalization of production and exchange.[3] There has also been some attempt to link the macrostructural dynamics of the world system to microlevel research on urban politics.[4] No attempt has yet been made to apply this type of analysis to the persistence of ethnicity and ethnic conflict in the new world order. This oversight reflects, in part, the persistence of certain widely held assumptions about the nature of ethnicity, particularly the notion that ethnicity is "ancient, unchanging, or inherent in a group's blood, soul, or misty past" (Conzen et al. 1990, 38). This primordialist conceptualization of ethnicity as a static, independent variable discourages examination of the fluid and contextual nature of ethnic identity and ethnic group relations, whether that context be local or global in scope.

Underlying the discussion about Miami as an international city is an assumption that globalization of the cultural, political, and economic arenas in Miami results from the presence of large numbers of people belonging to different ethnic groups. It is accepted, for example, if not expected, that Miami is the site of frequent ethnic parades, festivals, and ceremonies because Miami is the home of a variety of different ethnic groups desiring to celebrate their distinct cultural heritage. Similarly, Miami's ties to the world market, and Latin America in particular, are frequently attributed to a substantial presence of immigrants who maintain links both with their homeland and with fellow emigrants who have settled in locations throughout the world. Furthermore, the fact that local politics in Miami is so saturated with international issues is explained by reference to the large population of immigrants living in Miami for whom ethnic identity continues to be the most salient form of social identification and political mobilization.

This interpretation of the international dimensions of social, political, and economic activity in Miami is not inaccurate, but it is incomplete. Certainly ethnicity and ethnic attachments have played a critical role in the globalization of Miami, but the content of ethnic identities in Miami and the galvanization of ethnic sentiment for social, political, and economic gain are simultaneously influenced by the various processes operating at the level of the international system. Overcoming these conceptual weaknesses is critical, but numerous theoretical and methodological obstacles remain that inevitably complicate any attempt to link local-level interaction with global processes. Theories of the international system are by nature grand theories. Much of the grand theorizing that has thus far taken place is heavily criticized for imprecision and a failure to acknowledge the role of human agency. In addition to the levels-of-analysis problem, it is extremely difficult to distinguish cause-and-effect relationships between various overlapping and interlocking forces of social, political, and economic change. Recognition of the fluid and contextual nature of social identity can, however, enhance the study of ethnic phenomena by reversing the arrow of causality to explore the impact of international processes on ethnicity and ethnic relations in a metropolitan area.

Migration is one example of a process operating at the level of the international system that has profound implications for social relations at a local level. International migration brings people from different social, cultural, and historical backgrounds into close proximity. The stratification of these people into various groups does not necessarily or automatically reflect identities or interests transferred from abroad. Rather, it is the interactions among and between these people that define individuals as members of distinct ethnic groups. In Miami, ethnicity and ethnic relations must be viewed in the context of relatively recent and large-scale immigration to South Florida. The migration process did not simply transplant various ethnic groups from one location to another but was one of many interconnected processes that influenced ethnic identities and the nature of ethnic group interaction in Miami. As was shown to be the case with Cuban Americans in chapter 4, neither the content of ethnic identity nor the common concerns around which members of an ethnic group unite can be directly traced to their place of origin. As S. R. Charsley explains, "They are not simply the prolongation of pre-migration customs and patterns, but are the result of an interaction between these and the values and requirements of the receiving society" (1974, 355).

One implication of acknowledging the global and malleable nature of ethnicity is that ethnic relations in Miami cannot be accurately explained by mere reference to demographic characteristics such as a population that is 57 percent foreign-born. Where the immigrants came from, why they left, how they arrived, and under what circumstances they adapted to their new surroundings must also be taken into account. These factors profoundly influence the interaction between and among immigrants and established residents and shape the ethnic identity of individuals and groups. They also extend well beyond the confines of metropolitan Miami.

Ethnic relations in Miami are influenced not only by the movement of people across national borders but also by the international flow of goods and services. The local economy in Miami is tightly linked to the world market, particularly to the economies of Latin America and the Caribbean. Geographically the city is in an ideal position to benefit from increased levels of international trade and commerce, and trends in the global economy are regularly cited as explanations for Miami's transition from a sleepy southern town to a bustling international metropolis. This transformation has not, however, benefited all groups equally. Hispanics in Miami, by virtue of their language skills and established personal and professional contacts worldwide, were particularly well placed to capitalize on the potential advantages offered by an increasingly interdependent world capitalist economy. Other groups in Miami were not so well placed. This unequal and fluctuating set of opportunities and constraints that confronts various groups in Miami provides an illustration of how global economic trends can influence ethnic relations at a local level by altering the environment in which individuals and groups interact.

Ethnic tension in Miami, for example, is frequently attributed to direct competition among ethnic groups for scarce economic resources. Yet, existing analyses do not support this zero-sum portrayal of ethnic group interaction in Miami's labor market. What they do support is the extent to which Miami has been influenced by the global economic system. The result, as Portes and Stepick explain, is not direct labor market substitution of one ethnic group by another but "a new urban economy in which the immigrants raced past other groups, leaving the native minority behind" (1993, 43).

In addition to international migration and trends in the world market economy, the international political environment also influences ethnic relations at the local level. This is well illustrated by contributors to a 1981 volume on the transnational dimensions of ethnicity. According to the volume's editor John Stack, the resurgence of ethnicity throughout the world is tied to the global environment in two respects: (1) through the politicization of global communication and transportation networks; and (2) in accelerating patterns of political and cultural fragmentation. The world political system has been transformed by technological advancements that facilitate transnational ties among ethnic groups around the world. The global penetration of the domestic arena provides ethnic groups with greater opportunity to exchange ideas, information, wealth, and political strategies, and it results in a powerful "demonstration effect" such as occurred in the 1960s, when the global mass media fueled student political protest throughout North America and Western Europe (1981, 20). Linkages are also posited between global political fragmentation and ethnic groups in both the developing and the developed world. The pace of political, economic, and social change throughout the Third World allegedly exacerbates ethnic cleavages in those countries. In the West, the increasingly urban and bureaucratic nature of advanced industrial societies alienates the masses of citizens and fuels the need for communal attachments (24).

Stack's volume provides valuable insights into the role of ethnicity in a transnational world.[5] It also reveals, however, a tendency to attribute a great deal of independent explanatory significance to ethnicity without examining the content or construction of ethnic phenomena. Greater emphasis must be placed on the processes that result in social stratification and political mobilization along ethnic lines and that assign meaning and legitimacy to ethnic identity.

THE INVENTION OF ETHNICITY

Mandela's visit to Miami seemed to fuel an explosive clash of primordial sentiment between distinct ethnic groups. And at some level this was certainly the case. But neither the mobilization of groups in Miami along ethnic lines nor the symbols around which they rally can be taken for granted. Use of the categories "black," "Cuban," "Jewish," and "Anglo" assumes the existence of easily identifiable groups with shared interests and fails to recognize that the labels themselves mask a variety of distinct social identities that crosscut and overlap ethnicity. As already discussed, Cuban immigration to Miami has taken place in relatively distinct waves characterized by varied socioeconomic and racial compositions. The result is a Cuban population in Miami that is socially, politically, and economically very heterogeneous. There are now white Cubans, black Cubans, Jewish Cubans, old Cubans who speak little English and young Cubans who speak little Spanish, Republican Cubans and Cuban Democrats, and ample evidence to challenge the notion of a persistent communal unity.

The situation among blacks in Miami is similar to the heterogeneity and fragmentation of the Cuban community, with an additional complexity posed by the fact that *black* is obviously a racial distinction rather than a distinction of national origin or otherwise. Miami is home to Bahamian blacks, Jamaican blacks, Haitian blacks, as well as North American blacks. Interaction between these groups often has been minimal, characterized more by distrust or suspicion than by any sense of shared interests and common concerns. Historically, tensions have existed between Bahamian blacks and African Americans, and more recently there have been tensions between Haitian immigrants and the native black population in Miami. None of these divisions is extreme, but the cultural diversity of Miami's black population has certainly worked against the establishment of a common social or political agenda.

Despite this diversity, the tendency for individuals in Miami to identify themselves, and to be identified by others, as members of a particular ethnic group is widespread. Mandela's visit, along with a variety of similar incidents, also indicates that despite few notable exceptions, political reactions and opinions in Miami continue to divide fairly consistently along lines of race and ethnicity. In fact, when asked whether politics in Miami consistently divides along lines of race and ethnicity, 63 percent of the respondents in in-depth interviews in 1992 answered with an emphatic yes *(see fig. 5)*. What remains to be explained is why.

The Miami case provides evidence for both sides in the ongoing debate between analysts who explain ethnicity in terms of "deep historical and experiential factors" and those who maintain that ethnic cleavages arise because of "specific and immediate circumstances" (Glazer and Moynihan 1975, 19–20). The emotion that poured forth from various individuals and groups before, during, and after Mandela's trip to Miami, coupled with frequent references to deeply held values, kinship ties, and cultural attachments, provides evidence of a certain affective, primordial dimension of ethnicity. Cubans passionately recounted stories of friends and relatives who had been persecuted by the Castro regime. Blacks equated what was taking place in Miami with racial domination in South Africa, and asked, How dare they attack our link to the motherland? Surrounding events also indicate, however, that behind the very visible shouts and tears there was no shortage of individuals prepared to harness that energy in pursuit of social, political, or economic gain. Spurred on by the influential and dogmatic broadcasts of Spanish radio in Miami, many local leaders found themselves in a familiar struggle to be *el Cubanismo*, "the most Cuban," *Cuban* in this case defined as very patriotic and very anti-Castro. When Mayor Gelber decided to issue a formal apology, many individuals and groups supported his gesture, but just as many any others moved quickly to capitalize on the politically charged environment. And leaders of the

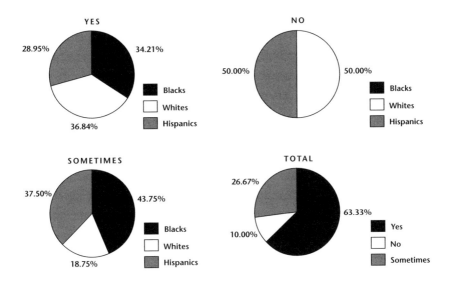

Figure 5. Summary of responses to interview question #17: Do politics in Miami consistently divide along lines of ethnicity?

Boycott Miami Now committee immediately recognized the social and political potential of an issue around which African Americans, Bahamians, Jamaicans, and Haitians could unite.

These circumstances prove that an exclusive focus on either primordial or instrumental factors is insufficient to explain the extreme complexity of ethnic phenomena. Instead, ethnicity is a dynamic force that evolves through the interaction of different groups in a context that fluctuates over time. The invention of ethnicity takes place through social and political discourse and draws heavily upon various symbols and ideologies. These symbols, however, are not merely static products of a primordial past; they are interpreted and reinterpreted so that they will be relevant to contemporary situations. Analyses of invented ethnicity must examine not only the symbols that provide content to ethnic identity but also the strategies through which symbols are assigned meaning, applied to concrete situations, and modified to changing contexts (Stern and Cicala 1991, xiii).

Chapter 4 detailed the invention of a Cuban American ethnic identity based on common heritage, shared suffering under tyrannical oppression, entrepreneurial spirit, and individual success. This identity drew heavily on various symbols linked to the international arena and was invented in a context heavily influenced by international issues, actors, and events. Emotional references to Castro and the evil threat of communist expansion have appealed to the exile sentiment of the Cuban community and have facilitated unprecedented social, political, and economic mobilization along ethnic lines. The constant manipulation of these symbols by local politicians, community leaders, and the media further legitimizes and strengthens their appeal, to the point that anticommunism and anti-Castroism are today part and parcel of Cuban American ethnicity.

Cuban American ethnic identity has been defined largely in terms of economic and political success and has, in turn, facilitated such success among Cubans in Miami. Blacks in Miami have not had the same level of success in constructing an ethnic identity that advances their social, political, and economic needs. In an analysis of blacks and ethnicity in the United States Martin Kilson argued that whites have denied blacks a viable ethnic identity primarily through authoritarian restrictions upon political participation. According to Kilson, ethnicity is an essential attribute of viable social status in American life and blacks have been deprived of that attribute as a result of (1) the historical refusal by white supremacist American society to accord blacks a quality of ethnic characterization comparable to that accorded white ethnic groups; (2) the lack of a true and viable black American heritage to shape and sustain a cohesive identity or awareness; and (3) a high degree of ambivalence among blacks with regard to the importance of black unity (Kilson 1975, 240–45).

Many blacks in Miami make claims in support of Kilson's thesis and point to numerous decisions by the Anglo power structure in Miami—the construction of highways through thriving black neighborhoods, an at-large election system that long diluted minority voting strength, a subtle divide-and-conquer strategy with respect to blacks and Cubans—that have eroded existing solidarity among blacks and obstructed the potential for future social or political mobilization along ethnic lines.

The response to Mandela's visit and the subsequent boycott represent an unprecedented form of social and political mobilization on behalf of the black community in Miami. As Gerard Jean-Juste explained, "Haitians,

Jamaicans and Afro-Americans here are slow to acknowledge that we are all of African descent. Today, we are proud to be African and want to fight to welcome Mr. Mandela" (Burkett and Andrews 1990). The snubbing of the South African leader, who represents the struggle against racial oppression worldwide, struck a very sensitive cord among blacks in Miami. Yet, the meaning and application of that symbol for metropolitan Miami occurred through the manipulation of the Mandela symbol by local leaders, politicians, and the media in pursuit of various social, political, and economic gains.

Evidence suggests that the manipulation of Mandela as a symbol was a relatively successful strategy on the part of certain black leaders in Miami. The predominant ethnic discourse of any group, however, is rarely accepted by all of its members. This is the case of Cuban Americans, such as one politician and Dade County employee who said of the political solidarity among Cubans in Miami, "Jorge Mas Canosa does not speak for me, he never did and never will" (interview, 16 June 1992). It is also the case among blacks with regard to the boycott. One prominent African American civic leader had this to say about the boycott and the principles upon which it is founded: "It makes no sense. I don't give a damn about Mandela. . . . There's no need to practice international brotherhood. Africa has never claimed me, I wasn't snubbed, and nobody in power in Africa ever stood up for my struggle" (interview, 2 July 1992).

The attempt to portray the boycott as an alternative to street-level violence through reference to a "Quiet Riot" is also contested by various members of the black population in Miami. "The boycott is not representative, absolutely not. It's not reaching the street. These are black lawyers working for white law firms. H. T. [Smith] has always had this total fixation with Mandela" (interview, 10 June 1992). Another African American civic leader remarked, "The boycott is only representative of those who are doing it" (interview, 18 June 1992); and a former black elected official referred to the "Quiet Riot" as "H. T. Smith's personal power trip" (interview, 27 July 1992).

Just as a "Quiet Riot" can take on symbolic significance in a city scarred by a history of civil unrest, Mandela evokes an emotional response among a local population bitter after years of racial oppression. Interestingly, however, Mandela, like Castro, is an international figure who is physically far removed from the local context of metropolitan Miami. Also like Castro, Mandela is a symbol whose meaning and relevance for Miami is heavily influenced by the international system. Cold War politics and a U.S. foreign policy focused intently on halting communist expansion assigned a great deal of legitimacy to the symbols and rhetoric of anticommunism that Cuban American ethnic discourse in Miami comprised. Similarly, as a world culture of democracy allegedly swept the globe, South Africa came under increasing international pressure to dismantle its apartheid system. The fact that Nelson Mandela is widely recognized as a key figure in South Africa's democratic future enhances his significance and legitimacy as a symbol of the struggle for racial equality among blacks in Miami and around the world.

The symbolic and global nature of ethnic identities in Miami also characterizes the relationships, whether conflictual or cooperative, between ethnic groups. The struggle that took place in the context of Mandela's visit was not directly about jobs, territory, or positions of political power. It was an ideological confrontation focused on a single individual whose symbolic significance for one group was in direct confrontation with his symbolic significance for another. This has been the case in Miami whether the issue was the English language, communism, or the holocaust.[6] Many observers and participants also contend that any resolution of the Mandela dispute was paralyzed by the highly symbolic issue of an apology. Arthur Teitelbaum, the regional director of the Anti-Defamation League, asked: "Are expressions of pain and regret acceptable substitutes for the words 'I'm sorry'? The point has been made. Now what? Shall we be confounded because the boycotters have failed to obtain a coerced apology from the mayor?" (Parker, 1991).

Ethnic group discourse in Miami does rely heavily on symbols, many of which are drawn from issues, actors, ideologies, and events operating at the level of the international system. Once appropriated to the local level, the symbols utilized by any particular ethnic group and the discourse to which they give rise interact closely with the symbols and discourses of other groups. Ethnicity, in other words, is a negotiated phenomenon. Eth-

nic symbols and the strategies to endow them with meaning exist in a particular context and evolve through interaction within and between groups. As Stephen Stern and John Allan Cicala write, "Choosing an ethnic expression, applying it to diverse situations, and transmitting it through time and space are based on decision-making and community interplay that require a great deal of creativity and inspiration" (1991, xii).

Group discourses in Miami frequently intersect, overlap, and inform one another, and during this process the appropriation, manipulation, and reinterpretation of various symbols is widespread. Certain symbols that are popular within one group may be borrowed by another in an attempt to legitimize their own ethnic discourse. Cubans in Miami, for example, often compare the evils perpetrated by the Castro regime to the Holocaust in Nazi Germany, and they invoke Martin Luther King and the civil disobedience of blacks in the 1960s to defend their campaign against communism in Cuba (Navarro 1995a; Rieff 1987b, 71). Similarly, in response to the highly critical Americas Watch report detailing the Cuban exile community's attacks on free speech in Miami, Jorge Davila Miguel, a columnist for *El Nuevo Herald*, wrote: "What would happen in Miami Beach if someone started a magazine or a radio program which tried to 'put into perspective' the virtues of the PLO and Yasser Arafat or, in Liberty City, the values of apartheid? The reactions of outrage might be considered justified" (Miguel 1992).

When African American columnist Robert Steinback defended Mandela against what he viewed as very unjust and inappropriate treatment by many within the Cuban and Jewish populations in Miami, he pointed out that Mandela affirms Israel's right to exist even though Israel maintained solid business ties with South Africa and asked: "Has the Cuban exile community vocally expressed solidarity with those who fight for freedom in South Africa, or even with the plight of the black underclass in this country? Why should Mandela renounce the staunch support he got from Castro?" (Steinback 1990).

The 1992 battle over redrawing Florida's legislative districts was also characterized by a great deal of ethnic polarization and manipulation of symbols. Several Jewish legislators who were alarmed at the prospect of losing political clout amidst a burgeoning Hispanic population in South Florida resorted to emotional recollections of the Holocaust in an attempt to protect their districts. State Representative Elaine Bloom of Miami Beach complained to a three-judge panel that "no one cares about the Anglo population or the Jewish population in Dade County" (Nickens 1992). She and seven other lawmakers, five of them Jewish, filed the following petition with the federal court: "Jewish voters must be protected. Fewer than 50 years ago, European Jewry were victims of the greatest persecution the world has ever seen, the Nazi Holocaust . . . Jews have been discriminated against in the United States and the state of Florida" (Bousquet 1992).

Similar types of symbolic interaction take place in an atmosphere of cooperation. During a 31 May 1992 "Rally for Israel" in Miami Beach a Hispanic pastor from a local group, Amigos Cristianos de Israel (Hispanic Christians in Support of Israel), rose to the podium to proclaim to a predominantly Jewish audience: "You might wonder why I'm up here. I love you. Lots of other Christians out there love you and support you. We identify with your cause, your persecution, and your unwillingness to compromise." The audience applauded loudly. Once the pastor was seated, the Jewish Rabbi presiding over the ceremony returned to the podium, thanked him, and responded: "We, too, hope that someday soon Cuba will be free and democratic." The audience again erupted in applause.

Ethnic symbols in Miami are also appropriated and manipulated within groups. Sam Saferstein, of the New Jewish Agenda, adamantly defended Miami Beach Mayor Seymour Gelber's decision to issue a "Mandela Day" proclamation. He argued that to reduce Mandela's lifelong dedication to an issue of ANC aid from questionable sources was "ludicrous" and issued the following "reminder to Jews": "It was Czechoslovakia—then part of the Soviet Communist Bloc, labeled as U.S. enemy #1—that sold arms to Israel in 1948 which proved decisive in its war of liberation" (Saferstein 1992). Similarly, by referring to the boycott as a "Quiet Riot," organizers draw on a very potent symbol of resistance to construct an ethnic discourse that appeals to even the most radical elements of the black population, at the same time invoking the threat of civil disorder within the larger Miami community as a whole.

In certain cases, one ethnic group may also reinterpret the content of another group's identity through its own symbolic lens or attempt to impose its own ethnic discourse on that of another group. Amidst the controversy surrounding Mandela's visit Cubans in Miami struggled forcefully against the conflict's being portrayed in racial terms, arguing instead that "the Cubans, who have suffered communism, who know it because they have lived it, do not want for the people of South Africa the substitution of their present regime with a communist tyranny. The Cubans in exile want for that people the elimination of racial segregation and all the injustice that this implies, wishing for that nation the full prevalence of human rights and of political freedom" ("Racial or Ideological" 1990).

In addition to the appropriation, manipulation, and reinterpretation of various symbols, some groups in Miami attack or call into question the symbolic content of other groups' ethnic identities. One Cuban American interviewed in 1992 chastised the black community's "fixation" with Mandela: "I tell H. T. Smith, 'Yeah right, H. T., you're going back to Africa. What are you going to do with the Mercedes?'" (interview, 8 June 1992). One African American county official referred to the Cubans in Miami as "people who talk about fleeing a dictator now ruling a dictatorship" (interview, 10 June 1992). Another African American, employed by the mayor's office, complained: "Hispanics say they are patriotic—hah! They came here of their own free will. They don't accept our constitutions, they don't ask to be allowed in, don't give up the language, and don't give up the fight over there. What we do here has nothing to do with over there" (interview, 8 July 1992).

This very symbolic nature of ethnic group interaction and ethnic identity in Miami does not, however, negate the potency of these symbols as tools to be manipulated in pursuit of more tangible political, economic, or social gains. The Cuban community in Miami, for example, has been very successful at linking symbolic issues, such as anticommunism, to a more complete and substantive political and economic agenda (Stack and Warren 1990). In the case of the boycott, black leaders not only attached a variety of concerns to the original demand for an apology but also used both the boycott and Mandela in an attempt to forge a Pan-African ethnic identity in Miami among blacks of distinct cultural and historical backgrounds. Various black leaders spoke passionately about brotherhood and links to the motherland. One African American community activist, speaking about the Mandela incident and the subsequent mobilization of blacks, explained: "I call it the 'Cousin Theory.' We're all cousins. Where you're living now just depends on where the slave ship stopped" (interview, 30 October 1992). Furthermore, after years of animosity between African Americans and Haitians, immigration policy toward Haitians and police brutality against Haitians became top priorities of Boycott Miami Now, an organizational group made up primarily of North American blacks.

The success of these political strategies is debatable and certainly difficult to quantify. Cuban American leaders such as Jorge Mas Canosa do appear to wield a great deal of power. There is some indication, however, that issues such as the United States Information Agency's broadcast of Radio Marti into Havana are, for Cubans in Miami, becoming less relevant in the face of growing concerns over health care, education, and job security. Extreme emphasis on symbolic issues may also be counterproductive if nontangible values are secured in the absence of any alteration in the basic distribution of resources (Stack and Warren 1990, 13).

The "Quiet Riot" in Miami has focused attention on the plight of the black community, and at least among some blacks it enhanced a sense of dignity, pride, and ethnic solidarity. Other individuals within Miami's black community, however, questioned the effectiveness of the boycott strategy and the relevance of Mandela to their local plight. Furthermore, it remains to be seen whether Mandela is a symbol powerful enough to unite North American blacks, Jamaicans, Haitians, and Bahamians in Miami around a common political agenda.

Irrespective of any substantive gain, mobilization around ethnic symbols does serve to transform ethnic groups into political actors, not just at the local level but nationally and internationally as well. Castro and communism are symbols that have fueled, and continue to fuel, expeditions by exiles in Miami who hope to liberate the island. As recently as 4 July 1992 an invasion attempt by one group of Cuban American combatants was thwarted when their boat broke down inside Cuban waters. According to a report in the *Miami Herald*, "There they were, four would-be raiders dressed in military garb, standing ankle deep in water in a broken boat drifting toward Cuba. Yelling on the radio for the U.S. Coast Guard to come get them NOW!" (Hancock 1992a).

Jorge Mas Canosa, a private Cuban American citizen who does not cur-
rently hold, nor has he ever held, elected office in the United States,
engages in a variety of transnational negotiations normally associated with
elected officials and foreign diplomats. For example, the CANF, under Mas
Canosa's leadership, created Operation Exodus, a very successful private
immigration service that brings Cubans into the United States from third
countries. With funding from the U.S. government and private donors, a
staff of sixty-four directors and seventy trustees has "smoothed the way"
into America for more than eight thousand Cuban immigrants. According
to one official who supervises the program for the INS: "The foundation
does the casework. They get to choose the people we will consider" (Slevin
1992a). In reference to this program, Wayne Smith, the State Department's
senior representative in Havana during the Carter and Reagan administra-
tions, explained: "I do not know of any other political organization in the
United States that has ever received this kind of privilege" (Rohter 1995).

Jorge Mas Canosa and the CANF also lobbied hard to secure U.S. government support for UNITA (National Union for the Total Independence of
Angola) rebels fighting to overthrow the Marxist government in Angola.
In 1988 Mas Canosa traveled to Angola to sign a commitment of common
cause with UNITA, making the CANF the first private, tax-exempt organization in America to execute a treaty with an African rebel group (Slevin
1992a). And in August 1992 Mas Canosa traveled to Mexico City to meet
with President Salinas de Gortari. The meeting marked the first time since
1959 that Mexico, a faithful friend of Havana, had welcomed one of Castro's foes. One source reported that during the meeting Salinas made key
concessions on trade with Cuba in exchange for CANF support for the
North American Free Trade Agreement (Chardy 1992). Similarly, on 14
October 1992 a Public Broadcasting System special entitled "Campaign for
Cuba" reported that Mas Canosa had worked closely with Boris Yeltsin,
offering to lobby for U.S. government aid to Russia in exchange for the
withdrawal of military and financial support from Cuba.

The black community in Miami has yet to exercise the same degree of
influence locally, nationally, or internationally. The boycott, as well as
voter drives and other forms of political mobilizations that have taken
place around the Mandela issue, has caused the local power structure in

Miami to recognize blacks as a viable political force in Dade County. By adding immigration policy to the list of demands, boycott organizers in Miami have taken their claims to the level of the federal government. Expeditions by regional NAACP president Johnnie McMillian and other local African American leaders to Haiti, as well as increased contact between local blacks and the ANC as a result of Mandela's visit, also indicate the increased potential for transnational activity on the part of blacks in Miami.

CONCLUSION

All summer long the ghost of South African anti-apartheid leader Nelson Mandela has haunted Miami as surely as a bearded wraith named Fidel Castro has deviled the city for three decades. Like Cuban Miami's absentee archvillain, black Miami's imported superhero is now a touchstone and tuning fork for local reality, a lens required for viewing life at the end of America.

(Rowe 1990)

Today scholars of ethnicity agree on the need to study ethnic phenomena contextually, including further empirical exploration of how ethnic identity is formed and what processes activate ethnic identity in the pursuit of particular goals (Kasfir 1979, 95). Similarly, events now occurring around the globe demand that greater attention be paid to the emergence and resurgence of ethnicity in both the developed and the developing world. The Miami case, and particularly the events surrounding the visit of Nelson Mandela, provides an ideal opportunity to illuminate the essence of ethnicity and ethnic group relations in the context of a changing world system.

Miami's status as a global city is widely recognized by analysts and observers of various backgrounds, who tend to emphasize the impact of ethnic diversity on the internationalization of Miami. Large numbers of immigrants have created a multicultural social milieu; the ties those immigrants maintain to their native countries and cultures have facilitated commercial and financial linkages between Miami and Latin America in particular; and the presence of these newcomers has introduced new, international political issues and policy concerns into the local political arena.

Underlying this interpretation of the internationalization of Miami is the conceptualization of ethnicity as a variable that significantly impacts social, economic, and political activity in an urban area. Although this is an accurate assumption, it fails to recognize that ethnicity may also be a dependent variable. Just as ethnic diversity has influenced the social, economic, and political processes of globalization, so, too, have those processes influenced ethnicity and ethnic relations in Miami. They have done so not simply by diversifying the local population or by altering the economic conditions under which ethnic groups interact but also by injecting new symbols into ethnic political discourses at the local level and altering the context in which those symbols are assigned meaning.

The events surrounding Mandela's visit to Miami suggest that ethnicity is neither a preconscious form of cultural attachment nor merely a rational construct. The fluid and contextual nature of ethnic identity and ethnic relations in Miami requires that ethnicity itself be reconceptualized and that theories of the international system be amended to account for the role ethnicity continues to play in a new world order. The challenge, therefore, is to articulate the complex and dynamic set of processes that invents and reinvents ethnicity and to link those processes to an equally complex and dynamic set of processes that makes up the international system.

- Blacks as "ethnic"?
What does S— think?

6

CONTESTED REALITIES/ SHIFTING TERRAIN

Toward a Theory of Ethnicity in the Postmodern World

The most charming thing about Miami is that no one knows what it is.

John Keasler

We need to interpret interpretations more than to interpret things.

Jacques Derrida

Is Miami the "land of opportunity"? A "paradise lost"? A "sophisticated tropics" or a "banana republic"? Is it the "city of the future" or a "city on the edge"? Is Miami America's Riviera or America's Pretoria? Miami is all of these things—a composite of images that overlap and intersect, compete and collide. The city's boosters have capitalized on, even perpetuated, Miami's elusiveness and romanticized the city's ambiguity as a form of "magic." But beyond the glitz and the glitter, Miami provides a lens, albeit a bold and magnified one, through which to view other places, issues, and ideas of great contemporary significance. Clearly, both geography and history have conspired to construct a city like none other in the United States. Yet the significance of metropolitan Miami lies not in its particularities, fascinating though these idiosyncrasies may be, but in the broader implications such specificities hold for the theory and method of social research.

The single-minded student of race and ethnicity who approaches contemporary conflicts, in Miami or elsewhere, from a conventional standpoint quickly confronts a bewildering array of claims and counterclaims, grievances and assertions, heroes and victims. Most such claims exist in direct opposition to contradictory assertions, as any number of perspectives vie for attention and dominance within the "public mind." Further complicating the welter of contrasting images is the additional realization that neither the claims themselves nor the coalition of individuals and groups who give them voice remain constant for very long; they shift and turn, acquire new meanings and shed others, in the very process of their articulation. Circumstances such as these displace the analytical object from the comfortable domain of linear reasoning and positivist thought to pose numerous epistemological, theoretical, and methodological challenges for conventional social science inquiry.

Many attempts to interpret social, political, and economic phenomena in ethnically divided societies begin with the assumption that the stratification of individuals and groups along lines of ethnicity is rooted in deeply held values and primordial attachments. Social conflict is presumed to result from a clash between different cultures, as well as from a fierce competition over limited material resources that pits these distinct groups in a zero-sum struggle for economic, political, and social well-being. The approach presented here challenges these widely held assumptions, arguing that neither the issues or problems over which groups struggle nor the identities and interests around which members of a group coalesce are the direct or unmediated outcome of objective conditions and empirical facts. This study is guided by an alternative assumption, namely, that issues, problems, interests, and identities are not soundly anchored to an objective empirical reality but are themselves images of reality created through discursive processes that define or assign meaning to social phenomena; that is, they construct social reality.

This perspective does not deny the importance of class divisions, social hierarchies, and the concentration of wealth and political power; rather, it emphasizes an alternative and interrelated dimension of power. Power, in this case, is rooted not only in material production, capital accumulation, or political position but also in the discursive realm of image construction and identity formation. Discourse, power, and identity politics are not disconnected from material conditions, nor are they related in any direct or deterministic way. The point is to understand how different groups variously situated within Miami's social structure actively promote competing images of the city and themselves and why some images and identities achieve greater currency than do others. Critical to the exploration of the process—and the central focus of this analysis—is image construction.

CONSTRUCTED REALITIES

An examination of public discourses in Miami from 1960 to 1990 revealed a multitude of comments, complaints, problems, issues, actors, and threats. Specific claims, whether they were about job displacement, Cuban entrepreneurship, or Nelson Mandela, were surrounded by other claims that made reference to similar concerns, however loosely or problematically related. The outcome was a number of narratives or discourses that existed simultaneously, assigning specific meanings to the disparate elements, issues, and activities that social reality comprises. Neither the construction of these narratives nor the claims that provide their content were arbitrary. Rather, both were comfortably situated within particular configurations of social, political, and economic power and interests at specific points in time.

The Liberty City riots of 1980 focused local, national, and international attention on Miami, and the causes of the rebellion were widely discussed and debated among the media, politicians, community leaders, and local government task forces. This discussion highlighted various factors that contributed to the anger and frustration of blacks in Miami, including a lack of trust in a law enforcement system replete with examples of police brutality against black residents and diminished faith in a court system of judges and juries that seemed committed to looking the other way. Also relevant was a pervasive sense of hopelessness and despair in the face of low employment rates, high rents, and inadequate city and county services, all of which persisted despite longstanding promises by local politicians and community leaders to address these pressing concerns.

The riots of 1980 temporarily put these issues back on Miami's public agenda but simultaneously propelled to the top of that agenda the issue of immigration and its impact on the local African American population in Miami. A frequent claim that surfaced in this discussion and debate was one that attributed the riots to anger among blacks at the loss of jobs to Cuban refugees and frustration with growing labor market competition between new immigrants and established residents. That the 1980 riots occurred just weeks after the Mariel boatlift, following a long year of record arrivals of Haitian refugees, lent credence to this complaint.

An exploration of the emergence and legitimation of the job displacement claim was presented in chapter 3. Complaints about a job takeover dated back to the early 1960s, when the Cuban refugee influx coincided with both an economic downturn that brought high unemployment to the area and the spread of civil rights gains to South Florida, which increased the political and economic expectations of the local black population. The claim that the refugees would take jobs from U.S. workers reflected the frustration of an urban population suffering economic stagnation, the concerns of black leaders fearful that the newcomers would detract much needed attention from the African American cause, and the desperation of local officials attempting to secure adequate assistance from Washington to cope with the local impact of the refugee crisis.

Over time the complaints about losing jobs to immigrants were surrounded by a variety of other claims that held Cuban immigrants responsible for problems and indiscretions ranging from an increase in the incidence of gambling among African Americans in Miami to a local business environment characterized by crime and corruption. Whether the issue was the "120-decibel level of casual Cuban conversation" (Resnick 1990) or animal carcasses floating in the Miami River, Cuban immigrants were portrayed as a threat not only to the job base of local residents but also to the moral fabric of American society. The job displacement claim provided the cornerstone of a broader public discourse that defined immigration as a foreign invasion and the immigrants as unwelcome intruders.

The success of the Cuban success story was similarly related to the tug and pull of vested interests—local, national, and international. The image of Cuban immigrants as hard-working, patriotic survivors of communist oppression was constructed through a series of claims, comments, characterizations, and concerns that simultaneously served the social, political, and economic interests of various individuals and groups. The discourse on tyranny emerged from the claims-making activity of U.S. politicians, government officials, and the media and defined a reality that reflected and fortified U.S. foreign policy concerns during the Cold War. For Cubans in

Miami, this narrative expressed the psychological tumult inherent in immigration to a foreign land and the obstacles that the refugees encountered as they tried to gain acceptance and incorporation into American society. Statements made by the business elite in Miami calling for a thousand more refugees reflected their personal satisfaction as well as the financial gain accrued from the economic turnaround in Miami during the late 1960s and 1970s.

During the early 1990s the visit of Nelson Mandela and the subsequent black tourism boycott consumed public attention not only in Miami but in other U.S. cities as well. The controversy surrounding these events was widely interpreted as another example of pervasive ethnic conflict in Miami and as evidence of a particularly deep-seated hostility between Latins and blacks. As the analysis in chapter 5 reveals, the conflict was not directly about jobs, political position, or a clash of primordial ethnic values. What took place was largely a struggle over meaning. Mandela was a symbol whose ideological significance for one group was in direct confrontation with what he signified to another group. He was viewed by one as a symbol of liberation and by the other as a supporter of tyrannical repression.

Not only did the emergence and legitimation of public discourses in Miami mirror patterns of vested interests and symbolic attachments but the specific symbols and ideologies on which these different definitions of social reality drew also reflected the context and configuration of social, cultural, economic, and political resources available to particular groups at a given time. The discourse of Cubans in Miami as recent immigrants drew heavily on symbols of kinship, common ancestry, and shared traditions. The strength and potency of this cultural capital was fortified by a continual influx of new arrivals from Cuba. As the established resident majority, at least prior to the 1990s, non-Latin whites had access to the powerful symbols of U.S. citizenship, nationality, and language, all of which were skillfully manipulated by politicians campaigning for "American" seats, media editorials bemoaning the loss of spoken English in Dade County, and bumper stickers making passionate references to the American flag.

As a disenfranchised racial minority in Dade County, blacks not only suffered limited political and economic resources but also lacked access to the same sort of cultural and symbolic capital that was available to non-

Latin whites and Cuban immigrants. The structure of Dade County's local political and economic system has been characterized as unresponsive to blacks and cited as the reason for the explosive rioting (Stack and Warren 1992, 293). This same set of circumstances—or Miami's unresponsive and discriminatory political and economic structures—may also explain why the unprecedented political mobilization of Dade County blacks during the tourism boycott drew strength not from symbols of citizenship or American civic culture but from symbols and images that called to life the threat of social violence; hence the boycott's more common title, "the Quiet Riot," and the related appeals to "riot at the polls."

CONTESTED SYMBOLS

These narratives operating in Miami during the past thirty years and their constituent claims did not exist in isolation. Each definition of reality and the symbols it contained interacted with, informed, and often directly clashed with others. Cuban Americans, for example, readily admit that their shift from "exile politics" to "ethnic politics" was in part a conscious reaction to perceived discrimination by non-Latin whites in Dade County. At the same time, many non-Latin whites and blacks engaged in a discourse that directly challenged the Cubans' self-portrayal as humble, hardworking exiles banished from their homeland. Whereas Cuban Americans espoused patriotism, non-Cubans complained that the immigrants lacked respect for the principles of democracy. Cuban Americans told tales of their rise from rags to riches, and non-Cubans associated the Latin community with corruption and unscrupulous business practices. Whereas Cuban Americans emphasized their desperate flight from tyranny, one African American, drawing an implicit contrast to the importation of African slaves, remarked: "They [the Cubans] came here of their own free will" (interview, 8 July 1992). And while Cuban Americans complain very vocally about the Castro dictatorship, non-Cubans in Miami accuse the immigrants of behaving like dictators themselves.

When Nelson Mandela became black Miami's "imported superhero," much as Castro had long been Cuban Miami's "absentee archvillain," Cubans in Miami were quick to attack the symbolic content of a black ethnic discourse focused on Africa in much the same way that their own symbolic ties to Cuba were increasingly chastised. And in 1992 Jewish leaders from Dade County conjured up the Holocaust as a key issue in the battle to redraw legislative districts in South Florida. In this local environment saturated by passionate political appeals to culture and tradition the tendency to manipulate ethnic symbols and to mobilize around ethnic identity was contagious. A close look at these conflicts reveals that various issues, actors, and events in Miami acquire a meaning and political potency that is not easily explained by conventional analytical frameworks. Whether it be a battle over the county's official language, a city referendum on communism, or an apology from local politicians who would not welcome South African leader Nelson Mandela because he publicly supported Cuban President Fidel Castro, much of what constitutes social conflict in Miami is best described as a struggle over symbols, waged through symbols, and offering rewards that are little more than symbolic.

In many instances the confrontation between groups was very direct. In other instances, however, the use of discourses as weapons of attack and defense was more subtle. When some non-Latin whites praised the Cuban refugees for their willingness to embrace the ideals of hard work and self-sacrifice they implicitly characterized other groups (read: blacks) as less willing to do so. When Cubans emphasized the color-blind character of Cuban society, they implicitly blamed non-Latin whites for the racial hostility that plagued Miami. Furthermore, in accusing the Anglo elite of attempting to "divide and conquer" minority groups in Miami, both blacks and Cubans recognized that certain definitions of social reality, such as job displacement, served to pit blacks against Hispanics and deflected attention away from inequalities and injustices deeply embedded in the social, political, and economic structures of Dade County.

SHIFTING TERRAIN

The symbolic nature of group interaction in Miami does not negate the potency of these symbols as tools to be manipulated in the pursuit of more tangible political or economic gain. Discursive activity, in other words, is not inconsequential; nor do the images that it constructs remain constant. The competing definitions of social reality in Miami fluctuated over time.

Their constituent claims were not issued consistently or always by the same individuals or groups.

During the 1970s, for example, the civic and business elite in Miami portrayed the Cuban refugees as an economic and cultural asset to Dade County. The 1973 declaration of Dade County as a bilingual and bicultural county was viewed in part as a recognition of, if not expression of gratitude for, the contributions of the Cuban newcomers. By the 1980s, however, media reports, the editorial pages of the *Miami Herald*, and the overwhelming Anglo support for the anti-bilingual referendum indicated that this view had begun to sour. In the 1990s many non-Latin white leaders appeared eager to embrace, at least publicly, the virtues of multiculturalism. Yet, interview results showed that this group was still likely to blame social tensions in Miami on the rapid and continual influx of immigrants—more likely, in fact, than were many blacks.

Just as the attitude of the Anglo establishment toward the immigrants appeared to fluctuate, certain prominent figures within the African American community in Miami also changed their viewpoint not only about the impact of immigration but also about the general circumstances confronting blacks in Miami. As co-author of *The Miami Riot of 1980: Crossing the Bounds*, Marvin Dunn, a professor of psychology at Florida International University and a respected community leader in Dade County, discussed the Cuban influx into Miami as one of the factors that contributed to the Liberty City riots in 1980. He pointed specifically to a "devastating job takeover" experienced by blacks and emphasized the success of Cuban immigrants in diverting attention and resources away from Miami blacks (Porter and Dunn 1984, 195). Similarly, in a speech at a bi-lingual conference in Miami in May 1976 Dunn warned: "There are other signs which convince me that cultural conflict on a massive scale may soon be upon us. The fact is that there is hard and bitter competition, especially between low income blacks and Latins, for the few jobs that are left to many of the residents in our economically depressed community. Blacks who held the most menial jobs in this city had to share those jobs with Latins after the great Cuban influx" ("Looming Conflict" 1976).

Despite the fact that the 1980s seemed to fulfill Dunn's forecast, his public statements regarding the immigrant takeover changed during the 1990s. In 1991 Dunn wrote: "There are many misconceptions about black Miami. One of these is that all, or most, black Miamians are poor and have been muscled out of the job market by newly arriving immigrants, black, white, and particularly brown. This has been a lingering legacy from Miami's time of fire: the 1980s, when the city was rocked by a series of racial disturbances. Yet there has not been any compelling evidence to support such a view" (Dunn 1991, 151).

In 1990 Dunn joined several Cuban American scholars in preparing a Ford Foundation report on relations between established residents and newcomers in Miami. The report challenged the job displacement thesis and highlighted the recent economic and political gains of blacks in Dade County compared with those of both non-Latin whites and Cubans (Stepick et al. 1990). When interviewed for this study in 1992, Dunn said of the job displacement question: "That has always been overstated. We really know nothing definite" (interview, 30 June 1992).

During a 1984 rally in Miami to protest Mayor Ferre's decision to fire Miami's black city manager, Howard Gary, another well-known member of Dade County's African American community shouted before a large and angry crowd of blacks that "I'd rather be black in South Africa than be black in South Florida. In South Africa you know you're going to be treated like a nigger. In South Florida they treat you nice before you go to sleep at night, and you don't know what to expect in the morning."[1] During an interview in July 1992, this same individual not only stated that ethnic and race relations in Miami had vastly improved since the 1980s but also vehemently rejected any symbolic linkage to South Africa: "I don't give a damn about Nelson Mandela."

The Cuban success story was also characterized by fluctuating comments, claims, and concerns. During the 1960s and 1970s the social and political energies of the Cubans in Miami remained focused almost entirely on their anticipated return to the island. Complaints about Castro, warnings about the evils of communism, and laments about the agony of exile dominated discussion and debate among the Cuban refugees. By the 1980s Cubans in Miami had begun to exhibit social and political behavior more akin to that of traditional immigrant groups. Larger numbers of Cubans became U.S. citizens, voter turnout among Cuban Americans increased, and although deep concern over Cuba and Castro remained, Cubans in Miami began to take a more active interest in local political, economic, and social issues. In the 1990s, the public statements of some Cuban American leaders have been indistinguishable in both content and form from those of the Anglo establishment in Dade County.

The changing nature of public discourse in Miami responded to shifts in the social, political, and economic context of the local, national, and international arenas. Discursive activity, however, not only reflects but also reinforces and redefines established configurations of social, political, and economic interests. The claims, comments, and concerns detailed in chapter 3 not only defined immigration as a threatening invasion but also defined social reality in a way that reinforced the status quo, or the "mobilization of bias," in Miami. Similarly, the claims that contributed to the success of the Cuban success story simultaneously fortified the ideological strength of democratic capitalism and reinforced the myth of the American dream. The many rags-to-riches tales told by Cuban immigrants themselves served to explain, defend, and protect the status of a group that had made a relatively rapid transition from an exile population to an established social, political, and economic force in Dade County. In 1990, when the boycott organizers and others manipulated the symbolic strength attached to Mandela and South Africa, they altered the perceptions of identity and interests among previously unallied black groups in Dade County.

TRI-ETHNIC POLITICS

The processes that assign meaning to social issues and problems also construct or define individual and group identities and influence the formation and fluctuation of group alliances. Through the frequent utilization and manipulation of the terms *black, Hispanic,* and *Anglo,* for example, these categories, however devoid of empirical referents they may be, become identities endowed with independent explanatory significance. The discussion and debate surrounding various issues in Miami—immigration, Cuban economic success, Mandela—revealed a common tendency to separate the population of metropolitan Miami into three distinct groups—

blacks, Hispanics, and Anglos, or non-Latin whites. In fact, the use of the terms *Anglo, black,* and *Hispanic* seems almost unavoidable in any discussion of Miami, as the preceding chapters indicate. These chapters also indicate, however, that the categories themselves conceal as much as much as they reveal about the nature and complexity of social and political phenomena in Dade County. Subsumed under the heading "Anglo," for example, is a substantial Jewish population that increasingly resents the loss of its own ethnic distinctiveness. "Hispanic" is a social and political category that masks very relevant distinctions of class, race, religion, nationality, political ideology, age, and gender among the Latin population in Dade County. Furthermore, the category "black" in Miami often signifies little more than the skin color of a particular individual or group.

This invention of ethnic identities in Miami was accompanied by the construction or reconfiguration of alliances and divisions within and between ethnic groups. The public discourse on job displacement defined longtime foes—blacks and Anglos—as allies in a resistance against the Hispanic invaders. This particular us-against-them construction drew heavily on notions of citizenship, established residency, and a shared American, or more accurately U.S., culture. Language, in this case, was a particularly powerful tool for drawing the boundaries of group membership. Obscured by this definition of social, or ethnic, reality are (1) the long history of tension between non-Latin whites and blacks in Miami, which predates the massive influx of Cuban refugees; (2) the fact that many of the Hispanic "invaders" have resided in Dade County for at least as long as many blacks and non-Latin whites; and (3) the tendency in other contexts of both Anglos and blacks to emphasize their cultural differences and to challenge or reject the notion that they share a common heritage.

Although the discourse on displacement defined social identity in Miami along the lines of natives versus newcomers, the Cuban success story constructed an us-against-them dichotomy that defined Cuban Americans as one of "us" as opposed to one of "them." The willingness to accept Cuban refugees into the host society was influenced in part by the perception that these immigrants were white. This definition was useful to a white resident majority that wished to continue denying civil rights to black Americans, just as it was useful to a Cuban immigrant group that wished for acceptance in a racially divided and color-conscious society. This particular construction of social reality was problematic, however, to the extent that the use of race as a criterion for membership in a group was extremely ambiguous. Cubans as a group are not white, a reality that became increasingly clear with each successive wave of immigration. Furthermore, Cubans in the United States learned quickly that their status as one of "us" was a fragile one that competed continuously with elements of the alternative discursive formation discussed above.

Numerous analysts have argued that there is in fact no black "community" in Miami, and a great deal of social, political, and economic behavior in Miami lends credence to that contention. Use of the category "black," however, dominates discussions by the media, politicians, and government officials, both black and white. Mandela's visit in June 1990 illustrated the predominance of the tri-ethnic framework, as well as the capacity of labels themselves to take on a particular political significance when used and manipulated by those actors and interests with the greatest capacity to set or determine the public agenda. The African American leaders who organized the boycott, for example, added to their list of grievances a concern for the plight of Haitian refugees. At the same time they began to emphasize the common ancestry of black groups in Miami who came from distinct cultural backgrounds and who previously had been indifferent to one another at best and hostile at worst.

Constructed identities, like constructed issues, problems, crises, and threats, are ambiguous, fluid, and frequently contested. Some African Americans in Miami rejected Mandela as a symbol of their cultural identity, and some Cubans in Miami adamantly distanced themselves from the meanings leaders such as Jorge Mas Canosa assign to Cuban American identity. Anglos complain about being referred to as non-Latin whites, and Jews in Miami resent being subsumed under the heading "Anglo." In March 1990 the one African American on the Miami City Commission angrily challenged the nomination of a black Hispanic to a committee position designated for a black. Commissioner Dawkins demanded a letter from the nominee stating that he was indeed black. When told that the nominee identified himself as black and Hispanic, Dawkins replied: "I didn't ask if he's black and Hispanic. I asked if he's black" ("Dawkins"

1990). For weeks, newspapers, radio stations, and government chambers throughout Dade County were consumed by a raging debate over what constitutes blackness.

TOWARD A THEORY OF ETHNICITY

Conflict within and between social groups is certainly not unique to Miami, nor is the tendency to portray the conflict in ethnic terms. Contrary to the optimistic predictions of liberal pluralists and modernization theorists, advances in science, communications technology, transportation, and education have not resulted in peaceful political and economic development worldwide. Nor has global class struggle brought about the socialist revolution forecast by Marx. Instead, as Benjamin Barber (1992) explains, the world is simultaneously coming together and coming apart; and it appears to be coming apart along lines of ethnicity. The central debate is over whether these are fault lines, rumbling for centuries prior to an unavoidable quake, or artificial boundaries imposed upon the masses for the benefit of a small but powerful elite. In other words, do contemporary ethnic conflicts represent a resurgence of primordial identities rooted in the cultural attachments and shared values of an ancient past, or do they more accurately reflect the skillful political manipulation of a wealthy few who attempt to maintain their economic and political dominance in a world capitalist system deeply stratified along class lines?

The complexity of social relations in Miami and elsewhere is not accurately addressed by either set of explanations; it demands an alternative approach. By combining the insights of various and sometimes contradictory theoretical and epistemological frameworks and applying these to a sound case study, this analysis lays the foundation for a new theory of ethnicity and ethnic relations in a postmodern world. Key concepts in the study of social phenomena, including ethnicity, power, and social reality, and the relationships between them are reconfigured, and new concepts are introduced. The result is a useful step toward reconciliation of longstanding debates about the significance of structure, the constitutive capacity of language, and the role of human agency. This step not only sheds light on issues of great relevance to Miami but also provides a more helpful framework for examining the increasing complexity of social realities worldwide.

Many of the theoretical and conceptual insights utilized in this study are not new. Marxist scholars have focused substantial attention on how economic structures—the mode and social relations of material production—shape, or in more reductionist terms, "determine," cultural and political outcomes. Poststructuralists have long emphasized the role of language and discourse in creating meaning, and scholars from various intellectual backgrounds have criticized theorists from both of these schools for failing to take into account the capacity of individuals to act in and alter the world in which they live. Yet just as the diversity and universality of ethnic phenomena cannot be explained by isolated references to primordial ties or instrumentalist motives, the complexity of social relations cannot be neatly captured by one or the other of these predominant approaches.

Most of the key criticisms of Marx's political thought are by now well known and in many cases arguably overstated. The most notable of these critiques include (1) the charge of economic reductionism, whether it be the limited autonomy afforded the state and other political institutions and activities or the relative inattention paid to various forms of human and cultural consciousness that are not directly rooted in a relationship to the means of production; and (2) the charge that Marxism failed to fully anticipate capitalism's capacity to sustain itself as an economic and political system, in part by transcending state borders and globalizing relations of production and exchange. In response to these and other criticisms, generations of neo-Marxists, analytical Marxists, cultural Marxists, and post-Marxists have struggled to interpret, reinterpret, and extend various principles of Marxist thought. One component of Marxist analysis that appears particularly applicable to ethnic politics in Miami, although it also is incomplete, is expressed in Marx and Engels's famous statement in *The German Ideology:*

The ideas of the ruling class are in every epoch the ruling ideas: i.e. the class, which is the ruling material force of society, is at the same time its ruling intellectual force. The class which has the means of material production at its disposal, has control at the same time over the means of mental production, so that thereby, generally speaking, the ideas of those who lack the means of mental production are subject to it. The ruling ideas are nothing more than the ideal expression of the dominant material relationships, the dominant material relationships grasped as ideas; hence of the relationships which make the one class the ruling one, therefore the ideas of dominance. (Marx and Engels 1978, 172)

The previous chapters indicate consistently that the definitions or constructions of social reality that achieved prominence on Miami's public agenda were those that reflected and reinforced the interests of the city's political and economic elite. In other words, the images and the identities with the greatest staying power were those that resonated most soundly with the ruling ideas. This conclusion does, however, present certain problems. To posit that images and ideas, or what Marx called the "ideological superstructure," are a product, or the unmediated result of economic conditions, or the "base" does little to explain the processes by which material forces of production cause, determine, or produce ideas and images. In other words, to argue that job displacement reflects the vested interests of the Anglo elite in Miami does little, in and of itself, to explain how the definition was constructed, what its constitutive themes were, who promoted it, how it competed and interacted with other definitions, and what outcomes it produced.

The weakness of this argument is similar to critiques often leveled at Marx's treatment of the concept of class consciousness. Marx argued that workers, or the "proletariat," would have similar interests because of their shared relationship to the means of production. For the workers to become aware, or "conscious," of their similar class positioning was deemed critical to the advent of socialist revolution. Marx, however, devoted relatively little discussion to how this class consciousness would evolve or when and why other forms of human consciousness—nationalism, gender, ethnicity, race—might supersede or crosscut class identification.[2] Marx posited class consciousness as a product of material conditions without specifying how it was produced or accounting for why and how similar material conditions might produce divergent outcomes.

This study seeks explicitly to avoid these and other errors attributed to Marxist analysis. Power, for example, is approached as a multidimensional phenomenon whose exercise and location cannot be confined to the realm of the economic. Human consciousness is also viewed as multifaceted. Individual and group identity are fluid and fluctuating, and neither their origins nor their consequences can be confined to the realm of material conditions. But perhaps most importantly, this analysis, unlike Marxism, makes no attempt to define one form of consciousness, one type of identity, or one particular definition of social reality as true and another as false. The preceding analysis of claims-making activity in Miami indicates that irrespective of their grounding, or lack thereof, in empirical "fact," identities, images, and ideas take on a social significance and political consequence all their own. As Nelson Kasfir (1979) pointed out, even if ethnicity is believed to be a form of false consciousness, it is still consciousness—the origins and uses of which warrant empirical investigation.

In emphasizing the constructed and contested nature of reality and the autonomy of language, this study also borrows from the insights of poststructural and postmodern theorists. Yet the case study findings suggest that these insights, like those of Marx, must also be amended. Much of postmodernist and poststructuralist thought has its origins in Friedrich Nietzsche's insistence that "it is only as an aesthetic phenomenon that existence and the world are eternally justified." Facts and things, according to Nietzsche, are constructed by the human act of interpretation; and language, viewed as the primary realm of human experience, is figurative, nonreferential, and incapable of conveying objective historical knowledge, knowledge that Nietzsche argued could not possibly exist (Megill 1985, 2–3).

More recent works by French philosophers such as Michel Foucault and Jacques Derrida illustrate postmodernism's contemporary emphasis on the constitutive and nonreferential nature of discourse and language.[3] Foucault's most significant contribution is his recognition of discourses as "tactics and strategies of power and control." The whole of social and political reality—relations of production, reproduction, state power, and ideology—is defined as "a battle among discourses and through discourses." But discourses and their production of truth are intricately connected to power relations: "We are subjected to the production of truth through power and we cannot exercise power except through the production of truth" (Foucault 1980, 93). Without the same emphasis as Foucault places on power relations, social processes, and history, Derrida's work takes meaning and discourse to an even higher level of abstraction and relativity. Palmer contends that it was the writing of Jacques Derrida that propelled discourse to new heights of determination (1990, 33).[4] Much of Derrida's work provides a critique of structural linguistics and focuses on the extreme instability of language. Words, or signifiers, do not yield up meaning, or the signified, directly. There is, in other words, no direct or fixed relationship between words and meanings, and any attempt to establish the transcendental meaning of a signifier will only lead in an infinite and circular path to another signifier. One analyst offers the useful analogy of the answer to a small child's question or a definition in a dictionary: one sign leads to another, and so on indefinitely (Sarup 1989, 36). Although Derrida offers "deconstruction" as a method for reading, or interrogating, a text, meaning remains always ultimately undecidable.[5]

The work of these and other postmodernists has permeated the study of literature, politics, policy analysis, and anthropology and has also been the subject of substantial argument and debate. Opponents come from a variety of backgrounds and level a wide range of criticisms. Postmodernists have been accused, at worst, of being apolitical, ahistorical, and even amoral and, at the very least, of producing jargon-laden prose accessible only to those in the innermost circles (Callinicos 1989; Rosenau 1992). Palmer, a particularly harsh critic, describes postmodernism as a dangerous and misguided "descent into discourse" and argues that the widespread and seemingly uncritical acceptance of postmodernist and poststructuralist thought in the American academy has "plunged critical theory even further into the abyss of aestheticism" and "unleashed a terroristic assault on reality and a violent repudiation of history" (1990, 40).

In some cases, as with Marxism, these charges are overstated, but the postmodernist emphasis on signs, texts, language, and discourse has served in many of its manifestations to divorce social and political life entirely from material conditions. This analysis of ethnic politics in Miami, along with various other works, argues that recognizing the constructive capacity of language and the relativity of meaning need not entail separating discourses from the social and political conditions of their making or use. As

Judith Newton contends, systems of meaning inform and construct the material, but the material also acts upon systems of meaning (1989, 17). Similarly, according to Dominick LaCapra, "Meaning is indeed context-bound, but context is not itself bound in any simple or unproblematic way" (1983, 14). This analysis has also been informed by Foucault's conceptualization of power as decentralized and diffuse; in addition, it heeds Walkowitz's warning that "there is danger in representing power as so diffuse and decentered that there is no agency, and there are no oppressors" (Palmer 1990, 163). Edward Said makes a similar point when he praises the "extraordinary worldliness" of Foucault's work on discourse and power but argues that "a great deal of power remains in such coarse items as the relationships and tensions between rulers and ruled, wealth and privilege, monopolies of coercion, and the central state apparatus" (1983, 221). Foucault himself states that "power must be analysed as something which circulates, or rather as something which only functions in the form of a chain. It is never localised here or there, never in anybody's hands, never appropriated as a commodity or piece of wealth" (1980, 98). The approach presented here accepts that power circulates but also argues that power has locales, such as ethnicity, class, gender, or nation-state, however fluid and fragile these locales themselves may be.

The Miami case illustrates that realities and identities are socially constructed, frequently contested, and highly contextual. Meanings or definitions are assigned to social reality through discourse—accounts, claims, statements, analogies, metaphors and language about or pertaining to issues, problems, events, crises, and threats. At no point are these discourses or the realities they construct divorced from material relations of production, reproduction, state power, or political control, nor are they determined by them. The implications for the study of ethnicity and ethnic relations in Miami and elsewhere are broad. Rather than accepting as given either the identities of individuals and groups or the issues around which they struggle, this approach focuses attention on the processes that define certain social conditions as problems relating to or resulting from ethnicity and on the forces that make ethnicity a predominant form of social stratification and political mobilization. Issues of ethnic conflict and

ethnic identities are not viewed only as independent variables but are
treated in a manner that simultaneously takes into account their status as
dependent variables.

By recognizing the fluid and contextual nature of social identity and
social reality, this study heeds Horowitz's earlier advice to move the study
of ethnicity beyond metaphors of blood and stone to those of clay and
putty. The content, or the "clay," with which ethnic identities and ethnic
relations are constructed includes various symbols, concepts, ideas, and
themes, many of which draw upon the notion of shared experiences and a
common past. Rather than attempting to establish the truth or falsity of the
conditions and claims that provide raw material for ethnic discourses, this
approach focuses on how these conditions and claims are interpreted and
perceived, and how those interpretations and perceptions are manipulated, used, and changed over time. Yet, to emphasize once again, as "invented" or "imagined" phenomena, ethnic identities are not wholly devoid of
material referents; nor is ethnic struggle completely detached from material conditions. As Yelvington states in his paraphrase of Marx, "People
invent their ethnicity as they invent their history, but, not exactly in ways
which they please" (1992, 3).

In order to understand more clearly how this interaction between the
real and the ideal, or matter and the mind, relates to ethnicity and ethnic
politics, it is useful to think in terms of "a limited repertoire of discursive
resources." Identities, ethnic or otherwise, and images draw content from
the array of symbols and ideas available to particular individuals or groups
at a given time. Many of the constituent elements are firmly ingrained and
relatively stable themes of the dominant culture, such as the rights of citizenship, private property, and equality before the law. The salience of
other themes rises and falls in accordance with local, national, and international events, as evidenced by the declining relevance of Cold War themes
as a viable discursive resource and the growing legitimacy of Mandela as a
symbol of international acclaim. Still other images or identities draw content from symbols and ideas that stand in direct contradiction to hegemon-
ic values and cultural themes, for example, black Miami's "Quiet Riot." The
point is that the processes of image construction and identity invention are
situated amidst established configurations of political, economic, and social

power. Discourses, in other words, are closely linked to resources. Individuals and groups have varied access to resources such as money, wealth, and influence. These varying degrees of access determine not only the content and nature of group discourse but also the capacity of groups to advance their particular vision of social reality to a prominent position on the public agenda.

Ethnicity, then, like history, is profoundly influenced by structural forces, but never in a unilinear or deterministic way. Identities and realities, once invented, take on an independent explanatory significance irrespective of their basis in empirical "fact." The content of ethnic identity and the nature of ethnic group relations therefore not only reflect but also redefine and reinforce vested interests and power relations. Thus, identity itself is a resource, and language or discourse is a form of capital that is essential to the production of meaning in the same way that industrial capital is essential to the production of material goods. Analyses of the role of power and influence in social interaction must take into account the access of individuals and groups not only to material resources but also to "a limited repertoire of discursive resources." At the same time, the utilization and manipulation of discursive resources must be viewed, to borrow from Edelman's discussion of the "political spectacle," as "strategies, deliberate or unrecognized, for strengthening or undermining support for specific courses of action or for particular ideologies" (Edelman 1988, 11).

An additional finding from the Miami case, and one with broad implications for the comparative analysis of ethnicity and ethnic conflict worldwide, concerns the interrelationships between ethnicity and the international system, or what can be referred to as a "new international division of identity." A number of analysts are now calling attention to a troubling paradox in the contemporary world system: at the same time that processes of global integration are linking peoples and political systems around the world into ever tighter networks, patterns of disintegration and disassociation (primarily in the form of ethnic conflict) threaten to transform the new world order into one of chaos and disorder. This is the case not only in Miami but also in areas as diverse as Los Angeles, Chiapas, Bosnia, and Berlin. While Miami proudly demonstrated its global leadership role in 1994 by hosting the international summit on democracy in the Western

Hemisphere, many black Miami residents continued to complain of social and economic injustices that rivaled those of the "developing" world. As Europe moves closer to "unionization," London, Paris, and Berlin are plagued by xenophobic attitudes and racial violence. On the very day that the North American Free Trade Agreement, the historic agreement signed by the United States, Canada, and Mexico, went into effect, Mayan peasants in the Mexican state of Chiapas rebelled. And within months after communist regimes in the Soviet Union and Eastern Europe collapsed under popular demands for democratization, the newly independent republics disintegrated into ethnonationalist turmoil.

Understanding the current *disorder* in the *new world order* will require paying more attention to the close interconnections between these two apparently contradictory world trends. The Miami case shows that "Jihad" factors, or "a threatened Lebanonization in which culture is pitted against culture, people against people, tribe against tribe," do not simply coexist alongside or clash with the globalizing forces of "McWorld" (Barber 1993) but are instead intricately linked to those forces in a variety of complex ways. World capitalism, international migration, and global advances in science and communications technology profoundly affect cultural and political identity in Miami not only by diversifying the ethnic composition of the local population and altering the economic conditions in which groups interact but also by injecting new symbols into local ethnic discourses and altering the context in which those symbols are assigned meaning and legitimacy. In other words, the international system influences the discursive resources available to ethnic and racial groups in cities and locales, as evidenced by the fierce struggles waged in Miami over Fidel Castro, Nelson Mandela, and Yasser Arafat. The international system also affects the relative power and influence of those resources and, in the process, privileges particular forms of discourse over others. Again, although ethnic discourses built on Cold War themes now have limited political appeal; claims relating to national self-determination or the environment are potent tools for political mobilization and ethnic group empowerment.

The question remains, however, why the universalizing or homogenizing forces of the global arena produce different outcomes in different regions and locales. The Miami case suggests that institutional structures and policies, the political behavior of elites, and the availability and manipulation of discursive resources act as intervening variables in determining the outcome of ethnic relations in cities and locales. Ethnic diversity does not automatically translate into ethnic conflict, nor does competition for material resources adequately explain the bewildering persistence of ethnic hostility. Instead, the very identities around which people coalesce and the issues over which groups struggle must be viewed as social constructions, or social definitions of reality. The constructions are not arbitrary; they closely reflect and reinforce the tug and pull of vested interests and power politics. Analysts must focus, therefore, on how politicians, government officials, community leaders, political activists, and the media reinforce and in many cases "invent" ethnic identities, how the rhetoric or "claims-making activity" of these actors defines certain sets of circumstances as "social problems" and determines which problems gain prominence on the public agenda, and how each of the above processes or any combination of them is inflected by particular patterns of material relations, social processes, and political institutions.

CONCLUSION

The goal of social science, in its most basic sense, is to illuminate existing social and political realities. The pursuit of this goal has long been premised on the assumption of a world of facts with determinable meaning, people who react rationally to the facts they know, and analysts who act as neutral observers of facts and the final arbiters of accurate knowledge (Best 1989, xiii; Edelman 1988, 1). What this conventional approach fails to recognize is that facts can rarely be separated from values, meanings are multiple and changing, and observers and what they observe construct one another. What emerges from the dynamic interplay of actors, interests, and varying contexts is not an objective, monolithic reality that remains constant over time but a very fluid set of socially constructed and politically contested "realities." This emphasis on elusiveness and ambiguity does not portray a hopeless state of affairs for the analytical endeavor of social science, nor does it suggest abandonment of the continuous and systematic pursuit of knowledge. Instead, analysts must ask different questions, actively challenge deeply held assumptions, formulate alternative frameworks, and be willing to incorporate into those frameworks the very fluid and contextual nature of the social and political world.

This analysis illustrates the numerous insights to be gained by applying such an approach to the study of ethnicity and ethnic group relations. Miami also provides an ideal setting in which to elucidate the complexities of social reality in the postmodern world. Ethnic conflict is a topic of critical and growing relevance, and Miami, as many of both its supporters and its critics suggest, is likely to be a bellwether of social relations for other areas around the globe. Many of the demographic characteristics that have converged so dramatically in Miami during the past thirty years foreshadow predicted population trends for the metropolitan United States as a whole. This is particularly true with regard to the large numbers of Hispanics, a population anticipated to soon become the largest minority group in the United States. In other large metropolitan areas that have experienced severe social upheaval, including Los Angeles, New York, and Detroit, explanations similar to those that circulate in and about Miami have been put forth to account for the conflict. This is true in Germany, France, and the former Yugoslav Republic as well. Although the details of each case are unique, a careful analysis would likely reveal similar ambiguities and political nuances in the emergent definitions of social reality.

Furthermore, as the discussion of the globalization of interethnic relations in Miami indicates, ethnicity itself can no longer be viewed in a purely domestic context. Ethnic identities and ethnic interaction in a given locale are influenced in a variety of ways by the international system. This situation is particularly pronounced in metropolitan Miami but in no way unique to it. The upsurge of hate crimes against Arab Americans during the Gulf War and after the arrest of a Muslim suspect in the 1993 bombing of the World Trade Center illustrates dramatically the linkages between ethnic group relations and international politics. So, too, do the violent attacks on Asian Americans by unemployed automobile workers in Detroit who attributed their plight (and they were encouraged in this by irresponsible U.S. politicians) to Japanese success in the automobile industry.[6] Similarly, ethnicity as a form of social and political mobilization exerts an independent impact on the global arena. As the nation-state loses its significance as a unit of analysis in international political affairs, Miami is just one of many cases that indicate a growing need to recognize the role of ethnic groups as transnational actors in a changing world order.

As a metropolitan area built on image and myth, Miami is often described as a city that continuously invents and reinvents itself. The insight to be gleaned from the Miami case is that image is not merely a smoke screen to be penetrated by social science in its rigorous pursuit of empirical reality; image is reality, and reality is image, and both are in a constant state of flux. If social and political realities are to be better understood and perhaps improved upon, then social science must embrace image rather than continue in its efforts to circumvent image.

APPENDICES

NOTES

REFERENCES

INDEX

LABOR MARKET ANALYSIS

The current analysis grows out of an earlier investigation of the labor market impact of Cuban immigration to Miami. Census data on occupational status and mobility in the Standard Metropolitan Statistical Area of Miami from 1940 to 1980 were used to investigate the claim that Cuban immigration exerted a negative economic impact on blacks in Miami's labor market.

I originally hypothesized that the massive influx of Cuban immigrants in the 1960s and their subsequent incorporation into the local labor market would reverse a downward trend in the occupational inequality between whites and blacks. Using an index of occupational dissimilarity, I measured the percentage of either population—whites or blacks—that would need to be redistributed for the percentage distributions in each occupational category to be equal *(see fig. A1)*. The index itself was calculated by determining the percentage difference between whites and blacks in each occupational category, totaling those differences, and then dividing by two. The results indicated that, with the exception of a slight increase in 1950, occupational

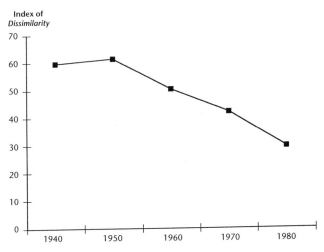

Figure A1. Occupational dissimilarity between whites and blacks in metropolitan Miami, 1940–1980. Source: U.S. Bureau of Census, 1940–1980, *Characteristics of the Population.*

dissimilarity between whites and blacks in the metropolitan Miami labor market declined gradually, without interruption, between 1940 and 1980.

I used census figures to document the changing occupational distribution of blacks in Miami from 1940 to 1980. Although various individuals and groups complained that the influx of Cuban immigrants during the 1960s halted or reversed the movement of blacks into middle- and upper-level occupational categories, the data do not support that claim. The percentage of blacks in professional and managerial occupations as well as in sales, clerical, kindred, and craft occupations increased between 1960 and 1980.

I also used a table published in the 1970 census to compare the occupational mobility of blacks and Hispanics in Florida and Georgia between 1965 and 1970. As a southern state with a large black population, Georgia provided a partial control for variables other than massive Cuban immigration that may have influenced the status of blacks in the labor market. The 1970 census included a question about the respondent's current occupation and his or her occupation five years prior. A table was then constructed to show the number of individuals that changed occupational categories between 1965 and 1970. A diagonal line drawn through the table identified those workers that remained in the same category; the percentage of workers above the diagonal line experienced upward occupational mobility, and those below the line experienced downward mobility. The results show no significant difference in the occupational mobility of blacks or Hispanics in Florida and Georgia.

Although these findings offer nothing in the way of a definitive statement on labor market competition in Miami, they do suggest that the rise of the job displacement thesis was not due to the gravity of the problem itself.

METHODOLOGICAL STRATEGY

This analysis of claims-making activity in Miami, Florida, was designed to identify the variety of comments, observations, complaints, and concerns that have characterized public discourse in Miami over the past thirty years. The data are drawn almost entirely from statements made during in-depth interviews and from claims that appear in the periodical and popular literature on Miami.

I conducted a total of sixty interviews in Dade County from May through November 1992. Using a reputational technique to select those individuals who were most cognizant of ethnic relations in Miami, I began with a list of key figures whose names appeared frequently in the media or who were suggested to me early on as valuable contacts by researchers working in similar fields at both Florida International University and the University of Florida. At the end of each interview, I asked interviewees to recommend other individuals whose knowledge of and experience in Miami would be useful to my project. I identified those individuals whose names were mentioned most frequently and made every effort to interview them. In most cases my efforts were successful. All of the Hispanics and all but one of the blacks I contacted agreed to be interviewed. Interestingly, non-Latin whites, or more specifically, Anglos, were not as frequently recommended, nor were they as willing to be interviewed. To some extent this supported portrayals of the Anglo elite in Miami as a shadow government, on the defensive. In all fairness, however, some of these individuals were not contacted until after the hurricane in August 1992, during which time their schedules were understandably tight.

I made a conscious effort to interview an equal number of respondents from each of three major ethnic groups in the Miami area. Of the sixty interviews I conducted, twenty were with blacks, twenty were with Hispanics, and twenty were with Anglos. Among the black interviewees there were individuals of Bahamian descent and individuals whose ancestors had migrated from North Florida and Georgia. Although respondents were not asked about this distinction, several mentioned it in the course of their interviews. This group also included one Haitian American.

The majority of Hispanics turned out to be Cuban American, although I did interview one individual from Nicaragua, one of Panamanian descent, and one from Puerto Rico. The Hispanic group also included one black Cuban. At least one-third of the Anglo respondents were Jewish, which roughly reflects the proportion of Jewish residents among the non-Latin White population in Dade County.

Although the respondents were not broadly representative of the community at large, the group was generally representative of the elite in Dade County. Respondents included politicians, attorneys, business people, journalists, community activists, civic leaders, elected and appointed government officials, city and county employees, as well as ministers, rabbis, and priests. If any occupational or professional category is underrepresented, it is the city and county commissioners. One commissioner refused to be interviewed; but in general these officials were not frequently nominated by other respondents. Several of the individuals interviewed explicitly suggested that real power and knowledge in Dade County lies not with the politicians but with the business community.

The local newspapers in Dade County provided a very valuable source from which to gather claims, particularly in terms of gaining a historical perspective. Among the written media, the *Miami Herald* is the predominant voice in Dade County. Something that appears to be unique to Miami is that the city's main newspaper daily publishes both a Spanish and an English version. In addition to the *Herald* and *El Nuevo Herald,* Miami is also home to a well-established black newspaper, the *Miami Times,* and the Hispanic-owned and -operated *Diario Las Americas.* A multitude of other, smaller papers cater to the Jewish population in Miami Beach as well as to other immigrant communities from throughout Latin America and the Caribbean.

The Miami–Dade County Public Library maintains a large and well-indexed collection of local periodicals. The *Herald,* the *Times,* and the *Diario* are all indexed jointly by subject headings. I completed a thorough review of these indexes from 1960 to 1991, focusing on the following subject headings: "race," "riots," "refugees," "public opinion," "Cuban," and "black."

Many other documents and sources also provided valuable data on claims-making activity in Dade County. National media coverage of Miami has been extensive, particularly during the last decade; and the city has been the subject of several insightful and well-researched popular works as well. Through the kindness and cooperation of various individuals and groups in Miami, I also had access to court depositions taken during the Voting Rights Act lawsuit and to transcripts, minutes, and videotapes of various conferences, meetings, and public hearings that addressed issues related to race and ethnic relations in Dade County.

Finally, the participant observation component of this research project was critical. As a stranger to the community (and the fortunate recipient of a dissertation research grant from the Graduate School of the University of Florida) I was able to devote myself entirely to observing Miami in much the same way that a cultural anthropologist observes a distant tribe. I sat in on task force meetings of the Dade County Community Relations Board, attended meetings of the city and county commissions, joined local political clubs, and participated in a wide variety of cultural celebrations and local festivities. Although less methodologically rigorous, living and breathing Miami for seven consecutive months enhanced my understanding of ethnicity and ethnic politics in Miami immeasurably.

INTERVIEW SCHEDULE FOR COMMUNITY INFORMANTS

Personal Questions

1. How long have you lived in Miami?
2. What is your occupation and/or involvement with civic affairs in Miami?

General Questions about Ethnic Relations in Miami

3. Has ethnic hostility in Miami increased, decreased, or stayed the same since the 1980s?
4. Between which groups is the level of hostility the greatest?
5. Why?
6. How would you describe relations between the other groups?

Questions Related to Immigration

7. What impact has immigration had on Dade County?
8. Have Hispanic immigrants taken jobs from black workers in Miami's labor market?
   If so, in what occupations or industrial sectors?
9. In your opinion, do [blacks/Hispanics/Anglos] suffer discrimination in the local workplace?
   If so, by whom?
10. Is language still a divisive issue in Dade County?
    Why?
11. As an ethnic group, how much solidarity exists between [blacks/Hispanics/Anglos]?
12. What are the issues that divide/unify this group?

Questions about the Boycott

13. Do you support/agree with the black tourism boycott?
14. What impact has the boycott had on Dade County—economically, politically, socially?
15. How have various ethnic groups in Miami responded?

Questions about Politics in Miami

16. Do you think [blacks/Hispanics/Anglos] are fairly represented by local government?

17. Does politics in Miami consistently divide along lines of ethnicity?

18. Can you provide examples of when it has?

19. Can you provide examples of when it has not?

20. What role do leaders or politicians play in either encouraging or discouraging ethnic polarization?

21. What impact do you think a move to single-member districts will have on ethnic relations in Dade County?

Concluding Questions

22. How would you describe interaction among Miami's ethnic groups outside of the political or economic sphere?—i.e., in schools, churches, civic affairs?

23. What do you think is the biggest problem now facing Miami?

NOTES

1. POSTMODERN MIAMI

1. On 29 October 1992 the Florida Planning Council sponsored a statewide conference in Miami organized around the theme "Rediscovery of America: Miami—Prototypical City of the Twenty-first Century."

2. Allman 1987 provides a fascinating discussion of Miami's plasticity and its often futile attempts to mimic other, more traditional urban showcases.

3. All of the interviews referenced in this book were conducted in Miami by the author between May and December 1992. Because of the subject matter and the positions of some interviewees, all respondents were guaranteed anonymity. Where relevant, an effort has been made to include information on the respondents' race, ethnicity, and position of power or knowledge.

4. The labor market debate is discussed in greater detail in chapter 3. For studies that present data refuting the job displacement thesis, see Card 1990; Cruz 1991; and Portes and Stepick 1993.

5. *Internal colonialism,* widely associated with the work of Robert Blauner (1972), Stokely Carmichael and Charles Hamilton (1967), and Oliver Cox (1948), views racial and class stratification as related systems of oppression. It emphasizes the institutionalization of racial discrimination and the social, political, and economic processes through which white dominance is maintained. The split-labor-market theory is another class-based theory of racial and ethnic antagonism. Split-labor-market theorists demonstrate how the ethnic and racial divisions among the working class serve the interests of the dominant class, or capitalists (Bonacich 1980; Greenberg 1980).

6. For a cogent summary of this debate, see Kasfir 1979.

7. The literature on modernization theory is voluminous. For seminal statements, see Apter 1965; Inkeles and Smith 1974; Lerner 1958; and Pye 1963. For an overview and contemporary defense of the literature, see Almond 1990.

8. See Fukuyama 1989.

9. Many Marxists are also engaged in efforts to defend and maintain the continued relevance of Marx in a new world order. One of the most widely read and most cited examples is Jameson 1984. Douglas Kellner not only praises Jameson's critical powers but also contends that one of the issues at stake in his work is "no less than the status of Marxism and the radical political project to which it is committed" (1989, 2). For Jameson and other cultural Marxists the world has indeed changed, but Marxism is no less

capable of explaining the postmodern condition than it was the modern. In other words, the "fragmentation, death of knowledge, and incommensurability" the term *postmodernism* is meant to convey is nothing more than the result of a new epoch in the historical progression of capitalist development, the "cultural logic of late capitalism" (Norton 1995, 60). For an insightful critique of Jameson's argument, see generally Norton 1995.

10. For examples of a primordialist approach, see Connor 1978; Geertz 1963; Greeley 1974; and Isaacs 1974. For an instrumentalist perspective, see Glazer and Moynihan 1975. For thorough and insightful discussions of both, see Kasfir 1979; and Young 1993.

11. For a detailed analysis of how communism fortified, if not invented, ethnic separatism in the Soviet Union, see Suny 1992.

12. For a recent application of the agenda-setting framework to a variety of policy areas ranging from sexual harassment to traffic congestion to AIDS, see "The Politics of Problem Definition" in Rochefort and Cobb 1994.

13. For a recent application of her theoretical framework to an analysis, see Nagel 1995.

14. Social problem theorists (Spector and Kitsuse 1987) and agenda-setting theorists (Cobb and Elder 1972) have recognized the need for and called for more empirical analysis to test and refine the theoretical propositions being advanced in their work. With regard to postmodernism, however, any attempt to empirically test or refine theoretical propositions in order to establish universal laws would be inconsistent with the intellectual endeavor of that body of scholarship (Rosenau 1992).

15. Sassen and Portes 1993 poses several research questions designed to examine whether the global city framework can be applied to Miami.

2. FROM "MAGIC CITY" TO "PARADISE LOST"

1. Throughout this book *Miami, Metropolitan Miami, Greater Miami,* and *Dade County* are used interchangeably, even though in actuality the city of Miami is only one of twenty-seven municipalities within Dade County. Others cities include Hialeah, Miami Beach, and Sweetwater. Where reference is made to the city of Miami proper or any other Dade County municipality, it is explained as such. This is standard practice in much of the literature on Miami; the reader interested in the specifics of metropolitan and municipal government structures in the Dade County area should see Stack and Warren 1992.

2. The term *Marielito* refers to the Cuban refugees who arrived in Miami in 1980 from the port of Mariel in Cuba. The controversy surrounding the 1980 boatlift severely tainted the image of these arrivals, and some Cubans in the United States consider the term a derogatory one.

3. Prior to desegregation, black entertainers who performed in nightclubs, hotels, and restaurants in Miami Beach returned to Overtown after their shows. Nightlife in Overtown flourished with after-hours entertainment by Nat King Cole, Cab Calloway, Harry Belafonte, and others (Hampton and Fayer 1990, 650).

4. The following developments resulted from the adoption of the Dade County Home Rule Charter in 1957: (1) a broad pattern of home rule for the county and its municipalities; (2) a council-manager form of government for the county; and (3) a new type of federal integration between the county and cities (Sofen 1961, 18).

5. Specific claims from Miami leaders and residents concerning the immigrant "invasion" are detailed in chapter 3.

6. In 1979 the president of Ecuador, Jaime Roldos, dubbed Miami the "Capital of Latin America," although similar references appeared in periodical literature throughout the decade (Levine 1985, 48).

7. Athalie Range was the first black elected to the Miami City Commission; she was followed by activist clergymen Edward T. Graham and Theodore Gibson. Johnnie Jones was the first black superintendent of schools for Dade County.

8. Anti-Castro terrorists were responsible for several bombings in New York and Washington throughout the 1970s (Americas Watch 1992).

9. This information was gathered during a personal interview with the assistant county attorney assigned to this case and from a review of the depositions of several key witnesses called by the defendants in *Meek et al.* v. *Metropolitan Dade County* (interview, 24 September 1992).

10. During his campaign Clinton expressed disagreement with President Bush's decision to return, without a hearing, Haitian refugees rescued at sea. Just weeks after the election media reports began to warn of an impending exodus from Haiti. The concern stemmed from a Mariel Coast Guard photograph showing seven hundred completed or partially completed boats along the Haitian coast (Marquis 1992). Subsequent reports indicated that there were in fact "few indications of an impending Haitian exodus" (Alvarez 1992).

11. Lozano's retrial was scheduled to be held in Orlando. After the Los Angeles riots Circuit Judge Thomas Spencer moved the trial to Tallahassee in hopes that that city's racial composition would facilitate the seating of a more diverse jury than the one chosen for the Rodney King trial. After Tallahassee protested the move and others contested the legality of Spenser's unilateral decision to relocate the trial, it was moved back to Orlando (Hamalludin 1992; Steinback 1992).

12. On 28 May 1993 a tri-ethnic jury in Orlando found William Lozano not guilty. In order to allow the Miami Police Department and the Florida National Guard to prepare for the possibility of civil disorder in Dade County, announcement of the verdict was postponed for four hours after the jury reached its final decision. Except for scattered incidents of street violence, Miami remained calm. The absence of major upheaval likely reflects Miami's well-honed policies and preparedness in the area of riot prevention and control rather than improved ethnic relations in the city.

13. During the early 1990s Johnnie McMillian, president of the local chapter of the National Association for the Advancement of Colored People (NAACP), was one of the

black leaders in Miami who became an outspoken critic of U.S. policy. She made trips to Haiti, organized protest marches, and wrote a series of editorials in the *Miami Times* callings on African Americans not to turn their backs on the Haitian refugees (McMillian 1992).

14. Even though it acknowledges the inaccuracy of the labels used to identify individuals and groups in Miami, this analysis is forced to use many of the same terms. *Hispanic, black,* and *non-Latin white* or *Anglo* are used in general discussion. More specific distinctions such as *Cuban, African American,* or *Jewish* are employed when necessary.

3. THE DISCOURSE OF DISPLACEMENT

1. For thorough analyses of the events and circumstances surrounding the Mariel exodus, see Bach 1985; and Clark, Lasaga, and Reque 1981.

2. The group Citizens of Dade United (CODU) claims more than ten thousand members nationwide—most but not all of whom are non-Latin whites—and continues to be very politically active in the Dade County area. The CODU membership application lists the organization's goals as follows: "Eliminate bilingual government; Retain the English Language and American culture; Deport illegal aliens; and Fight crime."

3. On 1 May 1980, during a May Day celebration speech in Havana, Fidel Castro issued the following statement: "Those that are leaving from Mariel are the scum of the country. Anti-socials, homosexuals, drug addicts, and gamblers who are welcome to leave Cuba if any country would have them" (Portes and Stepick 1993, 21).

4. For a more detailed discussion of the role of the media, see Parenti 1993.

5. An extensive literature exists on the topic of at-large versus single-member districts. See esp. Davidson and Grofman 1994; Davidson and Korbel 1981; and Guinier 1994.

6. Max Castro (1992, 99) refers to an evolving accommodation on the part of the Anglo elite to the new cultural and linguistic reality in Miami as "enlightened assimilation."

7. On numerous occasions, both black and Hispanic interview respondents suggested that what may appear to reflect an embrace of cultural diversity by Anglos is more likely driven by a purely political or economic rationale.

4. THE SUCCESS OF THE CUBAN SUCCESS STORY

1. This quotation, from a speech delivered by former United Nations Ambassador Jeane J. Kirkpatrick at a dinner in her honor hosted by the Cuban American National Foundation on 22 October 1982 in Miami, was published as *Cuba and the Cubans* (Kirkpatrick 1983).

2. One notable exception is Gustavo Perez Firmat's (1995) analysis of the collective identity of Cuban Americans in the United States. Some interesting work has also been done on the construction of Latino identity in the United States and on the use of the term *Hispanic.* See Oboler 1995; and "Politics of Ethnic" 1992.

3. Carlos Forment (1989, 48) criticizes Portes and Bach's analysis in *Latin Journey* (1985, 238–39, 342–43) for reducing ethnic solidarity—the "organizing principle" of the enclave—to narrowly self-interested, rational, market-based concerns. In that same work, however, Portes and Bach explain that Cuban immigrants' "achievement of independent economic status was significantly determined by the early support of family and friends" (1985, 216). Portes and Rumbaut also attribute the success of immigrant entrepreneurs, such as Cubans, to the fact that "relations between immigrant employers and their co-ethnic employees often go beyond a purely contractual bond" (1990, 20–21). In his most recent work, *City on the Edge,* with Alex Stepick, Portes emphasizes the prerequisites of an ethnic economy, a stable market, access to cheap labor, and access to capital (Portes and Stepick 1993).

4. On black Cubans, see Dixon 1982; on the Jewish Cuban community, see Marks 1992; and on Chinese Cubans in Dade County, see "Chinese Cubans in Dade" 1982.

5. The 1953 Cuban census classified 12.4 percent of the population as black and 14.5 percent as of mixed race (Fagen 1969, 21). For further discussion on the characteristics of pre-Castro Cuban society, see MacGaffey and Barnett 1962; and Nelson 1950.

6. The support that did exist for Montiel-Davis subsided significantly after she traveled with two hundred other exiles to Havana for semisecret talks with the Cuban government. A video clip released after the talks showed Montiel-Davis shaking hands with Castro and placing a kiss on his cheek (Fiagome 1994a).

7. See Stack and Warren 1990 for an insightful analysis of how politicians and community leaders in Miami have manipulated ethnic symbols for political gain.

8. Perhaps indicative of the growing political clout of Cubans, on 18 May 1993 a newly elected thirteen-member Dade County Commission, composed of six Hispanics, four blacks, and three non-Latin whites, voted unanimously to repeal the 1980 anti-bilingual referendum.

9. Various reports continue to surface about the growing political fragmentation of the Cuban American community and the emergence of different voices, including those that support dialogue with Castro. See, for example, Elliston 1995; and Navarro 1995b.

10. Certainly the exile community still has friends in high places, as indicated by congressional support for the Helms-Burton legislation to tighten the Cuban embargo (Rodousakis 1995, 3) and Senator Helms's explicit promise to Jorge Mas Canosa that "I'm going to do everything I can to make sure the United States stands with you" (Rohter 1995). Nor is Clinton or any presidential hopeful prepared to overtly alienate the powerful Cuban American lobby. But the point remains that in a post–Cold War world the political calculus has changed dramatically for all the actors involved.

11. Portes 1984 also demonstrates that the shift in political struggle among Cuban refugees from issues of exile to issues of permanent resettlement paralleled a significant increase in perceptions of social distance and discrimination from the host society (387).

12. For example, to emphasize the political fragmentation of Cubans in Miami or the United States can be viewed as a political strategy. The very act of defining Cuban Amer-

icans as a politically fragmented group weakens their potential power and influence and may actually serve to further the fragmentation as well.

5. MANDELA IN MIAMI

1. Six of the fifteen points that referred to a beneficiary group specifically used the term *African American;* the other nine used either *black* or *black-owned.*

2. Keohane and Nye's edited volume *Transnational Relations and World Politics* is perhaps the best-known work on the topic, and it has spurred a huge volume of related literature since its publication in 1971. See, for example, Krasner 1982.

3. The concept of a world system is most often attributed to Immanuel Wallerstein's *The Modern World System: Capitalist Agriculture and the Origins of the European World-Economy in the Sixteenth Century* (1976). For a comprehensive and insightful collection of works focusing primarily on the linkages between the United States, Latin America, and the Caribbean, see Sanderson 1985. Also see Johan Galtung's discussion of the transnational quality of dependency in Galtung 1971.

4. In Smith and Feagin's volume *The Capitalist City* (1987) contributors examine how various processes of economic restructuring—plant closures, plant start-ups, the expansion of service and other types of jobs—affect household and community restructuring at the local level.

5. For equally insightful but similarly flawed approaches to ethnicity and the international system, see Bertelsen 1977; and Suhrke and Noble 1977.

6. Throughout the summer of 1992, residents of Miami Beach engaged in a heated battle over whether the city of Miami Beach should fund the cost of maintaining and operating the Holocaust Memorial. Even though the memorial is located on city property, some critics argued that tax dollars should not go toward the upkeep of a religious monument. Public hearings on the matter were characterized by emotional references to the horrors of the Holocaust and accusations of Naziism among those opposed to city support for the memorial.

6. CONTESTED REALITIES/SHIFTING TERRAIN

1. The quotation is taken from an audio cassette recording of the 1984 rally. The cassette was loaned to me by one of the respondents selected for this study.

2. Laclau and Mouffe 1985 is widely cited as a post-Marxist work that takes up many of these questions.

3. This is an admittedly brief and simplified overview of the voluminous and diverse body of literature characterized as "postmodern." In fact, to mention Foucault and Derrida in the same sentence overlooks the very real differences and disagreements between the two. See, for example, Spivak 1992.

4. This section of the manuscript draws heavily on Palmer's (1990) thorough and insightful analysis of Marxism and postmodernism.

5. Derrida's best-known works include *Speech and Phenomena, and Other Essays on*

Husserl's Theory of Signs (1973); *Of Grammatology* (1976); and *Writing and Difference* (1978). For a very useful introduction to Derrida's work and to the work of other postmodern and poststructuralist writers, see Sarup 1989.

6. In 1983 two white automobile workers used baseball bats to beat and kill a Chinese American, Vincent Chin. Witnesses later testified that the two assailants were making obscene remarks about Asians and Japanese cars (Wu 1992).

REFERENCES

"Ads Exploited Ethnic Tension." 1985. *Miami Herald,* 21 August, 3B.

Allman, T. D. 1987. *Miami: City of the Future.* New York.

Almond, Gabriel. 1990. *A Discipline Divided: Schools and Sects in Political Science.* Newbury Park CA.

Alvarez, Lizette. 1992. "Few Indications of an Impending Haitian Exodus." *Miami Herald,* 22 November, 1A.

Amaro, N. V., and A. Portes. 1972. "Una Sociologia del Exilio: Situación de los Grupos Cubanos en los Estados Únidos." *Aportes,* no. 23: 6–24.

Americas Watch. 1992. "Dangerous Dialogue: Attacks on Freedom of Expression in Miami's Cuban Exile Community." 4 (7). New York.

Appleby, Joyce, Lynn Hunt, and Margaret Jacob. 1994. *Telling the Truth about History.* New York.

Apter, David. 1965. *The Politics of Modernization.* Chicago.

Arboleya, Carlos. 1969. "Cuban Influx Creates Jobs." *Miami Herald,* 22 February, 6A.

Arguelles, Lourdes. 1982. "Cuban Miami: The Roots, Development, and Everyday Life of an Emigre Enclave in the U.S. National Security State." *Contemporary Marxism* 5 (summer): 27–43.

Bach, Robert. 1985. "Socialist Construction and Cuban Emigration: Explorations into Mariel." *Cuban Studies* 15:19–36.

Bachrach, Peter, and Morton S. Baratz. 1970. *Power and Poverty: Theory and Practice.* New York.

Bahr, Howard, and T. Caplow. 1991. "Middletown as an Urban Case Study." In Feagin, Orum, and Sjoberg 1991.

Balmaseda, Liz. 1981. "Tossing Power with Pride." *Miami Herald,* 31 January, 1C–2C.

———. 1992. "Old Guard Sends New Message to Miami Cubans." *Miami Herald,* 24 October, 1B.

Barber, Benjamin. 1992. "Jihad vs. McWorld." *Atlantic Monthly,* March, 53–63.

Bean, F. D., B. L. Lowell, and L. J. Taylor. 1988. "Undocumented Mexican Immigrants and the Earnings of Other Workers in the United States." *Demography* 25, no. 1: 35–49.

Becker, Howard S. 1966. *Social Problems: A Modern Approach.* New York.

Bedwell, Don. 1967. "Miami Banks Welcome Cubans As Customers." *Miami Herald,* 26 March, 1A.

Bertelsen, Judy. 1977. *Nonstate Nations in International Politics.* New York.

Best, Joel, ed. 1989. *Images of Issues: Typifying Contemporary Social Problems.* New York.

Bilderback, Loy. 1989. "A Greater Threat Than the Soviet Union: Mexican Immigration As a Social Problem." In Best 1989.

Birger, Larry. 1965. "Banks Welcome New Amigos." *Miami News*, 28 November, 18A.

"Bishop Asks Miamians to Welcome Refugees." 1965. *Miami Herald*, 16 October, 6B.

"Black Brothers for Progress." 1969. *Miami Herald*, 23 February, 1A.

"Blacks Reject Suarez's Olive Branch on Mandela." 1990. *Miami Herald*, 27 June, 1B.

Blauner, Robert M. 1972. *Racial Oppression in America*. New York.

Blumer, Herbert. 1971. "Social Problems As Collective Behavior." *Social Problems* 18:298–306.

Bohning, Don. 1966. "Negro Cuban Exile Treads Warily in Miami." *Miami Herald*, 6 January, 4B.

Bonacich, Edna. 1973. "A Theory of Middleman Minorities." *American Sociological Review* 38, no. 5: 583–94.

———. 1980. "Class Approaches to Ethnicity and Race." *Insurgent Sociologist* 10 (fall): 11.

———. 1987. "Making It in America: A Sociological Evaluation of the Ethics of Immigrant Entrepreneurship." *Sociological Perspectives* 30, no. 4: 446–65.

Borjas, George. 1982. "The Earnings of Male Hispanic Immigrants in the United States." *Industrial and Labor Relations Review* 35, no. 3: 343–53.

———. 1983. "The Substitutability of Black, Hispanic and White Labor." *Economic Inquiry* 21:93–106.

———. 1990. *Friends or Strangers: The Impact of Immigration on the U.S. Economy*. New York.

Borjas, George, and M. Tienda. 1987. "The Economic Consequences of Immigration." *Science* 235 (February): 645–51.

Boswell, T., and James Curtis. 1984. *The Cuban-American Experience*. Totowa NJ.

———. 1991. "The Hispanization of Metropolitan Miami." In *South Florida: The Winds of Change*, ed. Thomas Boswell. Miami.

Botifoll, Luis. 1988. *How Miami's New Image Was Created*. Research Institute for Cuban Studies, Institute of Interamerican Studies, University of Miami.

Bousquet, Steve. 1992. "Coalition Fears Loss of Jewish Clout in Redistricting Plans." *Miami Herald*, 2 July, 1A.

Brigg, V. M., Jr. 1984. *Immigration Policy and the American Labor Force*. Baltimore.

Buchanan, James. 1977. *Miami: A Chronological and Documentary History*. New York.

Burkett, E., and S. Andrews. 1990. "Rhythms of African Pride Pulsate in Miami Street," *Miami Herald*, 29 June, 13A.

Bussey, Jane. 1992a. "Challenging the Embargo." *Miami Herald*, 9 August, 1K.

———. 1992b. "Miami's Lost Decade Slowly Comes to End." *Miami Herald*, 12 July, 1K.

———. 1992c. "South Florida Exports Expand 19.6 Percent." *Miami Herald*, 7 March, 3C.

Callinicos, Alex. 1989. *Against Postmodernism: A Marxist Critique*. New York.

Cannon, Margaret. 1995. *The Invisible Empire: Racism in Canada*. Toronto.

Card, David. 1990. "The Impact of the Mariel Boatlift on the Miami Labor Market." *Industrial and Labor Relations Review* 43 (2): 245–57.

Cardenas, Jose R. 1992. "Why Our Allies Are Wrong on Cuba Trade Issue." *Miami Herald*, 11 October, 5M.

Carmichael, Stokely, and C. Hamilton. 1967. *Black Power*. New York.

Casal, Lourdes. 1979. "Cubans in the United States: Their Impact on U.S. Cuban Relations." In *Revolutionary Cuba in the World Arena*, ed. Martin Weinstein. Philadelphia.

———. 1980. "Revolution and Race: Blacks in Contemporary Cuba." Working Paper of the Woodrow Wilson International Center for Scholars. Washington DC.

Castro, Max. 1992. "The Politics of Language in Miami." In *Miami Now*, ed. Guillermo Grenier and Alex Stepick. Gainesville FL.

Chapman, A. E. 1991. "History Of South Florida." In *South Florida. See* Boswell and Curtis 1991.

Chardy, A. 1992. "Miami Group Launches Coastal Raid on Cuba." *Miami Herald*, 14 October, 1A.

Chardy, A., and C. Corzo. 1992. "Torricelli Bill Backer Urges Exile Unit." *Miami Herald*, 25 September, 21A.

Chardy, A., and J. Reyes. 1993. "Cuban Exile Group Gears Up to Someday Overthrow Castro." *Miami Herald*, 6 February, 2B.

Charsley, S. R. 1974. "The Formation of Ethnic Groups." In *Urban Ethnicity*, ed. Abner Cohen. London.

"Chief Headly Stands Firm." 1968. *Miami Herald*, 22 September, 1G.

"Chinese Cubans in Dade." 1982. *Miami News*, 25 January, 3C.

Clark, Juan, J. I. Lasaga, and R. S. Reque. 1981. *The 1980 Mariel Exodus: An Assessment and Prospects*. Washington DC.

Cobb, Roger, and Charles Elder. 1972. *Participation in American Politics: The Dynamics of Agenda-Building*. Boston.

"Concern over Influx Grows." 1966. *National Observer*, 21 November.

Congressional Record. 1990. 97th Cong., 2d sess. Vol. 136, pt. 67: 8687.

Connor, Walker. 1978. "A Nation Is a Nation, Is a State." *Ethnic and Racial Studies* 1, no. 4: 377–400.

Conzen, K. N., D. Gerber, E. Morawska, and G. Pozzetta. 1990. "The Invention of Ethnicity: A Perspective from the USA." *Altreitalie*, no. 3: 38–61.

Cornelius, Wayne. 1982. *America in the Era of Limits: Nativist Reactions to the New Immigration*. San Diego.

Cox, Oliver. 1948. *Caste, Class, and Race: A Study in Social Classes*. New York.

Crockett, K., and G. Epstein. 1992. "South African Leader Cancels Miami Appearances." *Miami Herald*, 11 June, 1B.

Cruz, Robert. 1991. "The Industry Composition of Production and the Distribution of Income by Race and Ethnicity in Miami." Paper Presented at the Joint Meeting of the Association for the Study of the Cuban Economy and the National Association of Cuban-American Educators, 16 August, Miami.

"Cuban Program Boosts Dade's Economy." 1969. *Miami News*, 5 August, 11A.

"Dade Has Acted against Apartheid." 1990. *Miami Herald*, 14 August, 23A.

Dahl, Robert. 1956. *A Preface to Democratic Theory*. Chicago.

D'Amico, Robert. 1982. "What Is Discourse?" *Humanity and Society* 5, nos. 3–4: 207–29.

Davidson, Chandler, and Bernard Grofman. 1994. *Quiet Revolution in the South: The Impact of the Voting Rights Act, 1965–1990*. Princeton.

Davidson, Chandler, and George Korbel. 1981. "At Large Elections and Minority Group Representation: A Re-examination of Historical and Contemporary Evidence." *Journal of Politics* 43 (November): 982–1005.

Davis, Miller. 1967. "Jailed Exile's Backers Douse Freedom Torch." *Miami News*, 18 May, 1A.

"Dawkins: Is Nominee Black?" 1990. *Miami Herald*, 3 March, 1B.

Decker, Jonathan. 1995. "New Cuban Refugee Policy Floats Few Boats in Florida." *Christian Science Monitor,* 4 May, 3.

Defede, Jim. 1992. "What Magda Won." *New Times,* 25 November, 20–22, 24, 26, 28, 29.

Derrida, Jacques. 1973. *Speech and Phenomena, and Other Essays on Husserl's Theory of Signs.* Evanston IL.

———. 1976. *Of Grammatology.* Baltimore.

———. 1978. *Writing and Difference.* London.

Diaz, Guarione. 1991. *Ethnic Block Voting and Polarization in Miami.* Miami.

Diaz-Briquets, Sergio, and Lisandro Perez. 1981. "Cuba: The Demography of Revolution." Working paper, Population Reference Bureau. Washington DC.

Didion, Joan. 1987. *Miami.* New York.

Dillin, John. 1994. "Big States Want US to Pay Costs of Illegal Aliens." *Christian Science Monitor,* 3 February, 3.

"Dissident's Call for Dialogue Ignites Exiles." 1990. *Miami Herald,* 25 June, 1A.

Dixon, H. R. 1982. "Who Ever Heard of a Black Cuban?" *Afro-Hispanic Review* 1:10–12.

Dominguez, Jorge. 1992. "Cooperating with the Enemy: US Immigration Policies toward Cuba." In *Western Hemisphere Immigration and United States Foreign Policy,* ed. Christopher Mitchell. University Park PA.

Due, T. 1992. "New Miami Group: A New Black Power." *Miami Herald,* 1 March, 1J.

Dunn, Marvin. 1991. "Black Miami." In *Miami: The Sophisticated Tropics,* ed. Morton Beebe. San Francisco.

———. Forthcoming. *Black Miami: The History and Status of Blacks in Dade County, Florida (1896–1992).*

Edelman, Murray. 1964. *The Symbolic Use of Politics.* Urbana IL.

———. 1988. *Constructing the Political Spectacle.* Chicago.

Edwards, Tanja. 1992. "Beacon Council to Weigh Trade Missions to Africa." *Miami Today,* 25 June, 8.

Ehrlich, Paul, Loy Bilderback, and Anne Ehrlich. 1979. *The Golden Door.* New York.

Einstein, Paul. 1965. "To Help Cool Exile Tension." *Miami News,* 23 November, 1A.

Elliston, Jon. 1995. "The Myth of the Miami Monolith." In *Cuba: Adapting to a Post-Soviet World. NACLA: Report on the Americas* 29, no. 2: 40–41.

Epstein, G., and K. Crockett. 1992. "South African Leader's Visit Draws Criticism." *Miami Herald,* 5 June, 1B.

Erlich, Reese. 1994. "Study Revives Debate over Impact on Jobs." *Christian Science Monitor,* 2 May, 8.

"Exiles Saying Goodbye to Mañana." 1965. *Miami News,* 17 February, 1A.

Fagen, Richard. 1969. *The Transformation of Political Culture in Cuba.* Stanford.

Falcoff, Mark. 1995. "The Other Cuba." *National Review,* 12 June, 34–43.

"Fascell Demands Limit on Refugees." 1965. *Miami News,* 15 October, 1B.

Feagin, Joe. 1989. *Racial and Ethnic Relations.* Englewood Cliffs NJ.

Feagin, Joe, A. Orum, and G. Sjoberg, eds. 1991. *A Case for the Case Study.* Chapel Hill.

"Federal Program Aimed at Easing Unemployment." 1965. *Miami Herald,* 3 December, 1A.

"Federal Report on '68 Riots." 1969. *Miami News,* 12 February, 1A.

Federation for American Immigration Reform. 1990. "Immigration Report," June.

"Feeling Grows against Refugee Influx." 1965. *Miami Herald,* 17 October, 33A.

Fiagome, Clemence. 1994a. "Efforts to Remove US Embargo on Cuba Derailed by a Kiss." *Christian Science Monitor,* 12 May, 3.

———. 1994b. "Florida Sets out Welcome Mat for Exodus of Cubans on Rafts." *Christian Science Monitor,* 13 July, 4.

———. 1994c. "Shaking a Big Fist at Fidel." *Christian Science Monitor,* 7 September, 22.

Fichtner, Margaria. 1990. "Still Far to Go, Sisters Who Led Sit-ins in Sixties Still Seek Dignity." *Miami Herald,* 3 July, 2C.

Fiedler, Tom. 1992. "The Balkanization of Politics Strains South Florida's Social Fabric." *Miami Herald,* 12 July, 1C.

Fields, Gregg. 1994. "The Americas' Hong Kong." *Miami Herald,* 14 March, Business section, 7.

Filkins, Dexter. 1992a. "For Dade's Minorities, a New Era." *Miami Herald,* 22 August, 1A.

———. 1992b. "Metro Aims at Cuba Trade." *Miami Herald,* 21 July, 1B.

———. 1992c. "Suit May Change the Face of Metro." *Miami Herald,* 3 June, 1B.

Firestone, David. 1995. "Giuliani Criticizes Crackdown by Congress on Illegal Aliens." *New York Times,* 23 August, A1.

Firmat, Gustavo Perez. 1995. *Life on the Hyphen: The Cuban-American Way.* Austin.

"The Forgotten Many." 1982. *Economist,* 16 October, 21–23.

Forment, Carlos. 1989. "Political Practice and the Rise of an Ethnic Enclave: The Cuban American Case, 1959–1979." *Theory and Society* 18:47–81.

Foucault, Michel. 1972. *The Archaeology of Knowledge.* New York.

———. 1980. *Power/Knowledge: Selected Interviews and Other Writings.* New York.

Fox, G. E. 1971. "Cuban Workers in Exile." *Transaction* 8:21–30.

Fradd, Sandra. 1983. "Cubans to Cuban Americans Assimilation in the United States." *Migration Today* 11, no. 4: 34–42.

Fukuyama, Francis. 1989. "The End of History?" *National Interest* 16 (summer): 3–18.

Galtung, Johan. 1971. "A Structural Theory of Imperialism." *Journal of Peace Research* 8, no. 2: 81–117.

Gamson, William. 1968. "Stable Unrepresentation in American Society." *American Behavioral Scientist* 12:15–21.

Geertz, Clifford. 1963. *Old Societies and New States.* New York.

George, Paul S. 1978. "Colored Town: Miami's Black Community, 1896–1930." *Florida Historical Quarterly* 56:432–47.

———. 1979. "Policing Miami's Black Community, 1896–1930." *Florida Historical Quarterly* 57:434–50.

Gilder, George. 1984. *The Spirit of Enterprise.* New York.

———. 1985. "Making It." *Wilson Quarterly,* 9, no. 5: 70–75.

———. 1992. *Recapturing the Spirit of Enterprise.* San Francisco.

Giroux, Henry A. 1991. *Postmodernism, Feminism, and Cultural Politics.* Albany NY.

Glazer, N., and D. Moynihan. 1975. *Ethnicity: Theory and Experience.* Cambridge MA.

Glick-Schiller, Nina. 1992. "Postscript: Haitian Transnational Practice and National Discourse." In *Caribbean Life in New York City: Sociocultural Dimensions,* ed. Constance Sutton and Elsa Chaney. New York.

Goldfarb, Carl. 1990. "Mandela's Visit Prompts Rerun of Old Ethnic Battles." *Miami Herald,* 2 July, 1B.

————. 1992. "Miami Poverty Rate is Number 4 in Country." *Miami Herald,* 25 June, 8B.

Gordon, Milton M. 1964. *Assimilation in American Life.* New York.

Greeley, Andrew. 1974. *Ethnicity in the United States: A Preliminary Reconnaissance.* New York.

Greenberg, Stanley. 1980. *Race and State in Capitalist Development.* New Haven.

Greene, Juanita. 1963. "Anti-Exile Boos Fly at Mayor." *Miami Herald,* 16 March, 1A.

————. 1965a. "Miami Fears Effects of Cuban Influx." *Miami Herald,* 5 October, 1A.

————. 1965b. "Will Cubans Take Jobs from Natives?" *Miami Herald,* 5 December, 4H.

————. 1971. "Latins Could Muster Voting Power at the Polls." *Miami Herald,* 21 November, 8G.

Greenhouse, Steven. 1995. "How the Clinton Administration Reversed U.S. Policy on Cuban Refugees." *New York Times,* 21 May, A8.

Greenwood, M. J., and J. M. McDowell. 1988. "The Labor Market Consequences of U.S. Immigration: A Survey." Paper presented at the U.S. Department of Labor Conference on Immigration, Washington DC, September.

Grossman, J. B. 1982. "The Substitutability of Natives and Immigrants in Production." *Review of Economics and Statistics* 64, no. 4: 596–603.

Guerra, Alfonso. 1992. "Grateful for Passage of Cuban Democracy Act." *New York Times,* 7 October, 16A.

Guinier, Lani. 1994. *The Tyranny of the Majority: Fundamental Fairness and Representative Democracy.* New York.

Gusfield, Joseph R. 1981. *The Culture of Public Problems: Drinking-Driving and the Symbolic Order.* Chicago.

Hall, Stuart. 1988. "The Toad in the Garden: Thatcherism among the Theorists." In *Marxism and the Interpretation of Culture,* ed. Cary Nelson and Lawrence Grossberg. Chicago.

Hamalludin, M. 1992. "Churches: Our Demand Is for Justice." *Miami Times,* 14 May, 1A.

Hampton, H., and D. Fayer. 1990. *Voices of Freedom: An Oral History of the Civil Rights Movement from the 1950s to the 1980s.* New York.

Hancock, David. 1990. "Author: Exiles' Plans Out of Touch with Cuba's Blacks." *Miami Herald,* 22 February, 3B.

————. 1992a. "Exile Expeditions Worry U.S. Officials." *Miami Herald,* 13 July, 1B.

————. 1992b. "L.A. Unrest Could Happen in Miami, Professors Say." *Miami Herald,* 10 June, 2B.

Helg, Aline. 1990. "Race in Argentina and Cuba, 1880–1930." In *The Idea of Race in Latin America,* ed. Richard Graham. Austin.

Hochschild, Jennifer. 1981. *What's Fair: American Beliefs about Distributive Justice.* Cambridge MA.

Hoppe, Layne D. 1969. "Agenda-Setting Strategies: Pollution Policy." Ph.D. diss., University of Arizona.

Horowitz, Donald. 1977. "Cultural Movements and Ethnic Change." *Annals of the American Academy of Political and Social Science* 433 (September): 6–18.

"How the Immigrants Made It in Miami." 1971. *Business Week,* 1 May, 88–89.

Hufker, Brian, and Gary Cavender. 1990. "From Freedom Flotilla to America's Burden: The Social Construction of the Mariel Immigrants." *Sociological Quarterly* 31, no. 2: 21–35.

Huntington, Samuel. 1993. "The Clash of Civilizations?" *Foreign Affairs* 72, no. 3: 22–49

"Ignore Anti-Exile Statements, Catholic Official Here Urges." 1965. *Miami Herald,* 18 October, 1A.

Inkeles, Alex, and D. Smith. 1974. *Becoming Modern: Individual Change in Six Developing Countries.* Cambridge MA.

Isaacs, Harold. 1974. "Basic Group Identity: Idols of the Tribe." *Ethnicity* 1:15–41.

"It's Time to Ground the Airlift." 1969. *Miami Herald,* 18 February, 6A.

Jameson, F. 1984. "Postmodernism, or the Cultural Logic of Late Capitalism." *New Left Review,* no. 46: 53 92.

Jensen, Leif, and A. Portes. 1992. "The Enclave and the Entrants: Patterns of Ethnic Enterprise." *American Sociological Review* 57 (3): 411–14.

"Jobless Citizens Resent Cuban Hiring." 1960. *Miami Herald,* 2 December, 4B.

"Jobs Problem Cited against Haitians' Plea." 1963. *Miami News,* 17 September, 6A.

Johnson, H. 1988. "Bahamian Labor Migration to Florida in the Late Nineteenth and Early Twentieth Century." *International Migration Review* 22:84–103.

Jones, Charles O. 1984. *An Introduction to the Study of Public Policy.* Monterey CA.

Jorge, Antonio, and Raul Moncarz. 1987. *The Political Economy of Cubans in South Florida.* Cuban Studies Project Monograph. Miami.

Kasfir, Nelson. 1979. "Explaining Ethnic Political Participation." *World Politics* 31, no. 3: 88–111.

Kearney, Robert, ed. 1986. *Mostly Sunny Days.* Miami.

Keely, Charles. 1979. *U.S. Immigration: A Policy Analysis.* New York.

Kellner, Douglas, ed. 1989. *Postmodernism/Jameson/Critique.* Washington DC.

Kennedy, George. 1968. "Jury Says Outsiders Didn't Trigger Riot." *Miami Herald,* 13 November, 18A.

Keohane, Robert, and Joseph Nye, eds. 1971. *Transnational Relations and World Politics.* Cambridge MA.

Kilson, Martin. 1975. "Blacks and Neo-Ethnicity in American Political Life." In Glazer and Moynihan 1975.

Kingdon, John. 1984. *Agendas, Alternatives, and Public Policies.* Boston.

Kirby, Paul. 1992. "Survey: Miami Has One of the Nation's Worst Homeless Problems." *Miami Herald,* 12 December, 6A.

Kirkpatrick, Jeane J. 1983. *Cuba and the Cubans.* Cuban American National Foundation, 7. Washington DC.

Krasner, Stephen. 1982. "International Regimes." Special issue of *International Organizations,* 36, no. 2.

LaCapra, Dominick. 1983. *Rethinking Intellectual History: Texts, Contexts, Language.* Ithaca NY.

Laclau, Ernesto, and Chantal Mouffe. 1985. *Hegemony and Socialist Strategy.* London.

Lahey, Edwin. 1967. "Industrious Exiles Making Good in Miami." *Miami Herald,* 21 February, 14A.

Lamensdorf, Marilyn. 1992. "Dade Trade Jumps 13 Percent and Rising." *Miami Today,* 12 March, 1.

Lamm, Richard, and Gary Imhoff. 1985. *The Immigration Time Bomb: The Fragmentation of America.* New York.

Lawrence, David. 1991. "Get on the Ball . . . Learn Another Language." *Miami Herald*, 24 March, 1B.

———. 1992a. "Dear Mr. Perot . . ." *Miami Herald*, 14 June, 3C.

———. 1992b. "No, Mr. Mas, Intimidation Won't Work." *Miami Herald*, 22 March, 3C.

Lerner, Daniel. 1958. *The Passing of Traditional Society: Modernizing the Middle East*. Glencoe IL.

"Lest Washington Forget." 1967. *Miami Herald*, 27 October, 16A.

"Let Exiles Handle Aid." 1961. *Miami Herald*, 18 January.

Levine, Barry. 1985. "Miami: The Capital of Latin America." *Wilson Quarterly* 9, no. 5: 47–69.

Liebman, Seymour. 1977. "Cuban Jewish Community in South Florida." In *A Coat of Many Colors: Jewish Subcommunities in the United States*, ed. Abe Lavendar. Westport CT.

Lindblom, Charles. 1990. *Inquiry and Change: The Troubled Attempt to Understand and Shape Society*. New Haven.

"Local Attitudes toward Cubans." 1983. *Miami Herald*, 27 November, 23A.

"Local Officials Giving Mandela a Low-key Welcome." 1990. *Miami Herald*, 20 June, 1A.

"Looming Conflict Predicted by Local Experts." 1976. *Miami Herald*, 23 May, 1B.

MacGaffey, Wyatt, and C. Barnett. 1962. *Cuba: Its People, Its Society, Its Culture*. New Haven.

Maingot, Anthony. 1986. "Ethnic Bargaining and the Non-Citizen: Cubans and Haitians in Miami." In *The Primordial Challenge: Ethnicity in the Contemporary World*, ed. John Stack. Westport CT.

Majone, Giandomenico. 1989. *Evidence, Argument, and Persuasion in the Policy Process*. New Haven.

"Making It in Miami." 1971. *Life*. September, 37.

"Mandela Backers, Critics Brace for Momentous Visit." 1990. *Miami Herald*, 28 June, 1B.

"Mandela Remarks Draw Fire in Miami." 1990. *Miami Herald*, 23 June, 1A.

"Mandela Speech Off-limits to Civic Leaders." 1990. *Miami Herald*, 15 June, 1B.

"Mandela's Visit to Include Union Speech and Little Else." 1990. *Miami Herald*, 9 June, 4B.

"Many Watch Tour, See Opportunity." 1990. *Miami Herald*, 28 June, 1A.

Marks, Marilyn. 1992. "Havana Heritage." *Jerusalem Report*, 5 December, 25.

Marquis, Christopher. 1992. "Haitians Preparing for Exodus." *Miami Herald*, 14 November, 1A.

Marquis, Christopher, and Paul Anderson. 1992. "Bush to Sign Cuba Bill in Miami." *Miami Herald*, 23 October, 1A.

Martin, Lydia. 1992. "Take Charge of Rebuilding, Jackson Urges Black Leaders." *Miami Herald*, 1 September, 16A.

Marx, Karl, and Friedrich Engels. 1978. *The German Ideology*. In *The Marx-Engels Reader*, ed. Robert C. Tucker. New York.

Mauss, Armand L. 1975. *Social Problems As Social Movements*. Philadelphia.

"Mayor Gelber Won't Seek Re-election." 1992. *Sunpost*, 21 May, 1.

McHugh, Kevin E. 1989. "Hispanic Migration and Population Redistribution in the United States." *Professional Geographer* 41:429–39.

McKay, James. 1982. "An Exploratory Synthesis of Primordial and Mobilizationist Approaches to Ethnic Phenomena." *Ethnic and Racial Studies* 5, no. 4:395–420.

McMillian, Johnnie. 1992. "We Cannot Turn Our Backs on the Haitian Boat Refugees." *Miami Times,* 13 August, 5A.

McNay, Lois. 1992. *Foucault and Feminism: Power, Gender, and the Self.* Cambridge MA.

"The Meat Riot." 1970. *Newsweek,* 29 June, 20.

Megill, Allan. 1985. *Prophets of Extremity: Nietzsche, Heidegger, Foucault, Derrida.* Berkeley.

"Metro Asks Health Aid for Cubans." 1967. *Miami Herald,* 30 September, 1B.

"Miami." 1988. *Newsweek,* 25 January, 22–29.

"Miami Cools Off." 1962. *Kiwanis Magazine,* May.

Miami Herald. 1992. *The Big One: Hurricane Andrew.* Kansas City MO.

"Miami's Most Powerful." 1988. *Miami Herald,* 31 January, 1B.

Miguel, Jorge D. 1992. "Miami a City 'Where Violence Reigns.' Are They Serious?" *Miami Herald,* 2 September, 31A.

"The Miseries of Magnetism." 1995. *Economist,* 4 March, 40–41.

Mohl, Raymond A. 1986. "An Ethnic Boiling Pot: Cubans and Haitians in Miami." *Journal of Ethnic Studies* 13, no. 2: 51–74.

———. 1987. "Black Immigrants in Early Twentieth Century Miami." *Florida Historical Quarterly* 65:271–97.

———. 1988. "Trouble in Paradise: Race and Housing in Miami during the New Deal Era." In *The Making of Urban America,* ed. Raymond A. Mohl. Wilmington DE.

———. 1990. "On the Edge: Blacks and Hispanics in Metropolitan Miami since 1959." *Florida Historical Quarterly* 69:37–56.

———. 1991. "The Settlement of Blacks in South Florida." In *South Florida. See* Boswell and Curtis 1991.

Molotch, H., and M. Lester. 1974. "News as Purposive Behavior: On the Strategic Use of Routine Events, Accidents, and Scandal." *American Sociological Review* 39, no. 1: 101–12.

Moncarz, Raul P. 1978. "The Golden Cage—Cubans in Miami." *International Migration Review* 16:160–73.

Moore, Carlos. 1988. *Castro, the Blacks, and Africa.* Los Angeles.

"More Cubans Expected to Enter Our Town." 1965. *Miami News,* 10 October, 1A.

Moreno, Dario, and Nicol Rae. 1992. "Ethnicity and Partnership: The Case of the 18th Congressional District in Miami." In *Miami Now. See* Castro 1992.

Morrison, Allan. 1963. "Miami's Cuban Refugee Crisis: Invasion of 100,000 Exiles Creates Grave Problems for Hard Pressed Negro Laborers." *Ebony Magazine* 18, no. 8: 96–102.

"Muslims in the United States Fear an Upsurge in Hostility." 1993. *New York Times,* 7 March, sec. 1, p. 1.

Muth, R. F. 1971. "Migration: Chicken or Egg?" *Southern Economic Journal* 37, no. 1: 295–306.

Nagel, Joane. 1986. "The Political Construction of Ethnicity." In *Competitive Ethnic Relations,* ed. Susan Olzak and Joane Nagel. Orlando.

———. 1995. *American Indian Ethnic Renewal: Red Power and the Resurgence of Identity and Culture.* New York.

"Nationwide Jobs-for-Exiles Drive Opens." 1962. *Miami Herald,* 12 October, 2A.

Navarro, Mirey. 1994a. "After Years in Exile in Miami, Nicaraguans Ponder Home." *New York Times,* 18 March, A1.

———. 1994b. "Miami Is Set to Embrace Summit of the Americas." *New York Times,* 5 December, A16.

———. 1995a. "New Policy on Cubans Met by Protest Drive." *New York Times,* 17 May, A10.

———. 1995b. "New Tolerance Sprouts among Cuban Exiles." *New York Times,* 25 August, A6.

"Negro Exiles Join to Seek Rights, War against Fidel." 1963. *Miami News,* 6 June, 1A.

"Negroes Resent Job Loss." 1961. *Miami Herald,* 18 October, 1B.

Nelson, Lowry. 1950. *Rural Cuba.* Minneapolis.

Newton, Judith. 1989. "Family Fortunes: 'New History' and 'New Historicism.'" *Radical History Review* 43, no. 2: 5–23.

Ney, John. 1989. *Miami Today—The U.S. Tomorrow.* Monterey VA.

Nickens, Tim. 1992. "Legislator Fears Court May Take District." *Miami Herald,* 30 June, 1B.

"No Joy in the Victory." 1992. *Miami Times,* 18 June, 4A.

"Non-Latin White Enrollment Down in Dade County Schools." 1983. *Miami Herald,* 18 December, 8M.

North, D., and M. Houston. 1976. *The Characteristics and Role of Illegal Aliens in the U.S. Labor Market: An Exploratory Study.* Washington DC.

Norton, Bruce. 1995. "Late Capitalism and Postmodernism: Jameson/Mandel." In *Marxism in the Postmodern Age: Confronting the New World Order,* ed. Antonio Callari, Stephen Cullenberg, and Carole Biewener. New York.

Oboler, Suzanne. 1995. *Ethnic Labels, Latino Lives.* Minneapolis.

"One More Warning Here." 1969. *Miami News,* 21 January, 1A.

Orum, Anthony, and J. Feagin. 1991. "A Tale of Two Cases." In Feagin, Orum, and Sjoberg 1991.

"Our Refugees from Castroland." 1962. *Saturday Evening Post,* 16 June.

Palmer, Bryan D. 1990. *Descent into Discourse: The Reification of Language and the Writing of Social History.* Philadelphia.

"Paradise Lost." 1981. *Time Magazine,* 23 November, 22–32.

Parenti, Michael. 1993. *Inventing Reality: The Politics of News Media.* New York.

Park, Robert E., and E. W. Burgess. 1924. *Introduction to the Science of Society.* Chicago.

Parker, Laura. 1991. "Miami Vise." *Washington Post National Weekly Edition,* 7 January, 15.

Parkin, Frank. 1979. *Marxism and Class Theory: A Bourgeois Critique.* London.

Parks, Arva Moore. 1981. *The Magic City: Miami.* Tulsa.

Parsons, Talcott. 1951. *The Social System.* Glencoe IL.

Pedraza-Bailey, Silvia. 1985. "Cuba's Exiles: Portrait of a Refugee Migration." *International Migration Review* 19:4–34.

Perez, Lisandro. 1986. "Immigrant Economic Adjustment and Family Organization: The Cuban Success Story Reexamined." *International Migration Review* 20:4–20.

Perna, Santiago Rey. 1984. "Cubanos y Americanos Negros." *Diario Las Americas,* 24 April, 5A.

Petrella, Ricardo. 1992. "High-Tech Apartheid in the 21st Century." *Miami Herald,* 9 August, 1C.

Piore, Michael. 1979. *Birds of Passage: Migrant Labor in Industrial Societies.* Cambridge MA.

"The Politics of Ethnic Construction: Hispanic, Chicano, Latino. . . ?" 1992. *Latin American Perspectives* 19, no. 4.

Porter, B., and M. Dunn. 1984. *The Miami Riot of 1980: Crossing the Bounds.* Boston.

Portes, Alejandro. 1984. "The Rise of Ethnicity: Determinants of Ethnic Perceptions among Cuban Exiles in Miami." *American Sociological Review* 49, no. 3: 383–97.

———. 1987. "The Social Origins of the Cuban Enclave Economy." *Sociological Perspectives* 30, no. 4: 340–72.

Portes, Alejandro, and Robert Bach. 1985. *Latin Journey.* Berkeley.

Portes, Alejandro, and Juan Clark. 1987. "Mariel Refugees: Six Years After." *Migration World* 25, no. 5: 14–18.

Portes, Alejandro, Juan Clark, and Robert Manning. 1985. "After Mariel: A Survey of the Resettlement Experience of the 1980 Cuban Refugees in Miami." *Cuban Studies* 15:37–57.

Portes, Alejandro, and Leif Jensen. 1989. "The Enclave and the Entrants: Patterns of Ethnic Enterprise in Miami Before and After Mariel." *American Sociological Review* 54, no. 6: 929–49.

Portes, Alejandro, and R. Manning. 1986. "The Immigrant Enclave: Theory and Empirical Examples." In *Competitive Ethnic Relations. See* Nagel 1986.

Portes, Alejandro, and Ruben Rumbaut. 1990. *Immigrant America: A Portrait.* Berkeley.

Portes, Alejandro, and Alex Stepick. 1993. *City on the Edge: Miami and the Immigrants.* Berkeley.

"Public Opinion Poll." 1980. *Miami Herald,* 5 November, 11A.

Pugh, Tony. 1993. "Opportunities for Blacks Pledged." *Miami Herald,* 13 May, 1A.

Pye, Lucian, ed. 1963. *Communications and Political Development.* Princeton.

———. 1990. "Political Science and the Crisis of Authoritarianism." *American Political Science Review* 84, no. 1: 3–19.

"Racial or Ideological Confrontation of the Cubans with Mandela?" 1990. *Diario Las Americas,* 29 June, 4A.

Reese, M., and V. Coppola. 1981. "A Cuban Ritual Disturbs Miami." *Newsweek,* 22 June, 44.

"Refugee Program Is Most Generous Ever." 1964. *Miami Herald,* 2 January, 6A.

"Refugees Called an Asset to Miami." 1967. *New York Times,* 2 October, sec. 1, p. 28.

Regalado, Raquel. 1990. "Opiniones de Lozano." *Diario Las Americas,* 25 January, 1B.

Report of the Governor's Dade County Citizens' Committee on the Liberty City Riots. 1980. Miami.

Report of the National Advisory Commission on Civil Disorders. 1968. New York.

Research Institute for Cuba and the Caribbean. 1967. *The Cuban Immigration 1959–1966 and Its Impact on Miami-Dade County, Florida.* Miami.

Resnick, Bob. "The Takeover Is Complete." 1990. *Miami Herald,* 18 July, 10A.

"Reverend Studies Cubans in America." 1966. *Miami News,* 13 August, 1B.

Rieff, David. 1987a. *Going to Miami: Exiles, Tourists, and Refugees in the New America.* Boston.

———. 1987b. "The Second Havana." *New Yorker,* 18 May, 65–83.

"Rift with Cuba May Resolve Exile Problem." 1961. *Miami Herald,* 6 January, 1B.

Rochefort, David A., and Roger W. Cobb. 1994. *The Politics of Problem Definition: Shaping the Policy Agenda.* Lawrence KS.

Rodousakis, Christine. 1995. "Efforts to Tighten Cuban Embargo Angers U.S. Allies." *Washington Report on the Hemisphere.* Washington DC.

Rodrigues, C. L. 1990. "When Cross-Cultural Equals Double Cross: How Developmental Aid Can Backfire." *Administration and Society* 22:341–57.

Rohter, Larry. 1991. "When a City Newspaper Is the Enemy." *New York Times,* 19 March, A8.

———. 1995. "With Voice of Cuban-Americans, a Would-be Successor to Castro." *New York Times,* 8 May, A1.

Rosenau, Pauline M. 1992. *Postmodernism and the Social Sciences: Insights, Inroads, and Intrusions.* Princeton.

Rosenberg, Mark, and J. Hiskey. 1992. "Florida and the Caribbean Basin Countries in the 21st Century: Is Geography Destiny?" Working paper, Florida Caribbean Institute. Miami.

Ross, R., and G. Staines. 1971. "The Politics of Analyzing Social Problems." *Social Problems* 20:18–40.

Rowe, Sean. 1990. "The Quiet Riot." *New Times,* 20 September, 12.

Russell, James. 1992. "Book Pays Homage to Cuban Entrepreneurs." *Miami Herald,* 24 November, 3C.

Saferstein, Sam. 1992. "Miami Beach Mayor Receives NJA Backing." *Sunpost,* 21 May, 20.

Said, Edward. 1983. *The World, the Text, and the Critic.* Cambridge MA.

Sanders, Jimmy, and V. Nee. 1992. "Problems in Resolving the Enclave Economy Debate." *American Sociological Review* 57, no. 3: 415–17.

Sanderson, Steven E., ed. 1985. *The Americas in the New International Division of Labor.* New York.

Sarup, Madan. 1989. *An Introductory Guide to Post-Structuralism and Postmodernism.* Athens GA.

Sassen, Saskia. 1991. *The Global City: New York, London, and Tokyo.* Princeton.

Sassen, Saskia, and Alejandro Portes. 1993. "Miami: A New Global City?" *Contemporary Sociology* 22, no. 4: 471–77.

Schattschneider, E. E. 1960. *The Semisovereign People.* New York.

Scott, George. 1990. "A Resynthesis of the Primordial and Circumstantial Approaches to Ethnic Group Solidarity: Towards an Explanatory Model." *Ethnic and Racial Studies* 13, no. 2: 147–71.

Select Commission on Immigration and Refugee Policy. 1981. *United States Immigration and the National Interest: Final Report and Recommendations to Congress and the President of the United States.* Washington DC.

Sheskin, Ira. 1991. "The Jews of South Florida." In *South Florida. See* Boswell and Curtis 1991.

Shils, Edward. 1957. "Primordial, Personal, Sacred, and Civic Ties." *British Journal of Sociology* 8:130–45.

Simon, J. L. 1989. *The Economic Consequences of Immigration.* Cambridge MA.

Simon, J. L., and S. Moore. 1984. "The Effects of Immigration upon Employment." Typescript.

Sjoberg, G., N. Williams, T. R. Vaughan, and A. F. Sjoberg. 1991. "The Case Study Approach in Social Research: Basic Methodological Issues." In Feagin, Orum, and Sjoberg 1991.

Sleet, Moneta. 1980. "Miami: Roots of Rage." *Ebony Magazine* 35, no. 1: 136–45.

Slevin, Peter. 1992a. "Jorge Mas Canosa: The Road to Havana." *Miami Herald,* 11 October, 1A, 21A.

———. 1992b. "60 Minutes Examines Mas Canosa." *Miami Herald,* 19 October, 10A.

Smith, H. T. 1992a. "Boycott Has Scored Victories but We Must Not Become Complacent." *Miami Times,* 16 July, 8A.

———. 1992b. "Hurricane Andrew Did Not Blow Away the Racists in Our Midst." *Miami Times,* 10 September, 1A.

Smith, Michael P. 1992. "Postmodernism, Urban Ethnography, and the New Social Space of Ethnic Identity." *Theory and Society* 21:493–531.

Smith, Michael P., and Joe Feagin. 1987. *The Capitalist City: Global Restructuring and Community Politics.* New York.

Sofen, Edward. 1961. "Problems of Metropolitan Leadership: The Miami Experience." *Midwest Journal of Political Science* 5, no. 1: 18–38.

Sollors, Werner. 1989. *The Invention of Ethnicity.* Oxford.

"South Florida's Melting Pot Is About to Boil." 1985. *Business Week,* 4 February, 86–87.

Spector, M., and J. Kitsuse. 1987. *Constructing Social Problems.* New York.

Spivak, Gayatri Chakravorty. 1992. "More on Power/Knowledge." In *Rethinking Power,* ed. Thomas Wartenberg. Albany NY.

Stack, John, ed. 1981. *Ethnic Identities in a Transnational World.* Westport CT.

Stack, John, and Christopher Warren. 1990. "Ethnicity and the Politics of Symbolism in Miami's Cuban Community." *Cuban Studies* 20:11–28.

———. 1992. "The Reform Tradition and Ethnic Politics: Metropolitan Miami Confronts the 1990s." In *Miami Now. See* Castro 1992.

Stein, George. 1983. "Some Gain, but Many Left Behind." *Miami Herald,* 18 December, 1M.

Steinback, Robert. 1990. "For Mandela, Miami Offers Few Memories." *Miami Herald,* 26 June, 1B.

———. 1992. "Ironies Remain Despite Moving Lozano's Trial." *Miami Herald,* 7 April, 1B.

Stepick, A. 1989. "Miami's Two Informal Sectors." In *The Informal Economy,* ed. A. Portes, M. Castells, and L. A. Benton. Baltimore.

———. 1992. "The Refugees Nobody Wants." In *Miami Now. See* Castro 1992.

Stepick, A., M. Castro, M. Dunn, G. Grenier. 1990. "Changing Relations among Newcomers and Established Residents: The Case of Miami." Miami. Mimeo.

Stern, S., and J. A. Cicala. 1991. *Creative Ethnicity: Symbols and Strategies of Contemporary Ethnic Life.* Logan UT.

Stevenson, James. 1975. *Cuban Americans New Urban Class.* Ann Arbor.

St. Paul, Omar. 1992. "Pastors Press Demands on Retrial for Lozano." *Miami Times,* 16 July, 1A.

Street, Frank. 1992. "Beach Groups Hear Heated Debates on Mandela." *Sunpost,* 4 June, 11.

"Suarez, Four Others Denounce Mandela." 1990. *Miami Herald,* 26 June, 1B.

Suhrke, A., and L. Noble. 1977. *Ethnic Conflict in International Relations.* New York.

Suny, Ronald. 1992. "State, Civil Society, and Ethnic Cultural Consolidation in the USSR: Roots of the National Question." In *From Union to Commonwealth,* ed. G. Lapidus, V. Zaslavsky, and P. Goldman. Cambridge MA.

Taeuber, K. E., and A. F. Taeuber. 1965. *Negroes in Cities: Residential Segregation and Neighborhood Change.* Chicago.

Tanfani, J., and P. May. 1992. "Dade Politicians Join We Will Rebuild." *Miami Herald,* 23 September, 1B.

"Think Again, Mr. Mandela." 1990. *Miami Herald,* 28 June, 21A.

Thomas, W. I. 1924. *The Child in America.* New York.

Thompson, Allan. 1995. "Economist, MP Criticize Immigrant Head Tax." *Toronto Star,* 6 March, A3.

"Those Amazing Cuban Emigres—Send Us 1,000 More." 1966. *Fortune,* October, 145–49.

"To Miami, Refugees Spell Prosperity." 1962. *Business Week,* 3 November, 92–94.

Torres, Maria de los Angeles. 1988. "Working against the Miami Myth." *Nation,* 24 October, 392–94.

"Towards Justice." 1992. *Miami Times,* 14 May, 4A.

"Two Local Groups of Lawyers Join Growing Boycott." 1990. *Miami Herald,* 28 July, 2B.

Tyler, Stephen. 1987. *The Unspeakable.* Madison.

U.S. Bureau of the Census. 1940. *Characteristics of the Population: Florida.* Vol. 1, pt. 2. Washington DC.

———. 1950. *Characteristics of the Population: Florida.* Vol. 1, pt. 2. Washington DC.

———. 1960. *Characteristics of the Population: Florida.* Vol. 1, pt. 2. Washington DC.

———. 1970. *Characteristics of the Population: Florida.* Vol. 1, pt. 2. Washington DC.

———. 1980. *Characteristics of the Population: Florida.* Vol. 1, pt. 2. Washington DC.

———. 1990. *Characteristics of the Population: Florida.* Vol. 1, pt. 2. Washington DC.

U.S. Department of Justice. 1990. Statistics Division of Immigration and Naturalization Service. *1990 Legalization Summary Public Use Tape.* Washington DC.

U.S. Department of Labor, Bureau of International Labor Affairs. 1989. *The Effects of Immigration on the U.S. Economy and Labor Market.* Washington DC.

U.S. Immigration and Naturalization Service. 1980. *Cubans Arrived in the United States by Class of Admission: Jan. 1, 1959–Sept. 30, 1980.* Washington DC.

U.S. Senate. 1961. Committee on the Judiciary. Subcommittee to Investigate Problems Connected with Refugees and Escapees. *Hearings.* 87th Cong., 1st sess., 6–13 December.

Wallerstein, Immanuel. 1976. *The Modern World-System: Capitalist Agriculture and the Origins of the European World-Economy in the Sixteenth Century.* New York.

Warren, C., J. Stack, and J. Corbett. 1986. "Minority Mobilization in an International City: Rivalry and Conflict in Miami." *PS* 19, no. 3: 626–39.

"The Welcome Wears Thin." 1980. *Time Magazine,* 1 September, 8–10.

Weston, Bonnie. 1992. "Cuban Rafter Rescues Head for Record Year." *Miami Herald,* 12 October, 3B.

Whitfield, Stephen J. 1993. "Florida's Fudged Identity." *Florida Historical Quarterly* 71:413–35.

"Why School Chief Said No to Cubans." 1965. *Miami News,* 17 October, 1B.

"Wide Political Gaps, Money Divide Miami's Cuban Exiles." 1960. *Miami Herald,* 3 December, 1C.

Wilson, K., and W. A. Martin. 1982. "Ethnic Enclaves: A Comparison of the Cuban and Black Economies in Miami." *American Journal of Sociology* 88, no. 1: 135–57.

Wilson, K., and A. Portes. 1980. "Immigrant Enclaves: An Analysis of the Labor Market Experiences of Cubans in Miami." *American Journal of Sociology* 86, no. 2: 295–319.

Winant, Howard. 1994. *Racial Conditions: Politics, Theory, and Comparisons.* Minneapolis.

Wu, Frank. 1992. "The Fallout from Japan-Bashing." *Washington Post,* 3 February, A11.

Wyche, Paul. 1968. "Before, During, and After; What Brought on Unrest?" *Miami News,* 8 August, 1A.

Yancey, W., E. Ericksen, and R. Juliani. 1976. "Emergent Ethnicity: A Review and Reformulation." *American Sociological Review* (41): 391–403.

Yelvington, Kevin, ed. 1992. *Trinidad Ethnicity.* London.

Yin, Robert. 1984. *Case Study Research: Design and Methods.* Beverly Hills.

Young, M. Crawford. 1986. "Nationalism, Ethnicity, and Class in Africa: A Retrospective." *Cahiers d'Études Africaines* 103, XXVI-3: 421–95.

———. 1993. *The Rising Tide of Cultural Pluralism.* Madison.

Zeitlin, Maurice. 1967. *Revolutionary Politics and the Cuban Working Class.* New York.

INDEX

African American Council of Christian
Clergy, 53
AFSCME (American Federation of State,
County, and Municipal Employees),
147
Agendas, Alternatives, and Public Policies
(Kingdon), 88
aid, federal, to Miami, 130
Allman, T. D., 41, 49, 121, 123, 132
Alvarez, Luis, 47
American Federation of State, County,
and Municipal Employees
(AFSCME), 147
American Political Science Association,
10
Americas Watch, 124–25
Amigos Christianos de Israel, 166
Anglos: becoming a minority, 58; deflec-
tion of anger, 94; dissatisfaction with
change, 47; as elite, 31, 36; ethnic
identity, 182–83; immigration concerns, 62–64, 81–82; Jews, 27, 57,
166; language issues, 48, 77–78;
police misconduct, 46; race hatred,
30; resentment of "Latinization," 77;
response to Cuban influx, 40; segregation, 28; tourists, 29
anti-bilingualism ordinance, 47
Anti-Defamation League of B'nai Brith,
57, 78
assimilation, 8–9
Assimilation in American Life (Gordon), 8
at-large voting, 45–46
attacks, on tourists, 112
authoritarianism, 10

Bahamians, and tensions with U.S.
blacks, 27
Barber, Benjamin, 21, 184
Batista, Fulgencio, 32, 120
Bay of Pigs, 110, 111, 129
Becker, Howard, 13
Bilderback, Loy, 81, 82
Black Brothers for Progress, 73

Black Miami (Dunn), 24
blacks, 15, 26, 30, 31, 75, 122
Bloom, Elaine, 166
Blumer, Herbert, 13–14
B'nai Brith, Anti-Defamation League of,
57, 58
boatlift, Mariel, 22, 56–57, 71, 85, 119
bombing, of Cuban Art Museum, 125
Bonacich, Edna, 104
Botifoll, Luis, 116
boycott, 53–56
Boycott Miami Now committee, 55, 151,
153, 154, 161
Boyd, Joe, 69
Brooks, Luther L., 69
Brothers to the Rescue, 123
Brown, J. O., 66
Burgess, E. W., 8
Burns, Patrick, 4
Bush, George, 111
Business Week, 130
Buthelezi (Zulu Chief), 153–54

Calle Ocho, 115
Canada, immigration policies of, 80
CANF (Cuban American National Foun-
dation), 48, 52, 102, 112–13, 169
The Capitalist City (Smith and Feagin), 212
n.4
Card, David, 85
Cardenas, Jose, 111
Carey, Barbara, 151
Casal, Lourdes, 126
A Case for the Case Study (Feagin, Orum
and Sjoberg), 19
Castro, Fidel, 107, 210 n.3
Catholic church, 109
la causa, 110, 134–35
census, 41, 50
Center for U.S.-Mexican Studies, 81
Central Intelligence Agency (CIA), 110
Cernuda, Ramon, 125
Chapman, Alvah, 36, 59, 82
Charsley, S. R., 157

Chin, Vincent, 213 n.6
Citizens of Dade United, 77, 210 n.2
City on the Edge (Forment and Stepick), 211 n.3
civil rights, 31
Clark, Steve, 38, 151
Clinton, Bill, 50, 110
Codina, Armando, 118
Colby, William, 82
Commandos L., 112
commerce, international, 42, 157
communism, 107
Congress on Racial Equality (CORE), 66
Constructing Social Problems (Spector and Kitsuse), 14
Cornelius, Wayne, 81
Creole language, 144
crime, 79
"Crisis Amigo," 64
Crouch, Stanley, 25
Cuban American National Foundation (CANF), 48, 52, 102, 112–13, 137, 169
Cuban Art Museum, bombing of, 125
Cuban Democracy Act, 111. *See also* Torricelli bill
Cuban Refugee Program of 1961, 108, 114
Cubans: attempts to liberate Cuba, 39; as cheap labor, 131; citizenship, 133; diversity of population, 103, 120; as early residents, 28; as exiles, 110; immigrants benefiting commerce, 35, 113, 131; and job displacement, 64–70; myths about, 119; paramilitary organizations, 39; as refugees, 32, 34, 70–71, 107, 109; residential patterns, 33; and riots, 72; waves of immigration, 106–7; as "white," 107
Cuba Survey, 111
Curry, Victor, 151

Dade County Community Relations Board, 68
Dade County Federation of Labor, 66
Dade Massacre of 1835, 26
Dahl, Robert, 95
Davila Miguel, Jorge, 165
Dawkins, Miller, 149
deconstruction, 188
de la Garza, Rodolfo, 120
demographics, 28, 41–42, 50, 126, 144
Derrida, Jacques, 172, 188, 212 n.5
De Yurre, Victor, 54
Diario Las Americas, 118, 202

Didion, Joan, 28, 74, 76, 78
dissimilarity, occupational, 199
diversity, of Hispanic population, 103, 121
Dominguez, Jorge, 136
Dow Chemical Company, 131
Due, Patricia, 150
Duncan, James, 68
Dunlap, Tully, 68, 130
Dunn, Marvin, 24, 53, 55, 76, 179

Eastern Airlines, 51
Ebony Magazine, 64, 75, 90
Economic Consequences of Immigration (Simon), 84
The Economist, 75
Edelman, Murray, 13, 92
enclave theory, 85, 104–5
English, official language campaign, 48
ethnicity, 12–21, 155, 157; symbols of, 165–68, 176, 178
European community, 51
exports/imports, 42
externalization, 92

Facts About Cuban Exiles (FACE), 48
Fagen, Richard, 121–22
Farris, Wayne, 64
Fascell, Dante, 69
Ferre, Maurice, 19, 36, 45, 180
Fitzpatrick, John J., 110
Florida International University, 35
foreign policy, of Miami, 146
Forment, Carlos, 16, 17, 104–5, 211 n.3
Fortune, 67, 114
Foucault, Michel, 16, 187, 189

Gary, Howard, 180
Gelber, Seymour, 152
Gerstein, Richard, 69
Gersten, Joe, 151
Gibson, Theodore, 65
Gilder, George, 115
Giroux, Henry A., 12
Glick-Schiller, Nina, 138
The Global City (Sassen), 21
Going to Miami (Rieff), 76
Goode, R. Ray, 71
Gordon, Milton, 8
Graham, Donald, 51
Graham, Robert, 72, 74
Greater Miami Chamber of Commerce, 44, 117
Greater Miami Urban League, 69
Greene, Juanita, 7, 66

Gross, H. R., 70
growth, of population and economy, 29
Gusfield, Joseph, 14, 95
Gutierrez, Armando, 152

Haitians: and Clinton inauguration, 51; first refugees, 34; and growth of black population, 42; and police brutality, 54; and political asylum, 65; and tensions with U.S. blacks, 27
Hallgren, Art, 68
Hardemon, Billy, 149
Headley, Walter, 37
Helms, Jesse, 211 n.10
El Herald, 44
High, Robert, 114
Hispanics: diversity of, 103, 121; percent of voters, 43
Holocaust Memorial, 212 n.6
Homer, Porter, 70
Hurricane Andrew, 58, 59

identity formation, 173, 181, 183, 187
image construction, 173–74
immigration, impact of, 5, 32, 61–63, 79–87, 144, 174
Immigration and Naturalization Service, 71
immigration policy, 55, 72, 80–85, 137–38
Immigration Reform and Control Act of 1986, 41, 81
imports/exports, 42
Indians, 25–26
Inquiry and Change (Lindblom), 13
instrumentalism, vs. primordialism, 10–11, 16, 104–5, 208 n.10
integration, 31
internal colonialism, 207 n.5
International Fraternal Union, 122
International Management Assistance Corporation (IMAC), 43
international trade, 42, 157
interviews, 207 n.3
interview schedule, 204–5
Introduction to the Science of Society (Park and Burgess), 8
IRCA (1986 Immigration Reform and Control Act), 41, 81

Jackson, Jesse, 59
Jews, discrimination against, 27
"Jihad," 11, 21. See also "McWorld"
job displacement, 64–70, 79–87
Johnson, James, 53

Johnson, Lyndon Baines, 72
Jones, Donald Wheeler, 66
Jordan Marsh, 51

Keasler, John, 172
Kennedy, John F., 111
Kerr, Edward, 65
Kilson, Martin, 162
Kingdon, John, 88, 90
Kirkpatrick, Jeane, 102, 210 n.1
Kitsuse, John, 14
Kiwanis Magazine, 64
Knox, George, 148
Konzen, K. N., 15
Koppel, Ted, 149
Kraus, Clifford, 125
Ku Klux Klan, 31
Kulp brothers, 4

LaCapra, Dominick, 189
Lamm, Richard, 82
Lang, H. Daniel, 69
Lasaga, Manuel, 43
Latin Chamber of Commerce, 35
"Latin connection," 35
Latin Journey (Forment), 211 n.3
Lawrence, David, 49
Lazell, J. Arthur, 109
liberalism, 9
Liberty City, 31; riots, 46, 174
Life Magazine, 115
Lindblom, Charles, 13
Little Haiti, 42, 144
Little Havana, 35, 115, 144
Little Managua, 144
Lockhart, Charles, 64
Lozano, William, 47, 52, 209 n.11, 209 n.12
la lucha, 39, 110
Luytjes, Jan, 76

Mandela, Nelson, 53–54, 142, 164, 176
Mannheim paradox, 18
Mariel boatlift, 22, 56–57, 71, 85, 119
Marielitos, 57, 78, 208 n.2
Martí, Jose, 145
Marxism, 8–9, 185, 186, 207 n.9
Mas Canosa, Jorge, 52, 113, 125, 137, 163, 169
Mauss, Armand, 14
Mayan rebellion, 192
McDuffie, Arthur, 46
McDuffie riots, 46, 74
McMillian, Johnnie, 93, 148, 170, 209 n.13

McNayr, Irving, 69
"McWorld," 11, 21. *See also* "Jihad"
media, role in defining problems and
    issues, 91–94, 109
Meeks v. Dade County, 51
La Mesa Rotunda, 51
Metrorail, 37
Mexico, 169
Miami Dolphins, 35
Miami Herald, 44–45, 52, 73, 153–54,
    202
Miami News, 115
Miami Partners for Progress, 154
The Miami Riot of 1980: Crossing the Bounds
    (Porter and Dunn), 76
Miami's New Group, 51
"Miami Syndrome," 96
Miami Times, 59, 153–54, 202
Miami Today, 61, 98
migration, 156–57
Milan, Emilio, 39
mobilizationism. *See* instrumentalism
The Modern World System: Capitalist Agricul-
    ture and the Origins of the European
    World-Economy in the Sixteenth Century
    (Wallerstein), 212 n.3
Mohl, Raymond, 77
Moncarz, Raul, 126
Montiel-Davis, Magda, 125, 211 n.6
Moore, Carlos, 122–23
multinational corporations, 42
municipios, 124
Mutual of Omaha Insurance, 131
myths, about Cubans, 119

NAACP (National Association for the
    Advancement of Colored People), 65,
    66, 148, 150, 209 n.13
NAFTA (North American Free Trade
    Agreement), 145, 192
Nagel, Joane, 15
National Association for the Advance-
    ment of Colored People (NAACP), 65,
    66, 148, 150, 209 n.13
National Union for the Total Indepen-
    dence of Angola (UNITA), 169
New Group, 51
New Jewish Agenda, 166
New South Magazine, 73
Newsweek, 145
New Yorker, 78
New York Times, 125
Ney, John, 61, 98
Nicaraguans, 50, 56, 77
Nietzsche, Friedrich, 187

Nives, Luciano, 39
Non-Group, 36–37, 44
North American Free Trade Agreement
    (NAFTA), 145, 192
El Nuevo Herald, 44, 165, 202

occupational dissimilarity, 199
O'Meara, D'Arey, 64
Operation Exodus, 169
Overtown, 28–29, 47, 75

Pallot, William, 68, 114, 130
Palmatier, Howard, 114
Palmer, Bryan, 17–18, 20
Pan Am World Airways, 51
parades, 144
Park, Robert E., 8
Patten, Arthur, 69
Pedraza-Bailey, Silvia, 124
Penelas, Alex, 112
People United for Justice, 149
Pepper, Claude, 69
Pereira, Sergio, 48
Perez, Lisandro, 126, 136
Perez Firmat, Gustavo, 210 n.2
Perot, Ross, 49, 146
Petrella, Ricardo, 51
pluralism, 8
police brutality, 54
political asylum, 65
"Political Construction of Ethnicity"
    (Nagel), 15
population growth, 29
Porter, Bruce, 76
Portes, Alejandro, 104, 211 n.11
postmodernism, 12, 20, 188, 207 n.9
poststructuralism, 12, 188
poverty, black, 36
primordialism, vs. instrumentalism,
    10–11, 16, 104–5 , 208 n.10
Pye, Lucian, 10

questions, asked of informants, 208–9
"Quiet Riot," 53, 153, 168

Range, Athalie, 208 n.7
Reagan, Ronald, 111
Recapturing the Spirit of Enterprise (Gilder),
    115
Regalado, Raquel, 118
relative deprivation, 89
Research Institute for Cuba, 114
Resnick, Bob, 77
Rieff, David, 76, 78
riots: Liberty City (1968), 4–5, 72, 174;

McDuffie (1980), 24, 46, 74; "rotten meat," 38; Watts, 4
Rivero, Felipe, 111
Rojas, Fernando, 112
Rolle, C. Gaylord, 65
Roman Catholic Church, 109
Ros-Lehtinen, Ileana, 44, 125
Rosquete, Gonzales, 112
Rothchild, John, 2
"rotten meat riot," 38

Saferstein, Sam, 166
SALAD (Spanish American League Against Discrimination), 2, 48, 134, 152
Salinas de Gorteri, Carlos, 169
Santería, 78
Schattschneider, E. E., 13
schools, 67
segregation, 30
Select Commission on Immigration and Refugee Policy, 82
The Semi-Sovereign People (Schattschneider), 13
Simms, Robert, 73
Simms, Willie, 151
Simon, Julian, 84
Smith, H. T., 150, 154, 167
Smith, Michael, 18
Smith, Wayne, 169
Sofen, Edward, 30
Sollors, Werner, 15
Soto, Osvaldo, 117, 152
South Africa, 80
Southeast Bank, 51
Spanish American League Against Discrimination, 2, 48, 134, 152
Spector, Malcom, 14
Spencer, Thomas, 153
The Spirit of Enterprise (Gilder), 115
Stack, John, 96, 158
Steinback, Robert, 165
Stephenson, Edward, 66

Suarez, Javier, 146, 149, 153
Summit of the Americas, 49
symbols, of ethnicity, 165–68, 176, 178

Teele, Arthur, 49, 59
Teitelbaum, Arthur, 78, 164
Thomas, W. I., 12
Time Magazine, 75
Torch of Friendship, 111
Torres, Maria de los Angeles, 120
Torricelli bill, 111, 112, 125, 146
tourism, 29, 43
tourists, attacks on, 112
trade, international, 42, 157
transmigrants, 138
transnationalism, 138
Transnational Relations and World Politics (Keohane and Nye), 212 n.2
tri-ethnic view of Miami, 55, 57, 59, 181
Tuttle, Julia, 144
Tyler, Stephen, 15

unemployment, black, 36
UNITA (National Union for the Total Independence of Angola), 169

Villareal, Armando, 125
Voorhees, Tracy, 108
voting: at-large, 45–46; Hispanic voting blocks, 43–44
Voting Rights Act, 45, 51

Wallerstein, Immanuel, 212 n.3
Walsh, Bryan, 79, 114
Warren, Christopher, 96
Weedman, William, 68
We Will Rebuild, 59
Whitehead, James, 69
whites, non-Latin. *See* Anglos
Wise, J. C., 53

Yelvington, Kevin, 190

RACE AND ETHNICITY IN URBAN POLITICS

Louis DeSipio
COUNTING ON THE LATINO VOTE
Latinos as a New Electorate

Sheila L. Croucher
IMAGINING MIAMI
Ethnic Politics in a Postmodern World